Sean Smith is the UK's leading celebrity biographer whose best-selling books have been translated throughout the world. His subjects include J.K. Rowling, Robbie Williams, Kylie Minogue, Justin Timberlake, Britney Spears, Jennifer Aniston and Victoria Beckham. Described by *The Independent* as a 'fearless chronicler', he specializes in meticulous research, leaving his west London home to go 'on the road' to find the real person behind the star image.

Also by Sean Smith

Cheryl

SEAN SMITH

POCKET
BOOKS

LONDON • SYDNEY • NEW YORK • TORONTO

First published in Great Britain by Simon & Schuster UK Ltd, 2009
This edition published by Pocket Books, 2010
An imprint of Simon & Schuster UK Ltd
A CBS COMPANY

1 3 5 7 9 10 8 6 4 2

Simon & Schuster UK Ltd
1st Floor
222 Gray's Inn Road
London
WC1X 8HB

www.simonandschuster.co.uk

Simon & Schuster Australia
Sydney

A CIP catalogue record for this book
is available from the British Library

ISBN 978-1-84739-317-3

Typeset in Baskerville by M Rules
Printed by CPI Cox & Wyman, Reading, Berkshire RG1 8EX

For my brother, Lincoln, and my sister, Alison –
life's good companions.

Contents

Cheryl

PART ONE

CHERYL TWEEDY

1

The Little Smasher

Reality television has changed the way we view our entertainment – maybe for ever. It has given wannabes a break that might never have come their way without the power of Saturday night television. It has also bred a misconception that somehow those few that win are just lucky, that they have walked in off the street to be discovered by Simon Cowell or Pete Waterman without putting in the hard graft or having any discernible talent. That may be true of the ones that give viewers a laugh in the early auditions, a rhythm-free bunch with no style and voices that only a mother could love. The idea that a winner, voted for by millions of people, in a talent show on television is in some way less talented than an artist discovered gigging in a seedy bar is, however, one of the more ludicrous by-products of these TV contests.

The Hollywood view of show business is that happy accidents do happen. In a typical film scenario Cheryl Tweedy would be a pretty Geordie girl sizzling the bacon in a Newcastle café when a record producer walks in and orders a full English. He would hear Cheryl singing 'Like a Virgin' over the frying pan and sign her up on the spot. It's the fantasy that fuels no-hopers applying for *Pop Idol*, *American Idol* or *The X Factor*. They may have the dream but they spent their childhoods playing football and computer games or watching soaps with a mobile phone glued to their ear. In contrast, the great majority of today's major stars have worked their socks off to get their chance. Britney Spears was on Broadway aged nine,

Robbie Williams was playing panto when his mates were kicking a football in the park, Kylie Minogue was a television actress at eleven and Cheryl Tweedy was so young when she started singing in London clubs that she needed a chaperone.

Cheryl's pursuit of stardom may not conform to a Hollywood stereotype but, nevertheless, her life would make a terrific movie. She may not have been the heroine of a Catherine Cookson novel, ground down by miserable circumstances, but she grew up in genuinely grim surroundings in a poor area blighted by drugs and unemployment.

The opening shot of the true *Cheryl: The Movie* would be of a pretty brunette with the elfin features of Audrey Hepburn struggling up the steps of Walkergate Metro Station in the east end of Newcastle with a baby boy in a pushchair and a happy little girl by her side. At the top of the stairs she gazes up and down the bleak Shields Road, past boarded-up shops and pubs, before crossing over and making for a discreet entrance by the side of a small parade of shops. A modest sign above the door reads: 'The Noreen Campbell Dance School'. Cheryl Tweedy, aged four, had arrived at her dance lesson with her mum and her younger brother, Garry.

Cheryl's dancing on a Thursday afternoon was the highlight of her week. She would throw herself enthusiastically into the class in the main ballroom, with its pink walls and huge mirrors, while her mum, Joan, clutching baby Garry, would squeeze into the much smaller cloakroom with the other mums to chat about life, their dreams for their children and how they might achieve them.

Dance classes for little girls are much the same wherever you are. Gail MacKay, one of her teachers, explains, 'It's all done in fun form. They are fairies, elves or pixies – all that kind of thing. Cheryl really was very good right from the start. But she always had the personality to go with it. She was a bubbly little girl. She didn't show off as such but she liked the "showing" part of dancing. And, she had another very important characteristic: she was very determined.'

Many times, Gail would sit down with her mother, Noreen Campbell, to discuss the children and, without fail, Cheryl's name would come up as their star pupil. She was only four but she had a love of performing that her mother, Joan, recognized at an early age. No one seems to have a bad word to say about Joan Callaghan. Cheryl was extremely fortunate to have had a remarkable woman in her corner when she was growing up. Gail observes, 'She was lovely, Joan, very friendly like Cheryl. I know she was keen for Cheryl to do well.'

Joan, known to her friends as Joanie, was just seventeen when she had her first child, a boy called Joe. The dad, Anthony Leighton, was only sixteen and lived a few streets away from her childhood home in Mindrum Terrace, just across from Walker Park, a typical urban space with a football pitch and a bowling green, a children's play area and picnic tables and the obligatory group of bored youngsters hanging out together after school. Walker was Joan's neighbourhood. These were her streets.

The area was almost entirely working class but, when Joan was growing up, the local men had the prospect of employment in the shipyards. Joe was named after Joan's father, Joseph Callaghan, who worked as a shot blaster, operating the equipment that used abrasives to clean the hulls of the boats down at the Walker shipyards. Anthony, whom everyone called Bing, started off as an apprentice welder when he left school, following in the footsteps of his father, John, who was a sheet metal worker. This was a time when boys followed their father's trade.

When Bing and Joan were teenage lovers, the Swan Hunter Group, which owned the famous Tyneside shipyards, was a thriving business employing close to 20,000 people. The eighties, however, saw the decline of the industries that had been the backbone of working-class communities throughout the United Kingdom – the coal mines, the steelworks, the car and aircraft plants and the shipyards. Nothing hits a community harder than unemployment, especially in its effect on young people with little to look forward to when they leave school. Walker suffered. Many of the young men turned to drugs, in particular solvent abuse. Glue-sniffing became the preferred hit in the poor neighbourhoods, a problem that would cruelly touch the lives of Cheryl and her family. A contemporary of Cheryl's observed, 'I think there's a big drug problem in Walker. I remember lots of glue-sniffers from when I was younger. Walker is a pretty deprived area, quite bleak and not much to do.'

Joan and Bing married in 1978, when she was nineteen and he was eighteen. They had two more children together, a daughter, Gillian, and another son, Andrew. Soon after their youngest was born, the couple split up, perhaps an inevitable consequence of too much too young. Bing had abandoned his career path and Joan had never had the chance to follow one. She met a local painter and decorator, Garry Tweedy, and he took on her three children. The new family of five moved into a house in Cresswell Street, a neat and tidy row of terraced council houses, a couple of hundred yards from Welbeck Road, which runs between Walker and Byker and not much more than half a mile from Mindrum Terrace. Joan and Garry had their first child, Cheryl Ann, on 30 June 1983 – one month after Swan Hunter went into receivership. They were not married and Joan signed the birth certificate Joan Callaghan. When their son, Garry junior, was born in September 1987, she signed the register as Joan Tweedy, but the couple were still not married.

Growing up in Cresswell Street may have been hard but it was not Dickensian. Cheryl has admitted, in retrospect, that it was 'very tough'. At the time she had no idea that her upbringing was any different from the next little girl's. She was not unhappy. She had baked beans and fish fingers for her tea, second-hand clothes to wear and McDonald's for a birthday treat. The girl next door, Susan, was the same age and a playmate. She still lives in the street and had her first child in 2008.

Cheryl took after Joan in looks. A future boyfriend once joked that Garry, who was much fairer, couldn't possibly be her dad and got whacked by Cheryl for his cheek. Cheryl told *Vogue* magazine in February 2009 that she was so dark and hairy as a child that she was nicknamed 'Paki' at school. Cheryl may well have had some exotic ancestry, because foreign workers drifted into the shipyards to find employment and would end up staying in the area and raising a family. Away from the playground, the reality was that Cheryl was a strikingly pretty little girl and Joan was constantly hearing from family and friends, perhaps in the cloakroom at Noreen

Campbell's, that she should enter her daughter for bonny baby competitions. She took the hint and found, to her delight, that Cheryl would invariably win. She took the trophy for one sponsored by Boots and another by Mothercare. She won a contest sponsored by the local Newcastle paper, the *Evening Chronicle*, entitled 'Little Miss and Mister'.

Joan decided to do something more and rang the Pat Morgan Agency and made an appointment to discover if Cheryl had any prospects as a child model. Pat Morgan was a glamorous South African-born ex-model and beauty queen. She had been crowned Miss Great Britain in 1978, which made her a local celebrity and enabled her to get her agency off the ground in 1985 in the upmarket Newcastle district of Jesmond. She would have had more opportunities in London but wanted to stay in the North-East. She had a large number of children on her books and had more phone calls from parents trying to promote their children than from anyone else.

The first thing any children's agent will do is to interview the mother. If the mother is a nightmare, then an experienced agent will instinctively know that taking on the child will be a disaster. Joan passed her 'audition' with flying colours and never failed to impress Pat with the support and time she gave her daughter: 'I thought Joan was quite incredible. She had quite a big family but she would always go with Cheryl to any job. She was very supportive without being pushy. You get an awful lot of parents who push their children and their kids never really want to do it.

'Her mother was very helpful and never one of those grabbing mums who are always on the phone demanding things. She was just normal, not glamorous by any means. She brought Cheryl; she helped Cheryl even if she had to bring her other kids with her.

'I always noticed that she was never one of those that if you rang up and said, "I've got a job for Cheryl tomorrow" she never said, "I might have a problem with that." She just got her there and didn't bother me with any problems. She never said she needed to find a babysitter or whatever; she just got her there and she did the job.

'In my opinion, she was a brilliant mum.'

While Cheryl was undoubtedly lucky to have such a well-grounded mother, Joan was equally fortunate to have a daughter who really wanted to achieve as a child. As Pat confirms, 'She had the perfect child. Cheryl wanted to do it – that was her. If work was going and Cheryl was suitable for it, she was always going to get it because she was the best one around. Cheryl just stood out head and shoulders above everyone else.'

Even as a small child, Cheryl was displaying the key elements that have contributed to her success as an adult: natural good looks combined with a desire to work hard. 'She was just so cute,' observes Pat. 'She had such a warm smile, so gorgeous with her big brown eyes and dimples. But she worked damn hard for a young child and she wasn't pushed to do it.'

Cheryl compiled an impressive portfolio as a child model, mainly modelling for children's stores and catalogues. The impressive MetroCentre just across the Tyne in Gateshead was the biggest shopping mall in Europe and presented many opportunities for promotional work. It would almost become a second home for Cheryl over the next twelve years or so. Joan recalled, 'She did loads of stuff for the agency, on catwalks and on stages. She would go to shopping centres all over the place.'

Her best-known job as a child was a television commercial for British Gas in which she shared a bath with her younger brother Garry and a yellow duck. It was very innocent, showing how much fun it was to have gas supplied to your home. The voice-over proclaimed: 'It's all on tap at your gas showroom now.' Joan observed, 'It proved she was a natural in front of the cameras. She was filmed being washed by her screen mother. She isn't embarrassed about it because she was just a little girl.' Cheryl also teamed up with Garry in an advertisement for the Eldon Square shopping mall in the city centre.

The biggest engagement Pat Morgan found for Cheryl was the National Garden Festival in 1990, which was on a huge site in the Team Valley that is now a housing estate. 'It was huge,' recalls Pat. 'There was a week and a half of fashion shows, including a lot of children's things. Cheryl was very important for us then. I remember it was an awful lot of work because we had to do hours and hours of rehearsal.'

Cheryl was already showing great discipline for a young girl. She responded well to rehearsal and tuition, provided it was something she actually wanted to do and not boring old schoolwork. Pat remembers: 'From a very young age, you just had to show her a routine once and she did it. She would just do the routine and then she helped teach the other little kids as well, keep them in line. It was just incredible to see such professionalism in somebody so young.'

This was a big year for Walker's 'next top model' because she entered another modelling competition promoted by the Newcastle *Evening Chronicle* with the visionary title 'Star of the Future'. She emphasized her cuteness by wearing a flowery top, a frilly skirt and her hair in pigtails. More than a hundred children were reduced to fourteen finalists.

The judge, Mike Whitehouse, manager of the local Children's World store, had no hesitation in awarding first prize to Cheryl, calling her a 'little smasher'. Cheryl won £150 worth of clothing vouchers – a decent prize at the time. Her mother recalled, 'It was a lovely day. She really enjoyed herself. As a kid, that was her thing – dressing up.'

The newspaper has never forgotten that it was the 'first' to spot Cheryl's potential. It would be churlish to point out that Cheryl had done so much for the Pat Morgan Agency that she was practically professional by then. Pat Morgan closed the agency in 1992, when Cheryl was nine. She remembers her star client as if it were yesterday: 'From a very young age you knew she was going to be something special. I didn't know what it was going to be because she seemed, as far as I could see, quite an all-rounder. But I would say she was just about the best child we have ever had through the doors.'

The money Cheryl earned from modelling work was a bonus but it was never going to be enough to feed a family of seven. Pat admits, 'They weren't making an awful lot of money out of modelling; definitely not.' Joan, however, was able to use what they did earn to pay for Cheryl's dancing.

Cheryl was such a busy little girl that it would be easy to forget that she also had to go to school. She had started dancing and modelling at the age of four; she had also donned a smart blue uniform to attend St Lawrence's Roman Catholic Primary School in Headlam Street, Byker. Cheryl has never mentioned the school in any interview but, as a non-Catholic, she was very fortunate to be given a place at a school that was such a haven within a grim inner-city environment. Priority for places was given to Catholic children, but once these were filled, admission was extended to others.

St Lawrence's has an unusual location for a school, within the famous Byker Wall, which is, in fact, a housing scheme running around part of the boundary of Byker. The Wall, designed in the mid-seventies, is an unbroken block of more than 600 bright blue flats and maisonettes, which were innovative in their day but are now a bit of an eyesore. The whole Byker Estate, of which the Wall forms part, was awarded Grade II Listed status in 2007 by the Department for Culture, Media and Sport for its outstanding architecture.

The school is in the heart of the estate. Cheryl and her mother would catch the bus along the Welbeck Road for a mile or so, get off in the centre of Byker and walk across a footbridge at the back of the library and local swimming pool. Parents do not drop their charges at the school gates because they walk straight off the street into the front doorway. The only giveaway that this is a relatively rough area is the electric fencing on the roof. The classrooms are right on one of the maze of streets serving the estate. The current headmistress, Miss Bernadette Lamb, who taught Cheryl as an infant, says, 'People always say it's a haven. It's a special school. It was like that when Cheryl was here and still is.'

St Lawrence's is very popular with former pupils and has its own appreciation group on Facebook. The headmistress at the time was a nun called Sister Bernard, whom the children nicknamed, for obvious reasons, the 'Penguin'. Cheryl's contemporary Clare Bulman recalls, 'She was very stern and all the children were scared of her. You did not want to get wrong off her! She didn't really teach classes as such but she was always involved in our assemblies or school masses at the local church. She seemed to mellow a bit as we got older but that may have been because she was looking forward to leaving. Even though she was stern, I wouldn't have had it any other way.'

Miss Lamb, who took over from Sister Bernard, was Cheryl's form mistress as an infant, aged five, and was a favourite teacher. 'She was very fair but strict,' observes Clare. Miss Lamb was a great fan of Newcastle football club and endeared herself to the children by helping to arrange visits from famous old players like Peter Beardsley and Lee Clark. She was also very hands-on and didn't mind joining in. 'You would never find Sister Bernard kicking a ball round with the kids.'

Football is the biggest talking point in Newcastle. No matter how famous Cheryl becomes she will never be as famous in the city as Alan Shearer. In the main assembly room of the primary school, pride of place is given to an Alan Shearer shirt even though he was never a pupil. Ironically, considering how her personal life would develop, Cheryl was not especially interested in sport as a child – playing or watching it. At least at St Lawrence's they never interfered with her outside activities. Miss Lamb knew about the modelling and the dancing and was happy to encourage it, believing it was important to develop 'the whole child' and not concentrate solely on academic subjects.

By the time younger brother Garry joined her at St Lawrence's, Cheryl was beginning to take her dancing even more seriously. She was well known at primary school for her dancing but, as Clare Bulman recalls, 'She was never big-headed about her talents as some of the other kids would have been.'

From the age of six Cheryl was bitten by the competition bug. Noreen and Gail would pick her up at home on Sunday mornings – because Joan didn't have a car – and drive her to stage festivals in local towns such as Ashington and South Shields. She would usually enter three or four sections within her age group. One would be ballet, then song and dance, stage and perhaps a fourth would be national or character dancing. Cheryl never went home without a trophy. 'She won a lot of cups,' recalls Gail. From a very early age, Cheryl became used to performing in front of an audience.

2

Dancing Princess

Cheryl decided she wanted to be a ballerina, as little girls often do. She was an exceptional dancer for her age but Joan decided Cheryl needed extra ballet lessons if she was going to realize her ambition. Joan heard of a school in Whitley Bay that sounded promising. The classes were run by a distinguished local teacher called Margaret Waite, who taught in the town for forty years until her retirement in 2003.

Joan told Margaret that she wanted to improve her daughter's ballet technique. Margaret recalls, 'There was a lot of hard work to do with Cheryl. But once we started, she was sailing.' Once a week, Cheryl and Joan would make the seven-mile journey on the train to the coast for some ice cream and arabesques.

Cheryl was once described as a female Billy Elliot, the hero of the magical film that became a hit musical on the West End stage. Billy is the miner's son who overcomes working-class prejudice and sexism to win a place at the Royal Ballet in a gloriously uplifting story. Cheryl's flirtation with this world, however, was to end in disappointment.

When she was nine, Cheryl was at morning assembly when Sister Bernard made an announcement to the school: 'Congratulations to Cheryl Tweedy on being accepted for a place at the summer school of the Royal Ballet.'

Cheryl's two-week adventure in London was nothing like she imagined it would be: 'I wanted to go home straight away.

Everyone was prim and proper and I was just a Geordie from a council estate. The parents all had money and we struggled just to get the cash to travel down to London.'

Cheryl was not prepared for life outside Walker. In her home environment she was a big fish in a small pond. Her primary school friends admired her. The mantelpiece at home was already groaning under the weight of her dancing trophies. She was the 'Star of the Future'! That eminence did not travel south down the A1. Her famous determination and drive seemed to desert her in the illustrious surroundings of White Lodge, the Royal Ballet's school in Richmond Park. Here she was a very small fish indeed.

Joan, as ever, had travelled with her daughter and was invited with the other parents to watch her child's last performance after the two weeks of classes. Cheryl would later reveal that she was the only one who waved to mum. Clearly Cheryl was very homesick during this extended period away from familiar surroundings. She may have had the dream of being a prima ballerina but, at this stage of her life, the harsh truth of what it would take was too much. Margaret Waite believes the course was 'too intense' for her star pupil. She observed, 'I think it put her off ballet. She realized it wasn't what she wanted to do, so she went on to other things.' Cheryl confirmed, 'It shattered my dream. But I didn't want to stand a certain way all my life and eat salad.' In other words, she did not actually want it enough.

One of the purposes of events like the summer school is to weed out those for whom the flame does not burn brightly enough. It's a hard and ultra-competitive world at a cruelly young age. There's no indication as to whether Cheryl would have been invited back to the Royal Ballet. She was surrounded by the very best young ballerinas in the country and had done very well to be accepted to the summer school. Her ambitions in ballet may have been extinguished by the experience but her dreams of being a performer remained and she was not the sort of little girl to dwell on disappointments.

Margaret Waite continued to teach other styles of dancing to Cheryl and, in particular, encouraged her stage work. Cheryl was one of the stars when Margaret took pupils to entertain the elderly at various old people's homes in the area. She used to pair her with another local girl, Andrea Riseborough, because the two youngsters gelled so well. She knew they were her best pupils but even Margaret must look back in astonishment at having two stars of the future in the same class. Andrea has gone on to find fame as one of the most acclaimed actresses of her generation, featured in *The Sunday Times* as one of the rising stars of 2009. On television she starred as Margaret Thatcher in *Margaret Thatcher: The Long Walk to Finchley* and took the lead role in *The Devil's Whore*.

The trouble with being an all-rounder and good at most things was that it was difficult to know what to specialize in. Cheryl had this problem. She decided to try acting. Her first tentative venture was with the First Act Theatre group, a well-respected company that started up in the early nineties to provide training for young people in all aspects of the theatre.

The group was set up by local director Barry Wilmot who, after years of running the youth stage school at the Tyne Theatre in the centre of Newcastle, was concerned that too many talented youngsters were slipping through the theatrical net because of the lack of opportunity. 'I was auditioning about fifty kids for one vacancy and I thought it wasn't right that there were all these kids desperate to do it and there was just nowhere for them to go and that's why I started First Act. No kid is refused; none whatsoever.'

Barry's very first production with the new group, *Seven Brides for Seven Brothers*, was an instant success. He was a bit short-handed so one of his assistants, who was working on the television series *Byker Grove*, volunteered to bring a couple of lads along to help. Anthony McPartlin and Declan Donnelly duly presented themselves at the Jubilee Theatre and worked backstage. Barry recalls, 'Looking back I always think it was funny that they weren't even in the show on stage. Ant and Dec were lovely lads and, both of them, instantly had that spark. They have never changed. They were exactly like they are on TV when they were kids.'

Cheryl is quite unusual among the current crop of Geordie stars in that she never appeared in *Byker Grove*, although her career path crossed with many who did. *Byker Grove*, which began life in 1989, told the stories of a group of youngsters at a youth club. Ant and

Dec, of course, found fame as PJ and Duncan. Jill Halfpenny, winner of *Strictly Come Dancing*, cut her dramatic teeth at First Act before landing the role of Nicola in the Geordie children's soap. Dale Meeks was at First Act before playing Greg and later joining *Emmerdale* as Simon Meredith. Barry's own daughter, Lynne, was there briefly before going on to a successful stage career in the West End and is currently appearing in the popular revival of *Oliver!*.

Cheryl might well have ended up in *Byker Grove* if she had been a few years older. One of the younger stars of the show, also a First Actor, was television presenter Donna Air, who is four years older than Cheryl. Donna was another name that Barry always remembered, although he is a little less complimentary about her talents: 'I always remember Donna because she was a very pretty girl even as a kid but she didn't have the spark.'

The Jubilee Theatre, where all the young hopefuls attended Barry's classes, was a beautiful Victorian theatre at the St Nicholas Hospital, a working psychiatric hospital in Gosforth. The location was not the most convenient for Cheryl, who, with her mother, would get a bus out to the upmarket suburb after school. Like many of the things Cheryl was to try, Joan had heard about First Act when chatting to other mothers as she waited for dance lessons to finish.

Barry Wilmot always remembered Cheryl: 'When you get an unusual name like Tweedy, it tends to stick in your mind. Cheryl stuck out even though I have worked with thousands of kids. She was very vivacious if you can say that about a kid. She was with us at a time when we were using a lot of older kids for the shows, so she was too young and I considered her too inexperienced to get in. It was obvious to me that she had been to a dance school because she had that sort of dance school aura. She had confidence.'

Cheryl enrolled to do one workshop a week at £25 for a course of ten weeks, which broadly followed the school term. When she first arrived, she found herself slotted into a group of twenty-five children she didn't know. All the classes are performance-based so Cheryl had to get on with it from day one. Barry explained, 'Even if we are not doing a show, the kids are performing every single week. It's great for confidence. It's also great for working with people you may not like and it's great socially.'

Cheryl particularly enjoyed the creative element of drama classes. As she grew older, she would always seize the opportunity to put her own stamp on things, whether that was writing songs or devising dance routines. She was very disciplined about her work and there was something quite satisfying about spending an hour telling the story of Humpty Dumpty from the point of view of the surgeon trying to put Humpty back together again.

Cheryl was in danger of spreading herself too thinly, trying to pack too much into her days. She had done two terms with First Act but decided against a third. Barry observed, 'It was a shame because she would have got into our shows, I'm positive of that.' Instead, Cheryl took an opportunity to appear on stage for the first time in a pantomime.

Her dance teacher, Margaret Waite, always did the choreography for the productions of the Whitley Bay Pantomime Society and Cheryl was one of a dozen of Margaret's pupils cast in *Aladdin* for the January 1994 production. The society had been going strong since 1964, performing an annual pantomime at the grand old Whitley Bay Playhouse. The theatre closed in 2007, having fallen into a bad state of disrepair, but an £8 million overhaul has returned it to its former splendour. The society is entirely voluntary, raising money for local charities and giving children their first experience of appearing on stage. Cheryl is listed in the billing as a 'tot' along with a dozen or so other youngsters. Margaret recalls that she had a lovely little solo in which she danced by herself in a jazzy style.

Cheryl was eleven when her life was first turned upside down. Her parents split up and she discovered that only Garry junior was her full brother. She also found out that her mother and father were not married. The revelations did not make her love her family any less. To their credit, Joan and Garry senior did not involve the children in their personal differences and Cheryl remained on good terms with her father. She was at an age when she could have been affected in a bad way but she revealed in the Girls Aloud book *Dreams That Glitter* that she considered herself to be one of the lucky ones and that there were lots of kids at her school whose parents were not together. She observed, wryly, 'Some kids hadn't even met their dads.'

The family remained close. Garry stayed in Walker, not far from Cresswell Street, while Joan took the children to a council house on an unprepossessing estate just off the Heaton Road. The area was more colourful than the drab, soulless rows of houses in Walker, which did not even offer pubs and cafés to cheer up the local population. It was not, however, a move upmarket, although Joan and Cheryl could walk to Morrison's on the Shields Road past the bingo hall, the amusement centre, numerous bookmakers, a rough-looking pub or two and Greggs the bakers.

The house in Langhorn Close was arranged over three storeys with a kitchen, toilet and bathroom downstairs, then the stairs up to the second floor where there was a sitting room and Joan's bedroom. Another flight of stairs led to Cheryl's bedroom – the untidiest room in the house – another bathroom and the boys' bedroom, which Andrew shared with young Garry. Cheryl has always looked out for her younger brother in a big sister sort of way. Garry junior followed her to the same schools and took part in modelling and dance classes. One family friend observed, 'He was always a very intelligent lad.' The two eldest children, Joe and Gillian, soon moved into their own homes, although they stayed local. Joe and his family still live on the estate. Three older siblings meant that Cheryl always had to stick up for herself, as her big brothers would lark about and hang her upside down from the nearest balcony. She had to learn how to fight from a very early age – a talent that would stay with her.

The family's happy, boisterous times did not last. Andrew, who, just three years older, is closest in age to Cheryl, officially became a young criminal at the age of thirteen when he was handed his first conviction for theft. Over the years he was in court so many times the family could be forgiven for losing count, for the figure is more than seventy convictions in the last fifteen years. Andrew's problem is a chronic addiction to glue-sniffing. Cheryl would lie awake into the early hours hoping he would make it home safely. He usually made it, infusing the whole house with the stench of glue as he stumbled to bed. Cheryl cannot stand the smell of glue. It may seem strange to mention the grim world of glue-sniffing and petty crime in the same breath as an innocent young girl dancing and acting, but this was the daily reality of Cheryl's life.

Cheryl's new home was convenient for dashing to all parts of the city to continue her 'education' in dance and performance. It was only five minutes' walk away from St Lawrence's but Cheryl was about to start at a comprehensive school that was much nearer the old house. Walker School (renamed Walker Technology College in 2000) had been on its site in Middle Street since the early 1930s and had a dated air about it when Cheryl joined in September 1994.

Cheryl found herself placed in Grainger House, named after one of the most famous men of Newcastle and familiar to anyone walking around the city. Richard Grainger was the builder turned property magnate responsible for much of the redevelopment of Newcastle city centre. When you step off the train at Central Station, you walk straight into the area known as Grainger Town. Walker School has two other houses, one named after Grainger's architect, John Dobson, and the other in honour of the locomotive pioneer Robert Stephenson.

By her own admission Cheryl was not that keen on school. Her dancing, however, was going from strength to strength. Ballet, after the experience of London, was no longer the way forward. She stopped making the journey to Margaret Waite's school when she was twelve and decided to concentrate on ballroom and Latin dancing competitions. Margaret had loved teaching Cheryl and was very disappointed when she moved on. She recalls that Cheryl had sailed through many of the certificates that youngsters can obtain. One of her final exams saw her being 'highly commended' in the 'pre-elementary' certificate. Margaret expected Cheryl to do well in the future and says, 'She was just a great little entertainer.'

Cheryl had reached the stage where she needed a partner to progress. Boys were always at a premium and nobody stood out as suitable at the Noreen Campbell Dance School, so Joan decided to try the Newcastle Dance Centre in Grainger Park Road, which was well known in the city.

The school is run by debonair Michael Conway, a contemporary and old friend of Len Goodman, the chairman of the judges on *Strictly Come Dancing*, and Michael's wife, Mavis Whiteside, whose parents, Florence Newbegin and Jack Whiteside, opened the centre seventy years ago when it was known as the Newbegin-Whiteside School of Dance. Florence Newbegin began teaching dance in Newcastle in 1931 when she opened her first school in the attic of her parents' house. The centre has been at its current premises since 1975.

Both Florence and Mavis were champion dancers and even danced against each other in the final of the British Professional Sequence Championships in 1963. Mavis won. Family tradition is quite common in dance. Mavis and Michael's daughter, Hayley Conway, is one of the best-known choreographers and teachers in the North-East and would later play an important role in Cheryl's development. She is the third generation, after grandmother and mother, to win one of the annual Carl Alan awards, the Oscars of the dance world.

Mavis Whiteside, still teaching in her elegant late seventies, remembers meeting Cheryl for the first time. 'She came in for an interview with the lovely face and the dimples and we said she should come to us. Then we found her a lovely boy partner.'

The lovely boy in question was a dapper youngster called James Richardson. Cheryl and James clicked from the very beginning. Together, they had a magic quality way beyond their years. Hayley Conway observed, 'James was incredible. He was a real live wire and he had these fabulous facial expressions. When he and Cheryl used to have their lessons there was a real buzz around them. You would see the other teachers looking over at them because they had star quality. James was very stylish and charismatic. Cheryl used to love that because she knew the job of the female dancer was to provide the glamour. Even when they were young, they wanted to dance like older couples. I think the best word to describe them is intense. They were very intense.'

The Friday evening lesson was a compulsory practice. Joan would come with Cheryl on the bus from Byker and settle down in the centre's coffee bar on the top floor while Cheryl danced with

James. Michael Conway always found time for a word with Joan: 'She was a wonderful little lady and always looked after Cheryl. She is what we would call a real good Newcastle Geordie.'

Downstairs, in the ballroom, James and Cheryl would practise for a competition under the watchful eyes of Michael and Mavis, who would walk around, correcting them as they swirled around the floor. Michael explains, 'Competitions are a serious thing and you have to practise. Dancing is a repetition thing. Cheryl came to us specifically as a competitor and she excelled in Ballroom and, in particular, Latin. It's all about what happens inside and how you project yourself. Cheryl was very pretty and very good. Just turn the music on and Cheryl would perform. It was like switching a light bulb on. You can't teach it. It's just there.

'The thing about Cheryl was that she was "with" you all the time. She was never away like some kids, looking out the window during class. She listened to everything you said. She used to get mad with James sometimes because he would do his own little bits, ad-lib dancing because he was a natural and confident as well.'

James and Cheryl took their dancing very seriously. They would also get together once a week for more practice at the Noreen Campbell Dance School in Walkergate. There they were often joined by another keen young couple, Amy and Chris, who were friendly rivals. Years later Cheryl would bump into Chris Park again when they were both finalists on *Popstars: The Rivals* – yet another example of the small world of the entertainment business, particularly in Newcastle.

Cheryl was fortunate to be paired with James. Together they were so accomplished that they won the prestigious Northern Counties Championship and countless other competitions. Joan would always make sure that Cheryl was immaculately groomed, and, as Hayley Conway puts it, 'dressed tastefully'. Hayley recalls, 'She used to look lovely with her jet black hair and olive skin. And James was very dark and dapper as well. A teacher can develop a dancer's technique but you can't teach style and panache. James was quite a quiet boy and Cheryl would say, "Come on James" to him but when they got on the floor they were amazing.'

When they were eleven, they went to compete in the finals of the juvenile section of the National Championships held every May in Blackpool, the Olympics of dancing and the biggest competition of its kind in the world. Cheryl and James reached the last sixteen at the famous Tower Ballroom, which was a fine achievement for a young girl from a poor background with no family connection to dancing. It's easy to forget, but before *Strictly Come Dancing* such devotion to sequins and salsa would have been regarded as supremely naff and Cheryl has always kept pretty quiet about her dancing prowess as a child – quite simply, she was a champion dancer. Michael Conway says, 'She oozed talent.' How would Cheryl fare now if she took part in *Strictly Come Dancing?* Michael is in no doubt: 'She'd murder them!'

Closer to home, Cheryl and James put on a demonstration as part of the Newcastle Free Festival held at the newly refurbished Theatre Royal in Grainger Town. The Grade I Listed building, which opened in 1837, is a Newcastle landmark and one of the great theatres of Britain. They danced salsa to traditional music played by a Peruvian trio of brothers called Apu (Sacred Mountain), who settled in Newcastle and regard the city as their home despite performing all over the world. They still play some days outside the Monument in the heart of the city.

Cheryl's partnership with James also gave her the opportunity to perform on television for the first time when they were chosen to appear on the Michael Barrymore primetime show *My Kind of People* in 1995 when she was twelve. History and controversy have tended to obscure the fact that Barrymore was, for a few years, the biggest name in light entertainment. The audition process for his shows was pretty similar to the talent contests and further evidence of how much Cheryl's early career was useful preparation for the reality television shows in her future. She and James had to undergo a rigorous audition process. Hayley Conway remembers it well: 'Initially, I think they chose them because they were like little professionals with their facial expressions and the passion of their performance. I think they thought it would be quite funny to see these little people behave like adults. But when they started to perform and get further along the audition process, I think everyone realized that it wasn't a joke and these kids were really talented.'

James, in particular, proved himself television gold. Michael recalls, 'James had some wonderful expressions. He really used to feel the music in his hand and Michael Barrymore picked up on this. He would imitate James and take him off. People thought they were so good, he had them back again.'

If they were eleven or twelve today, Cheryl and James would have been ideal material for the popular *Britain's Got Talent* show run by Simon Cowell. In 2008 a pair of chirpy youngsters called Cheeky Monkeys proved so popular dancing rock 'n' roll that they made the final. 'Cheryl and James would have wiped the floor with them,' says Hayley.

At the age of twelve, Cheryl and James's partnership hit the rocks for a reason that affects many young dancers. Girls of this age suddenly become taller than the boys and that is a disaster for a dancing team. Michael observes, 'It's a shame they grew up. It's happened to us a few times. The girls get to eleven or twelve and shoot away from the boys. The boys gradually catch them up between fourteen and sixteen but then it's too late.'

Cheryl tried teaming up with a couple of taller boys but did not really gel with them. It was time to call a halt to her career as a competition dancer. James Richardson decided against seeking fame and has settled in Cramlington, where he is a fitness instructor. For Cheryl, however, a new ambition was taking shape: she wanted to be a singer. Joan told Mavis Whiteside, 'Our Cheryl is going to be a pop star.'

3

Metroland

By the time she was a teenager, Cheryl Tweedy had amassed a wide range of experience. Not many thirteen-year-olds could boast her track record: she had been a successful child model, paraded in fashion shows, won many dancing titles, attended the Royal Ballet's summer school, appeared several times on television and been cast in musical shows. Cheryl was not at one of the fancy stage schools in London where future stars like Emma Bunton and Amy Winehouse were taking their first steps to stardom. Nor did Cheryl have the opportunities that came the way of major young talent in the United States. Stars of the future, including Britney Spears, Justin Timberlake and Christina Aguilera, spent the early nineties receiving a million-dollar show business education courtesy of the Disney show *The Mickey Mouse Club*.

Cheryl, meanwhile, was hopping on the number 12 bus to Walker School. She was also facing up to life without her elder brother Andrew. At the age of sixteen, he was jailed for the first time, receiving a six-year sentence for stabbing two students. He would serve four.

On the days when she did not fancy going to school, Cheryl would leave the house as usual, say goodbye to her mother and wander down to spend the day at her friend Lorna's house. Lorna Reid was her best friend. Like Cheryl, Lorna had a couple of older brothers and had grown up in the neighbourhood. She was taller than Cheryl and had curly, blonde hair. A male school friend observes, 'Lorna was attractive and that but I wouldn't put her in the same league as Cheryl. There's not many that could compete is there? But Lorna was nice. They used to go everywhere together, do everything just about, but Cheryl was the boss.'

The school uniform was the giveaway that Cheryl was supposed to be in class as she meandered along Heaton Park Road looking in the shop windows. She would often exchange a laugh and a bit of banter with Jason Mack, the boss of the furniture store. Jason recalls, 'Sometimes she would pop in and she would ask questions like, "How much is this and how much is that?" She was only about twelve or thirteen and she was a cheeky thing. I used to wag my finger at her and say, "What do you want to know that for, you live with your mam!" Or, "You should be at school, cheeky chops."' It was nothing more than a little exchange to put a smile on your face on a grey day. Cheryl could not possibly know then that Jason, in a few years' time, would have a profound effect on her young life. Then, he just recognized Cheryl as the kid sister of Joe Tweedy whom he used to bump into walking the family dog, Monty, a Staffordshire bull terrier, in the local park.

Monty was quite a character and was often trying the patience of the Tweedy family. One Christmas morning they came downstairs to discover all the presents round the tree in a dreadful state with the wrapping torn to shreds and the gifts lying all over the place. Early thoughts that burglars had ransacked the room were quickly forgotten when they spied a very guilty-looking Staffie. Cheryl, who loved Monty, later recalled, 'I think he was looking for his own present – some bones. He'd chewed off all the paper. He was mental.'

School continued to drag for Cheryl, impatient to pursue her pop star ambitions. Her school reports praised her ability but suggested she preferred talking to her friends to doing any work. Cheryl also recalled the headmaster, Dr John Brodie, once telling her, 'It'll be interesting to see what you do in your life, Miss Tweedy.' He could not have guessed.

Her prospects were certainly looked on with more enthusiasm by an ambitious local management company, AIM Music, run by two former college friends, Andrew Falconer and Peter White, who went to North Tyneside College. After graduating, they started performing together. 'We did a clown show and that's how it started,' recalls Peter. Originally they had formed a company specializing in children's entertainment called Bucket and Spade Productions but Drew, as his friends called him, wanted to branch into music with a view to discovering promising talent in Newcastle. He was struck by the success of Take That, who had come out of Manchester, and saw no reason why the North-East could not produce a similar boy band.

The two college friends were like Little and Large. Drew was short, quiet and unassuming. He wore glasses, T-shirts and baggy jeans. Peter, who had the air of a Big Friendly Giant about him, was making a name for himself as one of the best-known clowns in the area. 'I've got a huge head and a big beard' was his jolly way of describing himself. He was happy to let his partner develop the musical side of the company. He says candidly, 'To be frankly honest, music doesn't interest me whatsoever.'

Take That split in February 1996 so there was a vacancy at the top. Britain had also failed to produce a younger version of Madonna or Kylie so there was definitely a gap in the market for a young girl singer. The Spice Girls phenomenon began in the summer of that year so perhaps it was not a good time to promote a new girl band. Drew kept a close eye on talent contests and karaoke nights in case a star of the future reached for the microphone. He came across a very pretty teenager larking about with her friends at an open mic session at Metroland in Gateshead and promptly signed her up – Cheryl Tweedy was on her way.

Drew, who had also discovered a couple of local boy bands, was keen to bring his acts along gradually and hit upon the bright idea of arranging for them to appear on stage regularly at Metroland, which was the entertainment area of the MetroCentre in Gateshead. He realized that every weekend there would be a guaranteed audience for his acts and they could gain experience. He decided to approach Andy Bailey, the new general manager of the family entertainment complex and a man who did not suffer fools. Andy, who was in his late twenties, had cut his managerial teeth at a theme park in Essex. He freely admits that he is a 'bolshie sort of character' but he cared passionately about his 'park', as he called it, and was determined to make it a success.

Going to Metroland was like going to an enormous seaside pier in the middle of a shopping mall – Coney Island meets Brent Cross. The whole area covered nearly 80,000 square feet and included a funfair, an amusement arcade and slot machines – everything to keep kids amused while their parents went and spent some serious money at the shops. In August 1996 it went bust and was taken over by a company called Arlington Leisure, who brought in Andy: 'Metroland was in a shopping centre so it wasn't really a destination place like Alton Towers. Parents would drop their kids off and hit the shops.'

Andy was keen to improve the entertainment side and put in a new stage that he needed to fill. Right on cue, he was approached by Drew Falconer. Andy recalls, 'He offered me a fantastic deal. He wanted to get his acts on my stage so it was cheap. He would provide all the entertainment for weekends and school holidays. I can't remember exactly how many acts there were but the main two were Cheryl and a boy band called 3NM.

'It was totally non-profit-making from their point of view. It was perfect for both of us because we didn't have the money to spend on entertainment.'

The deal was struck for £80 per week for everything, although that amount was never paid because Andy always deducted the cost of providing meal vouchers for Cheryl and the other performers. 'I would provide food for everybody who was involved on any particular day. I would always ask who they were for and he would say, "3NM, Excape, Cheryl, Cheryl's mother" – that sort of thing. It maybe came to twenty vouchers so I would say that was going to cost me £40 and would deduct it from his fee.'

Cheryl began performing at Metroland during the October half-term in 1996 when she was thirteen. Peter White was working there as well, looking after the stage and entertaining the children. He and Cheryl became firm friends. He was very easy to get along with, was very solid and dependable and had a dry sense of humour that kept everyone's spirits up. Andy Bailey describes him as a 'lovely guy who doesn't rock the boat and is happy to take a back seat'. His partner, Drew, on the other hand, proved to be a bit of a headache for Andy Bailey: 'I spent a lot of time sorting out arguments between him and my senior staff.'

Peter White has a much more pragmatic view of his ex-partner: 'I was the good cop. He was the bad cop. A lot of people describe him as a bastard and, as I always said, "Yes, but he is the sort of bastard you want on your side."'

Metroland was no quiet Monday night at the local pub performing in front of two men and a dog. Andy observes, 'You would get a crowd ranging in size from a couple of hundred kids to 1,500. We used the acts most of the time as fill-ins during talent contests. We would hold Mister Metroland or Miss Metroland contests and these were very popular so those were the days when the audience was biggest.'

From the outset, he was impressed with Cheryl: 'She had a fantastic personality. She was very pleasant and polite, a very normal, everyday sort of girl. I would describe her as very unassuming. She never had a problem chatting to me – she wasn't a shy little girl. She got on well with everybody. Some of the kids who performed were up their own arse. I mean we would get fifteen- or sixteen-year-old kids who thought they were dead famous. We would have security escorting them to and from the rooms they got changed in and the kids would be screaming at them. One or two of them would be, like, a w***er, but never Cheryl.

'I was usually busy with other things but every so often I would watch some of the shows. Cheryl used to appear quite nervous to start with but then she would just get into it.'

Cheryl was getting used to performing in front of a thousand appreciative kids. She was also appearing at fêtes and fun days throughout the area. She was starting to get recognized – especially by young men – but, at the same time, she kept her eye on the main prize and made sure she improved.

Drew wanted to ensure Cheryl's act was as polished as possible and sought out a choreographer who would help devise the dance routines. The pop charts in the summer of 1998 were dominated by two new acts, who were fresh-faced, energetic and young – B*Witched, a group of Irish teenage sisters who reached number one with the catchy 'C'est La Vie', and a bouncy fifteen-year-old from Swindon, Billie Piper. It's easy to forget that Billie, as she was originally billed, was a huge teenage star with a 'chav' style imitated by thousands. Drew dreamed of that sort of success for his young protégée and started billing her as just 'Cheryl'.

Billie Piper was the template for Cheryl Tweedy. When Billie was born, her parents were sharing a two-bedroom flat in a dismal, grey three-storey block in Park South, a working-class council estate in one of the roughest areas of Swindon. Within a few months of her birth, the local newspaper carried stories reflecting the tough neighbourhood: a man was stabbed to death in the street by a crazed knifeman. The headline read: 'Nightmare at Knifepoint'. Another exclaimed, 'Petrol Bomb Night of Terror', recounting the circumstances of a Molotov cocktail being thrown into the garden of a disabled pensioner in the street. This was no place for a young baby.

Billie's father, Paul Piper, was a brickie turned builder who worked hard to improve his family's circumstances, while her mother, Mandy, sought to encourage her daughter's talents and ambitions at a very young age. Billie took acting classes as a child and started appearing on stage at the age of nine. She attended dancing classes twice a week at a local studio, where she had a reputation for taking it very seriously. She also had an agent and appeared in advertisements.

Billie's life was turned around when she won a place at the renowned Sylvia Young Theatre School in London, where her contemporaries included Amy Winehouse and Matt Willis of Busted. She lost her Swindon accent and became a highly polished young performer. She was 'discovered' when record company executive Hugh Goldsmith saw her in a commercial for *Smash Hits* magazine. He had no idea whether she could sing or not, but she had the look he wanted. He brought in a team of writers and choreographers to ensure that Billie was an instant success. Billie, like Cheryl, was, at this point, a far better dancer than singer.

Billie Piper from Swindon had youth, vitality and was devastatingly pretty with a smile that could light up the National Grid. Cheryl Tweedy from Newcastle also had these qualities. The Spice Girls had brought 'Girl Power' to the table but their teens were now behind them. Billie Piper was the real thing. Perhaps Cheryl could be the next real thing.

Drew Falconer heard of a go-ahead local choreographer who had worked with Ant and Dec and on *Top of the Pops*. It was Hayley Conway, who recalls, 'He called and said, "I've got this girl who is a singer, her name is Cheryl and I want to bring her along and I want you to do some choreography for her. And can you supply me with some backing dancers for her?"'

Hayley had no idea that this Cheryl was, in fact, the Newcastle Dance Centre's former champion dancer. She recalls, 'In she came and we just laughed. "I know you!" she said. Her manager looked puzzled but I told him that I did, in fact, remember Cheryl from dancing lessons and it was all "How are you?" sort of stuff. After that I said, "Let me hear your songs."'

Cheryl had all her own songs. She would work on original material with Drew's songwriting pals and make demos at a small studio in Ryton, on the western outskirts. It was part of the game plan to be the finished package: the songs, the choreography, the clothes, the image, the look. Everything needed to be just right. This strategy had worked for the Spice Girls, who had spent a year living in a grotty house in Maidenhead, rehearsing every day at nearby studios preparing to showcase their talents. Similarly, Billie Piper was introduced to the world as a carefully presented act. In the United States, Jive Records was spending $1 million preparing to launch Britney Spears on the world stage. No luck whatsoever was involved in these three acts starting off with huge number one records. Instead, it was the result of forward planning and intensive marketing.

That, hopefully, would be in the future for Cheryl. For now, Drew was determined to turn her into a star. Hayley says, 'I asked to hear her songs. She stood in front of the mirror, holding a water bottle as a microphone and just belted out a few tracks, just bopping around. I didn't know that she could sing that well. She was very hip hop-orientated then. Her hair was very dark and quite curly because perms and things like that were really in. She was wearing baggy clothing and she is not particularly tall so I remember her as this little whirlwind character. She just looked like every other kid in a tracksuit, apart from being very beautiful.'

Hayley was hired. She already knew that Cheryl could dance brilliantly so it was a case of devising the choreography for the half-dozen or so tracks that represented her showcase. Hayley decided to go with a sporty, American feel and brought in two of the teenage girls from the centre to act as backing dancers. They all wore big ice hockey tops and knee pads. 'I worked out about half a dozen routines for the girls and synchronized them with Cheryl and then they went to Metroland and practised them during one of her regular spots there.'

Cheryl was rehearsing for what might have been her big chance – a series of concerts starting in South Shields where she, and some other local acts, would be supporting Ultimate Kaos, a London boy band that had already enjoyed some chart success. Cheryl started popping over to the centre a couple of times a week after school to rehearse seriously for the event. Hayley always found her easy to work with, primarily because she took direction so well, a legacy of all that practice for competitions she had done in previous years. 'With some artists you literally have to say, "Lift your arm here, put your arm there, turn your shoulder this way, look that way." There was none of that. It just wasn't necessary. If I said to Cheryl, "Four walks that way, stand for eight counts, do something," she would just do it – no problem. Dancing is a lot about how you put things together in your brain and how you understand what your teacher or choreographer is asking you to do. Cheryl got it every time.'

Cheryl was, as a teenager, already displaying a no-nonsense approach. Hayley observes, 'If she didn't want to do something, she would say, "I don't want to do that". A lot of teenagers would beat about the bush but she would be straight in there. She was not rude at all but she would voice an opinion straight away.'

Hayley could not devise anything too elaborate or energetic for Cheryl to do because she had to sing and she always wanted to sing live. Hayley was impressed that Cheryl wanted to do that in the pop world where lip-synching was so prevalent. A rigorous dance routine is a sure sign that a singer is pretending to sing because it's physically impossible to do both. You cannot sing when you are gasping for breath and the silly attached headset microphones fool absolutely no one these days. They are never switched on.

Cheryl, however, was always keen to learn new dance routines and was particularly keen on hip hop moves. During one session at the centre she asked Hayley to show her some moves: 'I was the teacher but she made me dance for her. I told her that she couldn't do them because she had to sing but she said, "I don't care, just show me." She was very eager to try the moves and I had to try to slow her down.'

On the day of the event, Hayley, who was also working with another group there, asked Cheryl if she needed to rehearse again. The reply spoke volumes for Cheryl's confidence and the way she was all business when it came to performing. She said, 'No, I can do it. No problem.' This attitude has always served her well.

The pop world is an amazingly small one. Ultimate Kaos, the headline act, were a bunch of five street-smart black teenagers who had been discovered in 1992 by Simon Cowell, then on the lookout for a new Jackson Five. The lead singer, Haydon Eshun, was nine years old. Cowell originally called them Chaos and they released just one record in that first year, 'Farewell My Summer Love', a 1984 top ten hit for Michael Jackson. They failed to replicate his success, peaking in the UK charts at number 55.

A name change and some restyling saw Ultimate Kaos emerge two years later and begin to gain wider recognition, supporting Take That on tour, appearing on *Top of the Pops* and releasing their only album to date, *Kaos Theory*, in 1996. They proved more popular in Europe than in the UK, where chart success proved elusive, although one single, 'Some Girls', reached number nine. Haydon first met Cheryl when they were both fifteen. They immediately hit it off and had one or two dates but they were both very young and they were hanging out together more than anything else. Rumours would emerge about them having a real romance after Cheryl became famous, but that was in the future. She once admitted having a crush on Haydon when she was nine but nothing more than that.

Haydon, the youngest in the band, disappeared from public

view when the band split towards the end of 1999 but re-emerged in the hit reality series *Reborn in the USA*, in which forgotten pop stars sought to revive their careers. The winner was Tony Hadley, the lead singer of Spandau Ballet. Haydon came in a very respectable fourth. The series had some effect in that he was shortlisted to sing the UK entry for the Eurovision Song Contest in 2005 but missed out to Javine, the girl who, controversially, just missed being chosen for Girls Aloud. He is still only twenty-six, the same age as Cheryl, so it's not too late for stardom. He has now signed to indie label Greengrass Records and is recording again.

For the big concert Cheryl looked a million dollars and more. Hayley Conway observes, 'She was just so naturally pretty even wearing big jumpers and a hockey top. She didn't have any lipstick or anything like that and her hair was scraped back with a fringe but she had these lovely olive eyes and beautiful skin. It was like she was saying, "This is how I am. If you don't like me, then tough." But she was absolutely stunning.' Cheryl's ability to look good in anything was a bonus because there was little money around to spend on costumes. Fortunately, Hayley was adept at styling her girls with next to no budget. 'It's about belief. It was like putting a sack on and saying, "This looks good everybody, believe me", and everyone would go "Yes". Cheryl looked stunning.'

Another young singer in Newcastle at the time, Michelle Heaton, later of Liberty X, was at the concert and remembers Cheryl 'outshining' the headline act, Ultimate Kaos, and being rapturously received by the audience. That may have had something to do with her being a local lass. Newcastle has always been one hundred per cent behind Cheryl.

4

Something Special

Drew Falconer's plans for Cheryl stretched far beyond Metroland. When the hoped-for recording contract did not arrive after the Ultimate Kaos tour, he started booking her into gigs in London. Peter White, who found himself nominated as chauffeur to the budding star, recalls, 'A lot of promoters down in London seemed to want her to be another Billie Piper because she was that young.' Drew had friends who were promoters in the London area and they would arrange appearances at various clubs, usually in the West End or Covent Garden. Each one was a potential showcase because you never knew when a scout for a record company might be in the audience.

Cheryl was still just fifteen. Leaving Langhorn Close for a trip to perform in London, when all your friends are traipsing home from Walker School for a night in front of the telly, was an extremely glamorous prospect for a young teenager even if the reality was yet another slog down the M1 in the back of Peter's Rover, chatting to the designated chaperone for the night. Sometimes that would be elder sister Gillian, or perhaps a family friend. Occasionally, Drew would travel with them but usually he was happy to let Peter deal with it. Cheryl's mother, who had made so many journeys to escort her daughter to hundreds of classes, competitions and concerts, was happy to let someone else take charge for a change. A hug for luck and a wave at the back door and she could step back and let someone else take over while she cooked tea for her youngest son, Garry.

Team Tweedy had a happy routine. Usually Cheryl would be booked in for two nights at a couple of clubs. They would stay the one night between gigs, usually at a Travel Inn. Peter would sleep in one room while Cheryl and the chaperone for the event had another. Any money they made would be ploughed straight back into the cost of 'Cheryl', paying for petrol, the rooms and food.

After the gig they would always stop for a McDonald's. It was Cheryl's reward and a compulsory stop as far as she was concerned. She always ordered a McChicken with extra mayonnaise. Peter observes, 'If it didn't have extra mayonnaise, it went back.' Cheryl was a healthy teenager with a healthy appetite. Worries about her fluctuating weight were well in the future. The need for a McChicken did backfire once when they stopped in Wembley only to discover the car had been broken into and all the music stolen while they were eating.

Occasionally they had time for a treat. The funniest film of late 1998 was *There's Something About Mary*, starring Ben Stiller and Cameron Diaz, whose use of a special hair gel has become almost iconic. They had the chance to slip into a West End cinema before a club gig. Cheryl loved it. Despite that diversion, this was no easy path to success and Peter was acutely aware of Cheryl's age. 'She was very young and a girl at that age can be very impressionable. Girls get really excited about things and I tried to balance things for her. I was the man who always had to tell Cheryl that hopefully this was what was going to happen. Drew was more "this is *going* to happen".

'All I saw was a happy, wee lass having a reasonably good time. But I am sure at any point there were highs and lows. She put up with a lot to try to become successful. Going up and down to London, do this, do that – you know. She could be older than her years sometimes and then younger than her years sometimes. She was basically a kid but I think she always, in a way, knew what she wanted. To me it was too much pressure for anybody. I wouldn't wish on my own kids what she went through. I think it must have been an absolute nightmare. But I think she learned a hell of a lot about the business, the good side and the bad side. It probably made her a better person.'

Cheryl could not wait to leave school. Her career at Walker School was hardly distinguished – a mixture of detention, suspension and truancy. She scraped by academically by cheating. Her method was to look sneakily at the brainier pupils' homework books and copy out their answers. She revealed to *OK!*: 'The geeks used to try to hide their work but I was friendly to them and so they didn't mind.' She managed to avoid getting caught, claiming that she was too crafty for that. She was not so fortunate with other misdemeanours, namely fighting and swearing, and the detention centre was almost a second home.

She was suspended for fighting with a boy at school, explaining to *Top of the Pops* magazine, 'He spat at me, so I slapped him.' On another occasion she was sent home for two weeks after a furious row on the bus with a classmate who kicked her in the leg. Cheryl's colourful language in the ensuing argument led to a complaint by a member of the public: 'The boy didn't get in trouble. I wasn't impressed.' These two incidents reveal that Cheryl was not joking when she said she learned how to fight at the hands of her elder brothers. She has a keenly developed sense of sticking up for herself come what may and is fearless when riled. She does not back down and she does not apologize.

Walker's current headmaster, Dr Steve Gater, was not at the school when Cheryl Tweedy was in attendance. Unsurprisingly, he is fed up with being wrongly identified as her headmaster and misquoted as the oracle on all things to do with Cheryl when he has never taught her or met her. He does, however, hope that one day she will return to the school and offer hope and inspiration to the pupils there. The school has undergone great improvements in the last ten years and will soon be moving to a new site, where one of his ambitions is to expand the arts department. Children at Walker in the future may have the chance to explore their talents in a way that was denied Cheryl. She had to rely on the patience and persistence of her mother to ferry her around to classes all over the city.

Cheryl sums up her school career simply: 'I was awful.' If she had knuckled down academically then she would have liked to have become a member of CSI (Crime Scene Investigation): 'I'd have loved to have gone into forensic detective work. I find it fascinating, like which way the blood is splattered and stuff.' She celebrated her sixteenth birthday just as they were breaking for the summer holiday and did not hesitate in ditching her school uniform for ever. Always independent in spirit, she wanted to earn her own money. She never again wanted to ask the Man from the Provident for the money to buy some clothes. This loan agent, known to all as the 'provi man', would come to houses on the poorer estates and arrange loans for the residents, who would then pay it back weekly. A teenage girl like Cheryl would be an ideal candidate, not thinking twice about borrowing money in order to get the bus down to the Eldon Square shopping centre to spend it in one afternoon at Topshop or River Island.

Was there ever going to be a time when money, or the lack of it, was not going to be a major issue in Cheryl's life? She was still moving forward with Drew Falconer and AIM Music but not fast enough for her liking. And she was not making any real money from the trips to London and singing at Metroland. She needed a job. Her dilemma was to find something that would have enough flexibility to allow her to pursue her ambitions. Her best friend Lorna was already working part time at the newly opened JJ's café in the Heaton Road, just a few hundred yards from Cheryl's house. It sounded ideal. At least she might earn enough money to buy clothes for her stage performances.

JJ's was one of those friendly neighbourhood cafés that everyone loves, a million miles away from the frothy interiors of Starbuck's and Costa. No lattes, no skinny cappuccinos, no raspberry and white chocolate muffins. At JJ's, named after the owner's niece, a working man could start his day with a cup of tea and a bacon butty and feel that all was right with the world. It was a cut above the average greasy spoon and was awarded a prize as the region's Best Café, post-Cheryl, in 2002.

The café's owner, Nupi Bedi, remembers the first time he met Cheryl in July 1999, just after her sixteenth birthday: 'She asked me for a job. I told her, "Make an application, write what you can do for me." All she said was, "I am so pretty that you are going to employ me." She really was a cheeky person, very cheeky and funny. She got the job.'

Cheryl was not employee-of-the-month material but she never failed to brighten everyone up. She became custodian of the tea urn and coffee machine. Nupi laughs, 'She was the best tea maker ever.' Cheryl, however, was not that keen on waiting on tables, although she was very popular with the customers. Perhaps her reluctance to look after tables was not simply a teenage desire to do the minimum at work. Nupi noticed that despite the cheeky demeanour, Cheryl displayed a certain reticence. 'She could be very, very shy,' he observes. She had good reason to be shy with one particular customer who had an unsavoury fascination with her feet. She told Q magazine, 'I wore open-toed sandals and he said he loved my feet. He was about thirty, sweaty and had spit in the corner of his mouth. I ran home and my brother came out to find him. He would have killed him!'

Nupi owned another café, the Quayside Café, in Queen Street in the new development on the Newcastle side of the Tyne, across from The Sage, the impressive international centre for music. Cheryl would sometimes do shifts at the Quayside, where the clientele was much more office worker and tourist. Her sister Gillian would also work there from time to time and even mother Joan would earn a few extra pounds when money was tight. 'Gillian was a very pleasant young lady.' Nupi knew all the family and liked them. The sisters shared a mischievous sense of fun. Nupi remembers once giving them a lift: 'I had a van at the time and I told them, "You will have to sit in the back." And they were fine about it and both sat in the back. Suddenly I could smell something horrid. Cheryl had let a stink bomb off. They were laughing away.'

Cheryl has always been close to Gillian, who is four years older and who, like Joan, became a mother at a young age. Peter White always remembers her as being fun when she joined them on trips to London. Her house in the nearby Chillingham Road became a haven for Cheryl when she needed a break from home. Gillian was also a useful listener when Cheryl wanted to talk about boys. Soon after she started work in the café, she flirted with a young plumber working on a nearby building site. Steve Thornton started popping in to JJ's so he could chat with the girl he thought had 'the face of an angel'. After spending what he later described as a fortune buying sandwiches, he managed to persuade Cheryl to join him for a coffee and, subsequently, they started dating.

Their first date ended in a kiss but Steve would later make some extravagant sexual claims to the *News of the World*. He claimed she performed a seductive strip to the sound of Britney Spears' hit '. . . Baby One More Time'. On another occasion, he says she blindfolded him before revealing a cowboy hat and promising him 'the ride of his life'. All good knock-about stuff, although Cheryl says they only ever had three dates. Steve was never going to be the love of her life but they had good fun together until just before Christmas when Cheryl was tempted by someone she found far more attractive. She soon stopped taking poor Steve's calls and he says he was heartbroken.

Cheryl showed no sign of giving up her quest for stardom despite her big break remaining disappointingly elusive. She was consumed with music: singing, rehearsing, performing and writing song lyrics. Nupi recalls how much she seemed to totally love music and become alive with it: 'Everything was music. I remember one day she said, "I am going to sing to you." She actually sang there in the café and she was very emotional and I told her how really good she was. I knew she was going to make it then.'

Sometimes Nupi would give her a lift out to the studio in Ryton where she would rehearse and record material, which she would later try out at Metroland. One weekend she sang a new song called 'Something Special', which made the park's boss Andy Bailey sit up and take notice. He recalls, 'I remember so well her singing it on stage and I loved it. It was a really nice song so I asked her to put it on a CD for me. And that's what she did.'

This original recording by 'Cheryl' might be a valuable collectors' item today. The song sounds a little dated but, at the time, it was contemporary pop, the sort of record that Kylie Minogue might easily have made. Cheryl's voice is clear and strong and is powerful early proof that she was a very accomplished singer well before Girls Aloud and does not need four other girls to make her sound good. Hayley Conway was impressed when she heard her.

'Her voice was very strong and quite earthy, quite a deep voice. I think there was a hint of soul to it.'

Just in case all the plaudits from the people around her were going to her head, Cheryl always had Peter White to bring her back down to earth: 'I would always tell her, "I can't stand this sort of music."' Sometimes when Peter drove her to the studios he was roped in as an unofficial cheerleader. An engineer would jump up and down and exclaim, 'She's doing great' in Peter's direction. 'Aye,' would come the reply, 'it sounds all right to me.' Peter's sober, dispassionate approach was one of the reasons Cheryl never suffered from what he calls 'a swelling of the head'.

Cheryl was chuffed when Peter's fiancée, Kelly, who also worked at Metroland, asked her if she would be a bridesmaid at their wedding. Drew Falconer was best man and it was one of the last times that Team Tweedy got together for a celebration. Cheryl was joined by a 'little' bridesmaid, a young cousin of Kelly's, who, a couple of years later, unwittingly provided an insight into Cheryl's good heart. Peter explains, 'My mother-in-law was talking to her when she came down to visit Metroland after she became well known. She explained to Cheryl that my wife's little cousin had told friends that she knew Cheryl and that Cheryl had been at my wedding. Her friends had started bullying her about it so Cheryl sent her a signed picture and a little note saying that she was at the wedding and the little girl was not lying. It was a very kind thing to do and I thought it was great of her to do that. Cheryl could become quite emotional about things and would get upset. It's not put on.'

5

Jason

Cheryl had always had a bit of a crush on Jason Mack, although he never realized it. He was quite stocky and athletic, with a twinkle in his eye and a ready smile. He also looked young for his twenty-seven years. Cheryl was barely a teenager and too immature to do anything about it when she first bumped into Jason on those days she decided against school. By the time she was sixteen, however, she had the cheek and the confidence to have a go. Jason was in a local bar one night, a few weeks before the millennium, when his mobile phone rang. To his surprise, it was Cheryl, who had never phoned him before. He recalls, 'I don't even know how she got my number. But she just phoned us up and asked if I would come up and see her at her mam's. So I left the bar, went to her mam's and she was there with her sister Gillian and it just went from there really.'

Chivalrously, Jason does not want to say what went on that night but it was the start of what would be the first proper love affair of Cheryl's life. It's a slightly grey area as to whether she was still going out with Steve Thornton at this point but she was soon established in an exclusive relationship with Jason, who was eleven years her senior. The age gap made no difference.

If she had known that Jason was already dabbling too much in drugs, perhaps Cheryl might have thought twice about making the call. His liking for cocaine was already having a detrimental effect on his business and private life. His last relationship had suffered because of it: 'I was living with a girl in Byker but things started to get out of hand with the cocaine and that's when the relationship sort of fell to bits. I was just coming in from work, getting a shower, getting a shave, going out, snorting coke, drinking, going for meals and it just fell to bits and I wasn't really bothered at the time.'

Getting together with the prettiest girl in the neighbourhood was the boost Jason needed. He explains, 'I didn't have any money at the time. My last relationship was on the rocks, my business was on the rocks so I was just on the slippery slope when I got with Cheryl.' He can hardly believe it today, observing, 'She could have had her pick of any man, yet chose me.'

Jason and Cheryl celebrated the new millennium full of optimism for their future and decided to see in 2000 at an all-night rave. They set off from the house in Heaton for the party in a warehouse on the quayside, which was fast becoming the most fashionable area of Newcastle. Cheryl walked through the door and immediately had second thoughts. 'She didn't like it,' recalls Jason. 'It had cost about £30 for a five-minute taxi ride. But when we got there, she went, "I want to go home. I want to see my mam for the New Year." So we got another taxi back home and ended up having a party at her mam's.' Family has always been of primary importance for Cheryl and it was no surprise that she realized she wanted to spend the occasion with her mother and her sister. Lorna came round with her two brothers, Darren and Robert. Joe popped in with his partner, Kerry Stewart. Andrew was still in jail.

After the New Year's celebrations, life soon took on a grim reality as Cheryl realized that there were three in her new relationship: Jason, herself and cocaine. Cheryl was not shocked by drugs but her experience with her brother Andrew had led to a lifelong, passionate hatred of them. Jason remembers that she had also already lost one school friend to a drugs overdose. She was not, however, going to give up on Jason. Instead, perhaps naively, she wanted to change him for the better.

Right away, she started to nag Jason: 'You don't need it, man. Why do you need that when you got me?' She had a point there, as Jason recognized. He agreed to put a stop to the coke and the couple settled into a reasonably comfortable routine. They had little money so they would stay in and watch TV or grab a DVD from the local store. Jason says, 'We used to sit and watch the soaps – *Coronation Street* and *EastEnders* – just like normal people.' They didn't go out much, occasionally venturing to the notorious Bigg Market, the hub of Newcastle nightlife, with Joe and Kerry. Cheryl did enjoy a drink and a cigarette but nothing excessive. 'I recall her drinking vodka and coke but I think it made her bad. She wasn't a big drinker.'

From the outset, Jason spent most of his time at Cheryl's home and says that he never had any problem with her mother, despite the age difference between himself and Cheryl. 'Her mam knew us; she had seen us about and knew who I was. She knew I lived local and knew Joe. I think she just accepted it.'

When Joan met Jason she, too, had no idea of the state he was in. Ostensibly, he was one of the more successful and eligible lads who lived locally. He was going off every day to his own business and all seemed well. He would pop into JJ's café for his breakfast when Cheryl was working. She always used to make sure her man had an extra bit of bacon on the sly to keep his strength up.

'I would go round to Cheryl's house just about every day, every night. As soon as I had finished work, I would go back to Cheryl's. I would always have my tea there. And I would have a bath.'

Jason still remembers settling down in front of the television to watch the very first episode of a new series called *Pop Idol*: 'We were just sitting watching it and Cheryl slapped us round the head and she says, "I'll be on there one day," and I said, "I don't doubt you, Cheryl." And she says, "I will. Watch. I'll be on there, one day. I will be famous." Those were her very words.'

Both families accepted that Jason and Cheryl were in a serious relationship. He was invited to leisurely family barbecues on weekends, sometimes at her father's house down near the old shipyards in Walker. Other times they would go to one of Joan's sisters who also lived locally. He enjoyed her family's company. Cheryl asked him to go with her to the crematorium when her nanna, Garry's mother, died.

One Sunday, they were invited for lunch at her mother's ex-husband Bing Leighton's home in Walker. Bing was now a well-known tattooist in the area and after the meal the three of them stayed in the kitchen discussing tattoos. Cheryl had decided to have her first tattoo and she had already picked out the design after spending hours agonizing over the choice. She wanted a tribal butterfly band, which was large, impressive and painful to have drawn on her lower back. She had also chosen one for Jason's upper arm, insisting that he have her name put on it. Jason describes it as resembling a red devil woman, a temptress in boots and suspenders. 'She picked it because it looked like her.' Underneath Bing drew the word 'Chez', for Cheryl.

In her home environment Cheryl was a typical teenager. She was very untidy, forever leaving clothes where she dropped them, and mixing in clean clothes with dirty ones. A friend who often visited recalls that the house would reverberate to her mother shouting, 'Cheryl, get this room tidy!' The room in question was decorated with posters on the wall of artists like Craig David and Kylie, as well as her favourite boy band, Damage. They were five young black singers from London who presented an urban alternative to the anaemic charms of Boyzone and Westlife. She especially liked their cover version of the classic Eric Clapton love song 'Wonderful Tonight'. Musically they reflected Cheryl's taste. Michelle Heaton recalled that Cheryl was really into R&B and liked to look 'the fly girl'.

While always the prettiest girl in the room, the teenage Cheryl was not the perfectly poised and groomed woman of today. She preferred to wear tracksuit bottoms and trainers and, most definitely, nothing pink. She wore very little make-up, perhaps a little lipstick or eyeliner if she was going out with her mother and sister or meeting up with friends, but she never spent two hours in front of a mirror. Jason used to say to her, 'You don't need make-up, man, you're beautiful enough.'

Cheryl's ambitions to be a performer remained undiminished. Peter White observes, 'It didn't matter where she was, she enjoyed performing.' It all seemed so certain. She revealed in *Dreams That Glitter*: 'There was just always something inside of me, almost like I knew that was my destiny, like there was no other option. I never had a Plan B . . .' Hayley Conway also felt that Cheryl had this sense of invincibility: 'She believed she could do anything. She had an absolute belief that this will be.'

She had begun appearing less at Metroland as London began to loom larger in the game plan. Jason became used to wishing her luck before she left for a trip south. But while Cheryl continued to seek her breakthrough, things were about to go downhill again for Jason. He was down to his last couple of thousand pounds but scraped together enough to buy out his partner in the furniture store and set about kick-starting the business. Nothing went right, however, and within a couple of months he was broke. He admits, 'I basically went from having everything you could think of to living on a giro. I had never lived on a giro. I found it hard to live like that. Cheryl stuck by us when I didn't have a penny, not a penny.'

In a simple, yet frank admission of how his perceived failure affected him, Jason started taking drugs again. This time around, however, it was not cocaine: 'I started taking heroin because I wasn't getting any further forward.'

At this stage of his descent into drugs, Jason did not consider himself to be a full-blown junkie and was able to do some work, helped by his family. He managed to save a little money for Christmas 2001. He gave Cheryl £500 to go and buy herself something nice. Christmas Day arrived and Jason asked Cheryl what she had bought with the money, expecting her excitedly to reveal new clothes, jewellery and perhaps a CD or two.

'She said, "I'll show you" and handed me three neatly wrapped presents. The first was a Lacoste jumper worth £150. The second contained a Lacoste shirt worth about the same. The third was a Henry Lloyd designer jumper worth, again, at least £150. They were all for me. She had spent all the money on me.'

Cheryl had even used the change to buy some Versace Blue Jeans cologne for Jason. 'She liked that. She liked the Red Jeans for her and the blue one for me. It was my stocking filler.' Fortunately, Jason had already bought some smaller presents for Cheryl so she did not go empty-handed that Christmas.

Cheryl had turned seventeen and clearly doted on Jason but, still very young, her existence was turning into a living nightmare, which she has described as Groundhog Day, living the same day every day. Jason's world was becoming completely consumed by drug-taking. He had become a habitual user. After two or three months, people she knew started to tell Cheryl what was going on and Jason is convinced that so-called friends were trying to split them up.

Perhaps inevitably the rest of her world began to collapse. Her natural confidence and invincibility were cracking. The stress and strain of her relationship with Jason was a contributory factor but the fact that she was no nearer stardom was too. Friends noticed that she would get depressed, questioning whether she would ever make it. She was a teenage girl with a heroin addict for a boyfriend, making teas in a local café. She watched Will Young celebrate winning *Pop Idol* in 2001 and wished it was her. She could be forgiven for believing she was being left behind.

The Metroland gigs dried up altogether when Andy Bailey decided to end his deal with Cheryl's mentor, Drew Falconer. He is reluctant to reveal his reasons: 'I cancelled the agreement for various reasons that I don't want to go into. There were a lot of rumours going around and I am definitely positive they were not true. One of the problems was, for example, you would have a talent contest and so and so didn't win, immediately there was trouble. It was wrong but that's life. To be honest, I didn't have a lot of choice really but to drop him because of the parents and I was getting a lot of problems towards the end. It was getting worse and worse. There were rumblings for quite a while but it was just sort of rumblings. But, as time went on, eventually it was a case of we have got to draw a line here, Metroland has got to get disassociated with this.'

Metroland had served Cheryl very well. She had, in a way, served her apprenticeship in these boisterous, noisy surroundings. She learned to appreciate an audience, a quality that served her well on her trips to London and would continue to set her apart in the future when she achieved stardom. Peter White observes, 'After a show, she wouldn't be the sort of person who would like walk away and say to someone, "You lowlife, I can't talk to you." She had time for everybody who spoke to her.' She still came in to see old friends, especially Peter, who continued to work there until the venue closed for good in 2008. She was 'chuffed to bits' when his wife Kelly became pregnant.

She and Drew also parted company. The whole business is shrouded in mystery. She has never named him or talked about him in interviews. He has never talked about her or taken a bow as the man who guided her first tentative steps towards stardom. He does not feature in any Girls Aloud literature or television documentary about her rise to fame. Andrew Falconer is the man who discovered Cheryl Tweedy and nobody knows. He left the North-East altogether and went to start a new life in Blackpool. All his former partner Peter White will say is: 'Me and Drew haven't spoken for years. I haven't a clue how it fell apart between Cheryl and Drew. I have got a lot of issues but I won't go into them because I don't want to drag them up again.'

Leaving Drew Falconer was the least of Cheryl's concerns at this stage. Her personal life was swamping any professional life she hoped to have. The qualities she loved in Jason, especially the ability to laugh and have fun, were becoming a distant memory. He recalls sadly, 'There must have been something she liked but that went. When I started taking drugs, she said that I changed into a different person. I was down in the dumps a lot. I was in my own little world and nothing mattered.'

Shockingly, Jason now says that there were about a dozen crack dens within a half-mile radius of Cheryl's house. It is an astonishing, grizzly statistic and one that reveals the heartbreaking difficulty Cheryl faced trying to keep her boyfriend away from temptation. She was facing an impossible battle.

Every time Jason went out to smoke crack he would be offered a new phone number for a dealer. At any given time, he says he would have twenty numbers in his phone so that if one supplier was temporarily out then he could just try another ... and another. Cheryl desperately tried to help but the cycle was never-ending. 'Every time I left the house,' explains Jason, 'I wouldn't get to the end of the street before the phone would go and she would want to know what I was doing. She just wanted to keep us away. She knew that I was sneaking away to these places but she just couldn't catch us while I was doing it.'

Cheryl's own health started to suffer, so distressed was she at what was happening to Jason. He observes, 'She wasn't eating. She wasn't sleeping for worry, in case she had to identify me on a slab somewhere. She lost that much weight that people actually thought she was taking heroin with me.' Cheryl described herself at this point as a 'walking corpse', as the bathroom scales registered five stone eleven pounds. She was prescribed anti-depressants by her doctor, who arranged for Cheryl to see a counsellor to discuss her problems. She has revealed that she became clinically depressed.

By this time Jason had found a flat round the corner and Cheryl would sit indoors with the curtains closed, worrying away the hours and completely down. They were still spending a lot of time at her mother's house and Joan was becoming more alarmed about her daughter. She was no stranger to the anguish drugs could cause but this was the first time crack had come into their lives. The arguments and her daughter's declining health prompted her to confront Jason.

'We were having a big argument one day and her mam says to Cheryl, "You get out. I want to speak to him." Her mam sat us down and she says, "Jason, you've got a problem. What's the matter? Why are you like this?" And I wanted to tell her but I couldn't. Even her ma had seen the change in us. And she says, "I've heard the rumours. Is it true?" And I told her lies. I says, "No, it's not" instead of saying "Aye, it is." They call it the devil's dust because it steals your soul. It just takes everything away from you.'

As summer approached in 2002, the situation at home was getting progressively worse. The rows were bigger. The breaking point came when Jason went missing for a week. Cheryl knew he was spending his days in a drug den smoking crack. While he was gone, she noticed that some of Jason's clothes were missing, specifically the designer clothes she had bought for him at Christmas. He had taken them to sell to buy more heroin.

On his return she confronted him. Jason recalls, 'She just basically says, "It's me or the drugs. Take your pick 'cos I can't put up with it any more." So I walked away and that was it.'

Cheryl has had many reasons over the years to despise drugs

and all that they stand for. Here was another. She was rejected by a man she had loved in favour of heroin, in favour of a dingy drug den where death lurked in the corner. Joan went round to Jason's flat and packed up her daughter's belongings. Jason posted the few photographs he had of Cheryl through their letterbox and that was that. Their relationship was at an end.

PART TWO

GIRLS ALOUD

6

What If We Get In!

It was time for Cheryl to take stock. If she had been asked to fill in a questionnaire about her life when she turned eighteen, celebrating her birthday in an all-you-can-eat Chinese restaurant, it would have gone something like this: Job – No, although there was always Nupi and JJ's café and she had started working part-time as a cocktail waitress on the Tuxedo Princess, a floating nightclub on the Tyne. Career – In the toilet. Prospects – None. Boyfriend – Not ready for anything serious, although she was dating a barman who worked at the club. General demeanour – Fed up. Other remarks – The only way is up.

At least her health was improving. She was regaining the weight she had lost during the stress over Jason; her skin was getting back its lustre and her eyes their sparkle. Nights in front of the telly with younger brother Garry, Joan and Steve, the man in her mother's life who everyone thought was sound, was not exactly the exciting time she had foreseen for her late teens. Joan, however, caught the end of an advertisement for a new reality pop competition called *Popstars: The Rivals*. Cheryl sat glued to the TV screen so that she could get all the details the next time the ad appeared.

Although it feels like these sorts of shows have been around for years, this series would be only the third of its kind in the UK. The first, in 2001, was simply called *Popstars*. The original version of the show that would eventually become a worldwide phenomenon was developed in New Zealand in 1999 and reached British screens a couple of years later. The format has changed very little down the years – a panel of three judges plays good cop and bad cop to a series of nervous or insufferably smug contenders. After six weeks three girls and two boys were chosen to be the members of a new British band called Hear'Say. The power of television was never so well illustrated as when their easy listening 'Pure and Simple' became the fastest-selling debut record of all time.

The relatively short lifespan of Hear'Say, who split up for good in October 2002, just as the new show was getting into its stride, was used by some as an example of the flaw in the genre. Some commentators even suggested that reality pop shows were dead. They were mistaken. All the millions of viewers watching *Pop Idol* and, subsequently, *The X Factor* show the format to be almost unbeatable. It guarantees ratings and a massive-selling number one hit record. Everybody is happy. Hear'Say even had a number one album, *Popstars*, at the same time as their single – a rare double. The principal flaw of Hear'Say, in retrospect, was in the make-up of the group. Combining boys and girls just does not work in the long term. For some reason the general public does not seem to support mixed groups. The most successful pop groups of recent times are either boy bands like Take That and Westlife or girl bands like the Spice Girls. The problem is probably one of image creation. Hear'Say never properly created an image in the way that the Spice Girls had Girl Power or Westlife are nice Irish balladeers.

Another problem for Hear'Say was that the five original members did not gel together well and one, the actress Kym Marsh, mother of two young children, quit the group after less than eighteen months. Kym and the other two girls in the band, Suzanne Shaw and Myleene Klass, have enjoyed success post-Hear'Say while the boys, Danny Foster and Noel Sullivan, have, so far, sunk without trace. With hindsight, the lessons learned were that an all-girl group would have been better and that they needed to present a united front to the public – all for one and one for all.

Much was made of the success of the five runners-up in *Popstars*, who formed their own group, Liberty X. They included Michelle Heaton from Newcastle whom Cheryl knew from her days at

Metroland and would have expected to surpass in her pop career. Liberty X lasted for five years and had a string of hits, including one number one, 'Just a Little'. Once again the girls, Michelle and Jessica Taylor, wife of England cricketer Kevin Petersen, have outshone the boys. Coincidentally, all these reality winners prolong their fame by appearing in yet more reality shows, among them, Jessica – *Dancing on Ice*; Myleene – *I'm a Celebrity . . . Get Me Out of Here!* Suzanne – *Dancing on Ice*; and Michelle – *Celebrity Big Brother*.

Popstars was followed in 2001 by the first series of *Pop Idol*, which launched record company executive Simon Cowell on television. The whole world loves a villain and Cowell's slightly pantomime Mr Nasty persona soon found a place in the hearts of viewers who could not wait to hear a new put-down. Perversely, he became the biggest winner from the programme, ahead of the top three contestants on the show – Will Young, Gareth Gates and Darius Danesh – although they all had number one hit records within six months of the grand final.

Pop Idol, *Popstars* and *The X Factor* may all seem to be cut from the same cloth but they are, in fact, three different franchises. No sooner had Will Young finished the final bars of 'Evergreen' than auditions were under way for the next incarnation of *Popstars*. Someone seemed to have learned the lesson of the first series that mixed groups don't work because the new idea was to have auditions running for a boy band and a girl band and then put them in competition against one another. At the end of the run, two groups would be formed, one all-girl and one all-boy, which would both release a record aimed at the lucrative Christmas number one market – there's nothing like some manufactured rivalry to tickle up sales. The other big difference between this show and the first *Popstars* series was that the final decision would be made by the voting audience.

The role of the judges is of paramount importance in reality talent contests. Viewers are easily led and a negative comment can have a decisive effect on 'the dream'. Post-Cowell, the judges have become more important than the contestants. They gather more headlines and attract more comment, as Cheryl herself would discover in the years to come. The initial rumour regarding *Popstars:*

The Rivals was that the boys versus girls theme would be played out by Chris Evans against Geri Halliwell. The two had been linked romantically at one time, which would have given the show an additional edge. In the end Chris did not take part. Instead, there were three judges: Pete Waterman, Louis Walsh and Geri.

Pete Waterman, who had been a judge on *Pop Idol*, was one third of the eighties hit factory Stock, Aitken and Waterman. A brash, gruff, yet sociable former Mecca Ballroom DJ, Waterman had set about bringing three-minute classic pop records back into people's homes. He explained, 'We have taken pop music back to the people who buy records, not the journalists who preach to people.' He wanted to appeal to listeners with 'Woolworth's ears'.

These days Stock, Aitken and Waterman are probably most famous for launching the UK career of Kylie Minogue. When Kylie, then a star of *Neighbours*, had come over to the SAW studios near London Bridge, Waterman had forgotten all about the meeting he had arranged with her. He wasn't even in London, but relaxing at his Merseyside mansion, when Mike Stock rang him to ask if a small Antipodean called Kylie rang any bells. 'She's in town,' said Waterman helpfully, only to be told that she was sitting in reception and had to be on her way back to the airport in a few hours. 'She's expecting to do something with us now.' Without thinking, Waterman replied, 'She should be so lucky!' The rest, as they say, is history. It is one of pop's great stories and one Waterman never tires of telling.

Pete Waterman was to be the manager of the boy band. In charge of the girl band would be mischievous Irishman Louis Walsh, who had guided the careers of both Boyzone and Westlife. He recruited the members of Boyzone in 1993, advertising for prospective members of an Irish Take That. The subsequent open auditions, widely reported in the Irish press, gave him experience of this kind of talent show bedlam. He had also appeared as a judge on the Irish version of *Popstars* in 2001.

The world of these judging panels is a very small one. Pete Waterman, for instance, was an old associate of Simon Cowell from the eighties when Stock, Aitken and Waterman helped Cowell launch the career of Sinitta. It was Cowell who originally signed

Westlife to Sony BMG, installing Walsh as manager. He also persuaded Ronan Keating of Boyzone to act as joint manager, a neat commercial gimmick guaranteed to generate a few more column inches of precious publicity.

The third judge, presented as the mediator between the two combative male managers, was feisty former Spice Girl Geri Halliwell. Geri has received so much media attention over the years that her achievements have been overshadowed. At the time of *Popstars*, she had notched up six number one records with the Spice Girls and a further four as a solo artist. She was the first big-name judge to appear on a television talent contest. At this stage, Simon Cowell was not a TV superstar and it was Geri that set the precedent that Dannii Minogue and Cheryl herself would subsequently follow.

Besides her celebrity, Geri brought experience of auditioning to the table. She had lived the agony and the ecstasy of rejection and ultimate success when she was accepted as one of the Spice Girls. The auditions for the Spice Girls, which involved answering an advertisement and then turning up with hundreds of other hopefuls, were almost a forerunner for *Popstars* without the television element. Ironically, Geri broke all the rules to make her way into the final five. She had missed all the auditions leading up to the shortlist but managed to blag her way in. The Spice Girls' first manager, Chris Herbert, who set up the auditions, recalled that Geri was the weakest link both as a singer and a dancer: 'We wanted to create a band as a unit, so it did not matter so much if, individually, they weren't so strong.'

Cheryl was accepted for one of the London auditions of *Popstars: The Rivals* in Wembley in early August 2002. It was a long day. Her first job was to go into a big room to register and be given a sticker with an identification number – just like The Prisoner. Cheryl was L786, which means she was the 786th person to register in London. If, for instance, she had chosen to audition in Glasgow, her number would have begun with the letters GO. Cheryl was well back in the queue. The hopefuls gathered in a huge waiting area where they were called in blocks of ten and then filed in to audition in front of a panel consisting of two producers and one of

Pete Waterman's staff. Chris Park, who was GO018 and made the live finals, recalls, 'We sang to them and if you were good or horrific you got through. If you were just all right, you missed out. It was a funny mixture – ridiculously tone-deaf comical ones and others who they thought might have a chance of winning.'

They went back to the room to hang around until an executive from the programme came through to announce the numbers that had passed this initial stage. And then Cheryl faced yet another long wait for the chance to impress the real judges. The television audience does not see any of this. They only see the cheers of excitement as if it's all one big party. The whole day is more tedious than queuing to see a doctor at a hospital casualty unit, although the longer the wannabes sat around, the more tense the atmosphere became. The show's presenter, Davina McCall, hovered around to speak to any of the day's 'stories' that the show's researchers might have uncovered – in particular, this was when she pounced on any sob story of contestants hoping to triumph for the memory of their dead granddad or pet dog, or to make a better life for their dear mother or three children.

Pete Waterman's reaction to his first sight of Cheryl Tweedy is almost as legendary these days as his 'She should be so lucky' remark about Kylie. When Cheryl left the room after being told she would be seeing them again in London, he said, 'You would need to be dead if you didn't think she was stunning. My God!' Pete was more taken with Cheryl's looks than her singing abilities, and told her, 'You have the most beautiful eyes and skin I have ever seen in my life.'

Cheryl was well turned out for her big chance. She wore a new white floral patterned top that hugged her bust, topped with a heavy-set cross choker necklace that looked decidedly clunky. Her hair was styled in a straight and unelaborate way, and she smiled. She sang the S Club 7 number one 'Have You Ever', which was not the sort of music the R&B fan would normally have had anywhere near the sound system at home. She certainly would not have performed a strip for her boyfriend to this lukewarm chart topper. It was, however, a clever choice of song – not too demanding, current and a hit for a manufactured band. Cheryl confessed that she was almost sick with nerves before she performed. She was asked to sing only one verse. She sang it prettily without rocking the boat, which may well have been exactly why she proved to be such a strong candidate for a group. She concentrated on looking at the judges, ignoring what the viewers never see – the two cameramen and the sound engineer.

Louis Walsh was all smiles and said, 'I want to put you through' before there was any real discussion on the matter. He did ask her if she really wanted to be a pop star, to which Cheryl replied that it was all she had ever wanted. He also cautioned that it was lots of 'early mornings, late nights and bullshit'. Geri helpfully added, 'It's not glamorous.'

Outside the room, one of the programme's team took all Cheryl's details and then gave her a letter that was her 'golden ticket' onto the show. She was told to try to avoid any waiting press at the door because the producers liked to be in total control of any publicity for the show. Other than Pete Waterman's now famous remarks, Cheryl's audition day was uneventful and she slipped out without being troubled by Davina. Chris Park, however, was just what Davina was looking for when he auditioned in Glasgow. The judges did not like his choice of song, 'Run Around Sue', a sixties dance hit for Dion. Geri and Louis had never heard the song before and sent him away to come up with another. Davina followed his progress throughout the day and grabbed him again when he was successful with his new song, 'It's My Life' by Bon Jovi.

Cheryl went back to Newcastle and waited for something to happen. She had made a good start because only about thirty were chosen from her audition day. About a week later a letter arrived, with a return train ticket, telling her that she would be required for a week-long audition process in London in September and to be prepared. Cheryl said goodbye to Joan, who wished her good luck, and took the metro three stops to Newcastle's Central Station. She was standing just by the main entrance when a good-looking guy approached and asked her for a light. It was Chris Park. Neither of them recognized each other from their dancing days at the Noreen Campbell Dance School.

Chris recalls, 'I got dropped at the station by my mum. I walked up to the station to have a cigarette. Mum didn't know I smoked so I just said I was going to get a drink and would be back in a minute. There was this girl standing at the front of the door, a little dark girl, and I asked her for a light. It was Cheryl. I didn't know it was Cheryl. She gave me a light and I didn't say where I was going. We were talking for a minute while I had a cigarette. I told my mum I had just seen this girl and I went, "There she is" as she walked past. My mum didn't recognize her either. She hadn't seen her in years either. The thing I most remember is that she only had a tiny, little wheelie case so I thought she wasn't going where I was then. I had this great big case! I got on the train and didn't think anything more about it. When I reached London, I had been told to look for someone with a sign PSTR [*Popstars: The Rivals*]. As I approached the driver, I spotted Cheryl coming from the end of the train. She pretended she didn't remember me from earlier. So I said, "You're auditioning for this, then." And we still didn't recognize each other. Newcastle Station, on the train, King's Cross Station – nothing.'

They didn't see each other again that day, but travelled in separate people carriers with other hopefuls to the hotel near the Gloucester Road in Kensington that would be home for the week – unless the judges gave you the early bath and then you would be on the next train home. More than one hundred boys and girls had been selected to go through the rigorous process of singing and dancing. This number would gradually be reduced to thirty by the end of the week. Some, mainly those who decided to get drunk and have a singsong the first night in the hotel bar, would be easily discarded, but for the others the competition was very fierce.

First-day auditions at Imperial College, London, were terrifying. The contestants all sat in rows in the type of seats you have at school, while the teaching staff – Louis, Pete and Geri – were on a raised platform looking down at a small stage at the front. Normally the 'audition room' was occupied by university students listening to a science lecture. When Cheryl's number was called, she had to get up and sing her audition song in front of not just the judges but the other 111 hopefuls as well. Chris Park describes the experience as 'hardcore'. At least the guys were given plenty of vocal encouragement from the girls because the sexes were only in competition with each other. 'The girls wanted to see who could sing or who was good-looking. But the guys wanted you to fall flat on your face when you walked up the steps to the stage. It was quite bizarre.' At this stage everyone was still just a number.

One of the good TV tricks that these programmes always pull is the bluff. On this occasion, Pete Waterman announced that everyone had done extremely badly: 'Those who stay past tonight need to up their game five hundred per cent.' The judges then proceeded to read out a list of names and invite them to stand in the middle of the room. The implication was that this list of names was the chosen one. Cheryl Tweedy was not among them. Was she in or was she out? Pete put everyone out of their misery by saying that those named would be the ones going home. The remaining seventy-seven boys and girls were ecstatic, which, of course, is just what the producers wanted.

Cheryl had been to London to perform many times since her unfortunate experience at the Royal Ballet summer school but that did not make the week any less nerve-racking, especially as she seemed to be saying goodbye to prospective friends on a daily basis. On the very first night her room-mate packed her bag.

The next day was given over to freestyle dancing, which was good for Cheryl. She found it much easier than did a pretty Irish girl called Nadine Coyle whom she recognized as the girl disqualified on Irish *Popstars* the year before when she was found to be too young. If Cheryl had been smart, she would have noticed that staying in the same group as Nadine was an indication that she was going through. At no point during the entire show did there seem the slightest chance that Nadine would not make the final band. She later revealed that Louis Walsh himself had suggested she audition.

Cheryl was not enjoying the early starts, up and ready to catch the coach outside the hotel at 8.15 a.m. Fifty contenders were now left to face a day on which the ability to take choreography would be vital – again, this was one of Cheryl's strengths. Chris Park had noticed that the 'little dark girl' from Newcastle was a good dancer and later that day he learned why, when, for the first time, they were called by their names: 'I was like, "I know Cheryl Tweedy!" I mean Tweedy is an unusual name and it came to me where I knew her from.' Chris barrelled over to Cheryl and said, 'Did you use to dance? My name is Chris Park and I used to dance.' Cheryl replied, modestly, 'You used to win.' When she told Chris that Amy had been her partner as a young girl, it all came flooding back and he told her that Amy had been his partner too and then his girl-friend. They started chatting about Noreen Campbell and the good old days of the Shields Road. 'It was a surreal experience in the middle of *Popstars*,' observes Chris. For some reason Cheryl was not at her scintillating best during this week and was rightly worried when she was called to face Louis Walsh to hear if she had made the final fifteen. She admits to having negative thoughts, perhaps a legacy of the disappointments in the past when she thought she was within touching distance of success. Not for the last time the emotion of the occasion seemed to overwhelm her and she couldn't stop crying when Louis told her she was still in. She had made the final fifteen girls. Joan steadfastly refused to get carried away with it all, preferring to try to keep Cheryl's feet firmly on the ground. When Cheryl rang to tell her the good news, she replied, 'Oh, good.'

Cheryl was able to let her hair down for the first time at the end of the week when the producers threw a party for the thirty boys and girls who were left. All the booze was free and the hotel bar took a hammering. Cheryl found herself being chatted up by one of the boys, a handsome carpet-fitter from Leicester called Jacob Thompson, whose sparkly smile stood out among the crowd. Jacob began the competition sporting some bizarre facial hair, a goatee that did not suit him at all and which Geri Halliwell told him to shave off in no uncertain terms. His look was certainly improved when he did so.

He was a couple of years older than Cheryl and seemed more mature than a lot of the boys, some of whom were very young and wet behind the ears. Chris Park remembered Jacob being a good-looking bloke, 'nice enough but very quiet'. Another contestant said, 'There was just nothing to him, no substance to him. He was no more than a five-minute conversation.' Cheryl, however, fancied him. The setting was too public for anything much more than a kiss goodnight but the pair swapped phone numbers, promising to meet up soon.

Cheryl and Chris caught the train home together. The pressure was off and the whole experience could sink in. Chris let off steam by practically chain-smoking the whole journey back. Cheryl was not far behind, smoking like a chimney, trying to release the tension of it all. At one point she turned to Chris and practically screeched, 'What if we get in!'

Cheryl was taking everything so seriously that she even refused to tell Chris's mother if she was still in the competition. Chris explained, 'They drill it into your head that if you tell anyone you will jeopardize your chances. Cheryl was not going to risk it even though it was pretty obvious because we had travelled home together.'

All the contestants had to wait for news of whether they had made the final ten and would therefore sing in the live shows. Jacob proved a welcome diversion during this thumb-twiddling time. He caught the train up to Newcastle and they went out for beers. Jacob remembers that in the bar Cheryl started singing 'Let's Get the Party Started' by Pink, one of the biggest hits of the year. He also revealed in a kiss-and-tell article in the *Sunday Mirror* in December 2008 that they slept together that night at the house of one of Cheryl's friends. He gushed, 'Her body was beautiful. She's petite and perfectly formed like a little china doll.'

Much more interesting than a teenage girl having sex with a boy she liked was Jacob's revelation that Cheryl confided her distress about her elder brother Andrew's glue-sniffing and admitted that he had been in trouble with the police. Jacob recalls, 'I was touched that she cared about him so much.' Their conversation shows Cheryl's compassionate side and also her open, trusting nature. This was her first real date with a prospective boyfriend and she was already revealing family secrets. At least it would be six years before Jacob talked to the press, and by then Cheryl had faced up to far worse things in the media. How strange and unsettling it must be, though, to have former lovers talking about your sex life on the pages of a newspaper.

Cheryl has always been nice about Jacob: 'I thought he was lovely. His eyelashes are amazing and I love his light eyes and dark skin. He's got a nice bum and a fantastic body.' They obviously enjoyed each other's company over these few weeks. He visited Newcastle again and she travelled to see him in Leicester. Jacob had become a local celebrity in his home town and on their way back from the pub he was literally chased down the street by a group of starstruck girls – much to Cheryl's displeasure.

More importantly, however, Geri Halliwell was on her way to the North-East to tell Cheryl the judges' decision. They could have announced the final ten in London but that would have ruined this television opportunity. Geri asked a terrified-looking Cheryl if she wanted the good or the bad news. She proceeded to give her the bad: 'We thought that you really held back. We could tell that you did not give your all. As a performer, you're beautiful, you absolutely blew us away. You're absolutely stunning-looking and there were a lot of people that loved you. Do you feel positive about it?'

Cheryl, looking yet more uneasy, mumbled, 'I'd like to – not at the minute, no.'

Geri, having milked the moment mercilessly, put her out of her misery: 'OK, so that was the bad news, 'cos you're in!' Cheryl, relieved and shattered at the same time, showed her spirit by having a go at Geri: 'You shouldn't do that. That was really horrible. You shouldn't be allowed to do things like that to people.' Cheryl was being a little ingenuous on this occasion. They always do that – it's all part of the game.

Cheryl was on her way. Unfortunately, Jacob was not. Louis Walsh went to his home in Leicester to tell him. Jacob admitted that he had found it difficult to sing in front of everyone and that may have counted against him. Cheryl tried to reassure him that, of course, their relationship would not be affected.

The manipulation of these moments for television was never better illustrated than in the dramatic treatment of Kimberley Walsh, an aspiring actress from Bradford. Pete Waterman went to her home to tell her the bad news that she had not made the final ten. Kimberley had faced many audition rejections over the years and seemed well prepared to handle disappointment. That would not have been good television and the camera continued to roll as if the whole point was that she must cry. Eventually, she broke and dissolved in floods of tears.

That might have been the last anyone saw of Kimberley if it had not been for the discovery that one of the final ten was ten days too old. And, to make even better television, the girl in question was Hazel Kaneswaran, who was heavily pregnant and due to give birth just before or during the live shows. The discovery that she had turned twenty-five before 1 July 2002 was fortunate indeed for the producers, who faced the dilemma of trying to be fair to a pregnant woman while dealing with the total impracticality of her making the group. Imagine 'Sound of the Underground', the first single, featuring four foxy ladies and one mummy changing nappies. That was a real possibility because Hazel was very attractive and an accomplished singer.

Louis Walsh, who had 'dearly wanted' Hazel to be in the final band, was unimpressed with the turn of events: 'At the last minute producers found an excuse to get rid of her. They were well aware of her birth date. Hazel has a fantastic voice and brilliant attitude.' The suggestion that they already knew Hazel was too old casts doubt on whether Kimberley was ever seriously rejected or whether she had been selected as a TV moment right from the start.

Geri flew to Dublin to tell Hazel she was being thrown out of the show. Louis, meanwhile, went to Bradford to surprise Kimberley with the news that she had been chosen as a replacement. Finally, Kimberley arrived at the house the girls were sharing for the live shows. Cheryl opened the door to her, which was the cue for much screaming and whooping. In all, the Kimberley saga had given the programme four great pieces of telly. Hazel had a baby boy two weeks before the live finals began. She later became a well-known face on Irish television, judging the *You're A Star* talent show.

The drama of the final ten was not yet over. One of them, Nicola

Ward, a pretty blonde from Surrey, in a moment of short-sightedness, took exception to the small print on the contracts they had to sign. She protested, 'They are trying to make us sign our life away. The contract was outrageous. If we win, we have to sign up to an agreement that means they own us . . . It's not worth it.'

And with that Nicola Ward drove off into the sunset. Pete Waterman observed that she was too 'cocky' right from the start: 'She has complained about money but I ask you, who wouldn't want to be in her position at twenty-one? She could earn absolutely nothing and now she doesn't even have a job.'

Nicola's final words on the subject: 'At the end of the day, when you look at what's happened to Hear'Say – the last band produced by this programme – then I don't think I am giving up too much.' Ironically, she joined an all-girl band, Cookie, but also left that group abruptly.

The producers chose another Nicola as her replacement. Nicola Roberts from Runcorn in Cheshire thought she was being interviewed by Dane Bowers, host of the *Popstars Extra* show, about how being rejected had changed her life. Instead, he revealed she was going to the house. Nicola, a shy seventeen-year-old redhead, was found a bed in the room Cheryl was sharing with Aimee Kearsley, the youngest of the remaining contestants. Nobody realized the importance at the time, but the replacement girls, Kimberley and Nicola, were both from the North and bonded quickly with Cheryl.

Sadly for Jacob Thompson, there was no eleventh-hour reprieve. One of the male finalists, Peter Smith, was also too old but this was dramatically revealed during the live shows too late for Jacob or one of the other rejects to be recalled. Who knows what would have happened if Jacob had been chosen for the final ten? Inevitably, he was an outsider from the moment he was given the bad news.

7

Right Here Waiting

The *Popstars* home for the duration of the contest was light years away from the council house in Langhorn Close, Heaton, and was luxury that Cheryl had never known before. The £2 million house would be worth three times that now, even in these credit-crunching times. Just to rent it in 2003 would have cost £10,000 per month. The girls could start the day off with a leisurely swim in the pool or a visit to the gym and Jacuzzi. The mansion was on the private estate of St George's Hill, Weybridge, a celebrity enclave best known for an exclusive golf club where Cliff Richard's house could be seen from one of the fairways. It was not a cutting-edge location for girls with street cred but Cheryl loved it, and the peaceful surroundings had such a positive effect on her that this leafy part of Surrey would be her first choice when she later began searching for a new marital home. She had about three weeks in the house while the television series began and the audience caught up with the rehearsals.

Inside the house, it was chaos. Ten fiercely ambitious young women, no men and a swimming pool to leap into, clothed or unclothed, any time of day or night must have seemed like the hen party from hell on occasions. The place was a total tip, a larger reflection of how Cheryl kept her room at home in Newcastle. Nadine observed, 'It was a total nightmare, to be honest. Most of the time, you could hardly see the carpet in some of the rooms for all the clothes and stuff on them.' There's a wonderfully staged publicity picture of Cheryl, revealing a hint of cleavage, smiling at the camera while vacuuming the stairs – as if that was a regular thing!

Two female chaperones lived in to try to keep the peace and make sure no men sneaked in, especially any of the boy finalists who were living nearby in Oxshott. They were also supposed to make sure nobody escaped, although Cheryl did join some of the girls for a night out at a bar in Weybridge where they met up with some of the boys. She later described it as the best night of the whole series, having a laugh with everybody, including fellow contestants Sarah Harding, Chloe Staines and Javine Hilton. The girls sank three bottles of wine before staggering home. Most of the time they had to make do with opening a bottle of wine at their luxury home, having a dip in the pool and putting the world to rights. Cheryl did manage to sneak out a few times to see Jacob, who would travel down to London. On one occasion they stayed at a very modest hotel in King's Cross after Javine, who was twenty and from Notting Hill, had volunteered to give Cheryl a lift across London.

More and more, tabloid newspapers treat reality shows as if they represent proper news, competing for front-page space alongside matters of life and death, terrorist threats, world disasters and cuts in the National Health Service. Fake reality, it seems, is an infinitely preferable accompaniment to cornflakes than real life. Contestants need to get noticed to enhance their chances of gaining public interest and, subsequently, their all-important vote. Kimberley and Nicola had head starts because they came into the house in a blaze of publicity. Nadine Coyle had a health scare when she discovered a lump that turned out to be stress-related. Another finalist, Sarah Harding, had been photographed topless for *FHM* magazine. She should not have worried. Geri Halliwell could have filled a library with topless shots taken before she found fame. Cheryl was in urgent need of some publicity, so a week before the live competition began her relationship with Jacob was revealed in the press. The dating of a maybe star and a not-this-time wannabe was hardly front-page material but it was better than nothing. Poor Jacob was described as a 'hunky carpet-fitter' despite having come so close to televi-sion stardom.

A spokesman for the programme wearily confirmed, 'Love did blossom at the London call-back in August and the pair have been seeing each other ever since.' The papers might have shown more interest if they had spotted the pair sneaking into the flea-pit hotel in King's Cross.

If Cheryl had had more PR savvy at this point, she might have paired off with one of those who had made the live shows. The baby-faced Jamie Shaw had a massive crush on her, saying, 'She's honest, thoughtful and very kind. Looks-wise, she's absolutely per-fect.' Jamie, however, was only seventeen and far too young for Cheryl. Many girls would be swept away by Jamie's little boy lost persona, especially when he showed a tendency to weep on the show – as did most of the boys – but Cheryl liked a more physical, earthy type of man.

A week later, Cheryl had her first experience of the fickle nature of the media when her old flame, Steve Thornton, was fast out of the blocks to tell all to the *News of the World* about their passionate fling. Under the saucy headline 'My Ranchy Nights With *Popstars: The Rivals* Cowgirl', he revealed that 'TV Babe wore Wild West hat for sex'. Blossoming love was interesting but Stetson sex frolics were much more attention-grabbing. The revelations may or may not have helped Cheryl to a few more votes from the lads over the coming weeks.

Cheryl was quickly on the telephone to give the plumber a piece of her mind in the best 'How could you?' fashion and he was suitably shame-faced about it. Every female star gets this sort of tabloid treatment and it never did the Spice Girls any harm. It was an early lesson for Cheryl about press intrusion, a subject she would become an expert on sooner rather than later. She was, for the moment, down-to-earth about it: 'People are reading it, but it's all forgotten so soon. It's fish and chip paper the next day, so who cares?'

In the first live show, Cheryl was asked to sing 'Baby, Now That I've Found You', the karaoke favourite by The Foundations that had been a hit in 1967. She looked more polished than at her audition, in a grey miniskirt, boots and flowery top. She moved smoothly if unadventurously. Vocally she began a little uncertainly before picking up the tempo as she went along. It was a safe if unspectacular performance from a very pretty girl. She did enough to sail through.

In the official Girls Aloud book, *Dreams That Glitter*, Cheryl says, 'I'd never actually sung live in front of anyone before, not even sung karaoke.' She must have forgotten the many times she had done so at Metroland; in the numerous London clubs where she had performed; as a well-received support act for Ultimate Kaos; or just singing for the passing crowds in front of the Monument in the middle of Newcastle city centre. Cheryl had been a performer for years, so her assertion is a little strange. She was, however, genuinely nervous. She used to be that way before going on stage in front of a thousand kids at Metroland. It's perfectly normal for a performer and something that the great majority never lose. Cheryl's confidence had also taken some knocks over the past couple of years so she needed reassurance to reclaim her old invincibility.

The songs were chosen for the girls, mainly by Louis Walsh, who, perhaps contrary to popular opinion, is very shrewd about this sort of thing. After the danceable Foundations hit, Cheryl found herself singing ballads. One finalist observed, wryly, 'Perhaps he wanted to guarantee she got through. Why take a risk with her and go out on a limb with a song?' In the second live show for the girls, two weeks later, she sang Shania Twain's debut hit, 'You're Still the One'. She loved the number, which had been her father's first dance when he married his girlfriend, Joanne. Cheryl was elegant and seemed older than her nineteen years in an off-the-shoulder red dress, her hair swept back to emphasize a pearl necklace and earrings. She looked beautiful if not quite so much 'one of the girls on a night out' as she had done the previous week. That may have counted against her when it came to the voting because she found herself in the bottom four. She sang in a tentative manner to start with and some dodgy tuning, once again, led to a slow start and a stronger finish. Fortunately, her professionalism shone through and she remembered to finish with a 100-watt smile.

Her mother, Joan, who was in the audience, observed, 'She was nervous but it was a bit easier this time as she had experienced this sort of pressure two weeks ago in the first show.' Joan described the competition as an emotional roller-coaster, which is one of the reasons why it is such compelling television. How do you react when you are chosen and then another girl has the heartbreak of missing out? Cheryl seemed to be in tears every time the camera caught a glimpse of her watching the drama unfolding.

The weeks of the live finals were not a free ride for the contestants. They were expected to work very hard. On the Friday morning, for instance, Cheryl was up at the crack of dawn to be picked up with the other girls to go straight down to the LWT studios on the South Bank to rehearse all day. First up would be the group number that would always open the show. All the finalists would have to do their best three or four times that morning so that all the camera positions could be worked out meticulously. After a quick lunch each girl would do her own number four or five times. There was really no excuse for messing up during the live show.

The judges were not in attendance on the Friday. Instead, some of the production team would sit in their seats and take some of the tension out of proceedings. 'You were crap', they would say, tongue-in-cheek, when one of the finalists had given their all. Chris Park observes, 'They used to take the piss all the time.' Sometimes they would have to go into the studio to record backing vocals for the performances. That could drag on until 4 a.m., so by the time they had been driven back to St George's Hill, it was practically time to get up again.

At least there was some respite when the girls met the popular boy band Blue during filming for *CD:UK*. The band was flavour of the year in 2002 and the boys were plugging their new album, *One Love*, which would be number one in November. A little publicity for both Blue and *Popstars: The Rivals* did no one any harm. The boys were living the dream and showed the confidence of having already 'made it'. One of the four, Lee Ryan, bounded up to Cheryl and said he thought she was 'fit', the sort of remark that would have lost him his teeth in the wrong parts of Newcastle.

Cheryl didn't seem to mind, declaring that for the first time in her life she was speechless.

Another of the four, Duncan James, was impressed by Cheryl, who he thought was 'simply stunning-looking, gorgeous', which was at least a degree better than describing her as 'fit'. Some rumours would surface over the coming months that Cheryl had been asked out by Duncan but nothing came of it.

Another outing for mutual publicity took the girl finalists to the launch of Westlife's greatest hits album, *Unbreakable* at Zuma restaurant in London. Any show with Louis Walsh is bound to feature Westlife at some stage and the famous boy band happily posed for photographs with the girls, all of whom seemed to have become much more glamorous in a few short weeks. Cheryl, grinning away in a skimpy black top and skirt, discovered she enjoyed the taste of champagne much more than Newcastle Brown Ale. She even found time to dance with Gareth Gates, runner-up in the previous year's *Pop Idol,* who then seemed destined for a long career, having had three number one hits in 2002.

The day of the show was another very early start and straight into rehearsing with Davina McCall. The conversations were not a rehearsal for what lay ahead that evening but to carefully work out the 'marks', where the contestants would walk and stop, and stand and talk. After lunch Cheryl was handed her copy of the running order so she could see at what point she would perform. It would read something like – group song, Davina chat, adverts, singer 1, singer 2, singer 3, adverts and so on. They would work a pre-recorded clip in between – perhaps the Westlife party or another occasion when the boys all dressed as James Bond and drove sports cars while the girls wore diamonds and pretended to be Pussy Galore.

Halloween fell after Cheryl's second live show. The boys dressed up in 'Scream' masks and turned up at the girls' house to try to spook them, banging on the doors and making weird noises, before being allowed in for a party.

For the third live show, Cheryl was handed a very difficult song, the Sinead O'Connor classic 'Nothing Compares 2 U'. The notoriously prickly Irish singer had her finest hour with this Prince track in 1990 when she achieved her only number one. Sinead made the song her own with a quirky, emotional and haunting interpretation. For talent show contestants it should come with a government health warning. Joan thought it 'one of the hardest songs to sing'. Perversely, Cheryl sang with more panache than in previous weeks. Joan said she 'did it justice' but her performance failed to make the best impression on the voting public. She looked fabulous again; this time she wore a black corset – perhaps not her best colour. Cheryl was petrified that she might suffer a wardrobe malfunction because the tiny top seemed to have a mind of its own and would spring open without warning. A trip to the loo was called for just before she went on stage to apply yet more 'tit tape' to make sure her modesty was protected. Chris Park sums up what it was like to be a finalist on the day of the live shows: 'It's fine at rehearsals. It was just when it came to walking through the doors for the real show; it was like "shit!".'

The competition was now very strong and Cheryl was feeling the pressure increase as she got closer. If she was eliminated this week, just before the grand final, there would be an overwhelming sense of anticlimax. The bottom three were Kimberley, Aimee and Cheryl. Then Kimberley was safe and it was Cheryl against her young room-mate, whom the more life-hardened Cheryl had taken under her wing. Davina McCall, mindful that she was dealing with fragile young girls, was sympathetic and said immediately that she was going to 'put you out of your misery'. She revealed it was the closest vote of the series and that they were separated by just 1,218 votes. In terms of the hundreds of thousands of votes, this was the equivalent of a cigarette paper between them. Davina announced that Aimee was going home and the two girls dissolved into tears. Aimee was only sixteen and certainly looked younger than the remaining contestants. Cheryl was genuinely upset. 'That night I would have preferred to have gone through it so she didn't have to. She was only young. I was only nineteen myself but I'd taken knocks. I was stronger.'

Chris Park recalls, 'She was very, very upset because they got on very well and I think she would have liked Aimee to have been in the band with her. That's a big part of the process.' Cheryl's anguish for her young friend was completely genuine, although she snapped out of it as the prospect of the final loomed.

Throughout the series, Newcastle had been supporting two finalists, Cheryl and Chris. The signs were good for both. In the penultimate week Chris had secured most votes despite not being a favourite of the judges. He had the boy band credentials – spiky blond hair, an earring and too much tan from a bottle. On the finals show for the boys, he sang 'With a Little Help from My Friends' and could have done with a bit more. He just missed out on being in the band. Despite his disappointment at being over-looked, he did not mind too much, as plans were already in motion to form an alternative boy band from the losing five. And Chris was convinced they would be better than the five who had been selected.

The following week was the girls' final and friends in Newcastle were proactive in trying to get publicity for Cheryl. An old school friend from Walker, John Mulroy, persuaded the city council to let him hang a banner from the Tyne Bridge for a couple of hours over lunch. He enlisted the help of Joan and Nupi Bedi and the three of them were photographed waving above the forty-foot-long flag proclaiming, 'Vote For Cheryl Tweedy'. John rightly observed, 'Geordies support their own.' Afterwards, it was hung inside Nupi's Quayside Café. Home-town support is essential for success. As Nupi explained, 'I had the phone on repeat voting for Cheryl.'

Six girls had made it through to the live final on 7 December. Cheryl was joined by Kimberley, Nicola, Nadine, Sarah and Javine. The last named had made a big impression during the competition. She seemed to stand out from the other girls. She was taller, black and possessed a more powerful voice. She was a strong favourite to make the final line-up. The boy finalists, however, favoured Cheryl, Kimberley and Sarah, who had won their admiration by coping with particularly intrusive revelations from her ex-boyfriend.

On the big night, Cheryl was asked to sing the relatively unde-manding ballad 'Right Here Waiting', which is a very slushy song. If there were such an instrument as a feisty-ometer, then this would not register on the scale. Richard Marx had taken it to number two in the British charts when Cheryl was six. Cheryl loved R&B, harboured ambitions to be a street dancer, and here she was singing this old tosh. It was a song that she would have to mess up in a major way for it to harm her chances. One characteristic of her singing that was particularly evident on this performance was her Geordie vowels. She couldn't do anything about that and it might have resulted in some unfair criticism of her singing abilities. The judges were not particularly impressed. Pete Waterman said he 'felt for her' but did not explain why.

The judges, however, agreed on one thing. She looked fantastic in a purple waif dress, her hair flowing naturally to reveal some drop pearl earrings. Her stage presence had grown much more polished in the two months of the competition. She looked Hollywood and Vegas rolled into one. Geri said she looked 'gorgeous'.

Conspiracy theorists might argue that Cheryl was given a soft song to sing because the record company executives really wanted her in the band. Throughout the series the main emphasis seemed to be on Cheryl's looks not her abilities. Perhaps, vocally, she did not do herself justice in the live shows but it's all about survival. She was getting enough votes and that's all that mattered. Just as important, she had laid the foundations for an enduring image. She portrayed herself very much as an ordinary girl, modest, kind to the other girls and wearing her heart on her sleeve. In her final piece to camera, she said, 'I lived on a council estate all my life . . . I'm just a normal girl from Newcastle, that's all I am.'

Was Cheryl in trouble? The judges' remarks were probably the least enthusiastic to her. Nicola, who had not been in the bottom two, sang the Pointer Sisters' hit 'I'm So Excited'. Sarah performed Bonnie Tyler's 'Holding Out for a Hero'. Nadine nailed the Whitney Houston barnstorming number 'I Wanna Dance With Somebody', an ironic choice because she was arguably the best singer and the worst dancer. Geri observed, 'We all know she doesn't like dancing very much.' Kimberley could do little wrong with 'Chain Reaction', the Diana Ross dance favourite. Javine Hylton sailed through 'I'm Every Woman', the Chaka Khan classic and a fantastic song for a diva-to-be. These choices probably worked to

Cheryl's advantage. Her song was the only ballad on the show and, accordingly, stood out.

The producers cranked up the tension for the result. Davina milked it: 'The first person in the band is . . . Cheryl.' She had, in fact, received a huge vote, nearly 230,000 calls. When she heard her name, Cheryl sprang to her feet, punched the air and shouted, 'Come on!' Her reaction was just like her dad's when he had heard she had done well growing up. There's a time for snivelling and a time for joyous release and this was, most definitely, the latter. Cheryl has a very volatile personality, as the great British public were in the process of discovering. She described her feelings: 'I was just overwhelmed – it was fantastic. I woke up on Sunday morning and I burst into tears because I was just so happy.'

Nicola, Nadine and Kimberley followed her into the spotlight, leaving the blonde bombshell Sarah Harding against Javine Hylton for the final spot. Astonishingly, Davina announced Sarah's name, leaving Javine the loneliest woman on the stage. Davina told Javine, 'I don't understand this – you are too good for the band. You are a star in your own right.' At the time she was right. Javine did seem to have something extra and that was perhaps her downfall. Nobody felt sorry for her. She was almost overpraised so that the viewers thought she would make the band easily. Perhaps the public were not so sure about the prospects of the lovely Geordie from Newcastle.

Louis Walsh shrewdly observed, 'I think kids are watching so many of these shows now that they don't vote for the person they like most, they vote for the person they feel most sorry for. So I'm going to vote for Cheryl. I'm going to vote for Sarah . . .' Unsurprisingly, therefore, Louis revealed that he thought Nadine, Nicola and Javine were definites to make the band and, also, that Javine would subsequently have a big solo career.

Some rumours about voting problems did surface but the producers revealed that Sarah had managed 50,000 more votes than Javine and had always been ahead on the count. Chris Park, who a week earlier had been in the same position as Javine, observed, 'It's not who is the least popular. It's who's not the most popular. Everybody is popular and had big fanbases.'

Javine may have seemed like a big star in the making during this particular talent contest but over the seven years since *Popstars: The Rivals* she has hardly set the world alight. She was chased by record companies in the afterglow of the series but her debut single, 'Real Things', only reached number four in the charts the following July. The Cheeky Girls, the novelty pop duo who auditioned for the show, had four top ten hits in 2003. Javine was chosen to represent the UK in the Eurovision Song Contest in 2005, pretty much the kiss of death for any artist. Javine came third from last with the forgettable 'Touch My Fire'. Inevitably, she surfaced in a reality show, *The Games*, where she met MC Harvey of So Solid Crew with whom she now has a baby boy. She ended up winning *The Games* but it would have been much better for her career if she had won *Popstars: The Rivals*. In retrospect, perhaps the great British public got it right after all.

Afterwards, it was party time. Everybody was still shocked over the Javine elimination, but Cheryl had a more pressing matter that was threatening to make her moment of triumph a little uncomfortable. Jacob rang to congratulate her. He told the *Sunday Mirror* that she had promised to call him back but never did. Jacob was about to be dealt a hard lesson in life – boyfriends do not last long when fame comes calling. They become spare wheels very quickly. It happened with all of the Spice Girls. And it would happen to Girls Aloud. Cheryl had known Jacob only a few months since 'love had blossomed' and had barely seen him at all in recent weeks.

A week after the finals there was a special show at the studios and Jacob went along. He says Louis Walsh was polite but didn't really want to know. 'I literally had to beg a ticket to get into the studio to see the girls perform. That was humiliating considering I had been such a big part of the show.' He managed to blag his way into the backstage bar where a party was in full swing. He claims Cheryl cut him dead and asked him what he was doing there. He knew it was over: 'I didn't contact her again. I knew it was pointless. We were dead and buried.'

'I was ditched as soon as she became a star.' Jacob was getting a little ahead of the story. Cheryl was certainly not yet a star. She was one-fifth of a girl group who might come to something or might go the way of other talent show winners. For the moment, her mother, Joan, was able to highlight how much it mattered to her daughter: 'She has wanted this since she was four.'

8

The Girls

The five girls hugging excitedly looked like five members of the same band immediately. They were of similar height and shape, they wore their hair simply and they looked nice without being overstylish or made-up. It was a Saturday night and these five foxy girls were about to hit the town. That, in a nutshell, was Girls Aloud. Immediately after the result, they were ready for a host of publicity shots and, for the final, had been cleverly styled in a mixture of purple and white for maximum effect. Books and DVDs were rushed out with that image of joyful success on the cover.

The Spice Girls, up until then the most successful UK girl band of all time, were beset by personality clashes from the very outset. They were, however, put together to be individually different so that each one could appeal to a certain section of the potential audience. Victoria Beckham, for instance, was recruited specifically to appeal to the more mature, discerning man. She was encouraged to pout and be slightly apart from the others, projecting an element of disdain that indirectly led to her nickname, Posh. Girls Aloud, conversely, seemed to be very similar. They were five sides of the same pentagon. They shared a burning desire for success. Geri Halliwell had tried to explain it: 'It's the sparkle in the eye – something shiny coming from within.'

The series producer, Nicholas Steinberg, observed, 'The story is that they've come from nowhere, but the truth is they've all wanted it for a long time.' Louis Walsh was scathing about the ambition of many of the girls who entered the show, suggesting they were interested in make-up and sunbeds and had no idea what was required. That criticism could not be aimed at the final five.

The group that emerged from *Popstars: The Rivals* was far more chav than posh. Cheryl already roomed with Nicola Roberts and they got along well. Cheryl described Nicola as a 'typical Scouser' and felt they had a natural affinity – Geordie and Scouser. They were both girls who loved McDonald's, before the demands of forever wearing figure-hugging outfits put an end to that. Nicola was a couple of years younger but possessed the same sense of invincibility that Cheryl conveyed. She felt that it was her destiny to be a winner on *Popstars: The Rivals*. In *Dreams That Glitter*, Nicola reveals that she always knew she was going to be a singer and that it was a case of when and not if. Both girls had no Plan B.

Like Cheryl, she had no family connections to the music business. She was born in the non-starry small town of Stamford in Lincolnshire. She was the eldest of her mother's four children. Debbie was seventeen when she had Nicola, the same age as Cheryl's mum when she started a family. Her father, Paul, was in the RAF and the family lived on a tough council estate in Runcorn, Cheshire, about fifteen miles south of Liverpool. If she had been a few years older she would have auditioned for the Spice Girls; she had to settle for adopting Geri Halliwell as her childhood idol and being called Ginger Spice at school. Nicola is very much the fiery redhead.

Cola, as her friends called her, did not begin her pursuit of stardom as young as Cheryl. She was ten before she caught the performance bug and started attending dance classes and entering singing competitions. She also was considerably more conscientious at school, managing an impressive ten GCSEs, two more than her idol, Geri. She seems to have led a protected, happy childhood in a close-knit family. Every summer holiday the family of six would head off to the West Country to stay in a caravan. She did not suffer then from the insecurities that would set in later when she stood next to her bandmates, whom she described as 'four of the most gorgeous girls in Britain'.

Her mother, Debbie, who worked as a dinner lady at Nicola's

primary school, was always hugely proud of her daughter's abilities and encouraged her to sing at all the family parties: 'She always sang with a hairbrush. Since she was eleven, she said there is nothing else she wanted to do. I think fate has got a lot to do with it. If something is meant for you, it will happen.' Unsurprisingly, it was her mother who phoned up to get the audition form for *Popstars: The Rivals*. Nicola left school at sixteen and travelled the Tweedy path to stardom by getting a part-time job as a waitress. She also enrolled in a local college to study Performing Arts and sang in a local band called Devotion.

Nicola had led a sheltered life by the time she left home for the luxury *Popstars* house. She had a steady home-town boyfriend, Carl Egerton, who was studying for his A levels. When she heard that she had secured an audition in Manchester, her father drove her all the way there from a caravan site in Cornwall and then all the way back afterwards so that they could continue their holiday. One can only imagine how wide her eyes opened when she heard about Cheryl's life as they chatted late into the night in their room – a family life blighted by her brother's glue-sniffing and jail time, a love life poisoned by heroin. Cheryl must have sounded like she was from Mars, not Newcastle. Nicola is a thoughtful, intelligent girl who can be loud and boisterous with people she knows yet reserved and lacking in confidence in unfamiliar surroundings.

Nadine Coyle, known as Nadz, was worried that she did not enjoy full public support because she came from Derry in Northern Ireland and not from the North of England. She grew up singing and dancing. Her mother, Lillian, swears that she knew Nadine was special when, at the age of two, she launched into a version of The Drifters' classic 'Saturday Night at the Movies'. At the age of six she was already competing in music festivals. Her father, Niall, used to sing locally. Every year he put on a pantomime for charity and would always cast his little girl, who everyone agreed had a lovely voice. She was a precocious talent and played Sleeping Beauty when she was thirteen, so she was used to performing in public before facing the ordeal of TV auditions. Money was tight at home because her father was unemployed but she, too, came from a loving family and was always close to her two sisters.

Being a talented performer in a smaller environment gave Nadine the chance to be noticed at a younger age. That was certainly the case when she auditioned for the Irish version of *Popstars*. Louis Walsh was one of the panel and thought the girl with the winning, toothy smile was a certain star of the future. She sailed through the show and ended up as one of the six band members of the new group, called, unoriginally, Six. If she had stayed in that band, the world might never have heard of Nadine Coyle because Six sunk without trace. Nadine, however, was swiftly thrown out when it was discovered she was too young for the rules of the competition. She had not sneaked in by just a few days – she was two whole years too young.

Presumably Nadine thought nobody would ever know. She was a shapely sixteen and had no trouble fooling everyone until it came round to stating her date of birth in a winners' profile interview for the show. She gave her real one. D'oh! Six speedily became Five and there was a hilarious moment when the five remaining winners came on stage with a cardboard cut-out with a question mark for a face in the place where Nadine should have been. Unquestionably, Six would have been a much better band with Nadine, who had great charisma and presence for a teenager. That did not seem to be the case when the show was aired because Six went to the top of the Irish charts with the fastest-selling single in the country's chart history – shades of Hear'Say – while Nadine and her family were shunned in her home town. Nadine Coyle has a strong personality and is fiercely independent. Her family's treatment after the Six scandal may well have led to her relocating everybody to California when Girls Aloud took off. She would later say of lying about her age, 'I did do the wrong thing, but given the same chance, I would do it again.'

Her exit from *Irish Popstars* made great television, which is exactly the point of these shows. Nobody in TV land would have cared if that had been it for Nadine, but Louis Walsh was sure she would have a big career and he became her champion when she successfully auditioned for *Popstars: The Rivals*. At seventeen, she was old enough to compete in the new show. Her ability to dust herself off and recover from the Six scandal within little more than six months is testimony to her strength of character. Six, who were also managed by Louis Walsh, split up in early 2003 just as Girls Aloud were getting into their stride.

Cheryl was not the first in Girls Aloud to have a footballer for a boyfriend. Nadine was dating Neil McCafferty, a then promising midfielder, whom she had met at a disco while still at school. He, too, had travelled over to London from Ireland when he was signed by Charlton Athletic in south-east London. He failed to break into the first team and had to watch from the touchline as Nadine's fame grew. Irish journalists suggested the young couple might become the Irish Posh and Becks but that would soon prove to be wildly optimistic. Nadine shared a room in the *Popstars* mansion with Kimberley and soon discovered they had football in common. Kimberley was dating a footballer called Martin Pemberton, who played in central defence for Stockport County, a few miles south of Manchester but light years away from Old Trafford. That was about as good as it got for Martin and while he battled on in the lower divisions he gradually saw less and less of his girlfriend.

He was twenty-six when Kimberley was getting her break and his age might explain why the boys in the competition seemed a little young to the stage school girl. She was a mature twenty-one when she came out with the classic putdown: 'They're all good-looking. If I was a young girl, I would be quite impressed.' Kimberley is a Yorkshire lass, born in Bradford, whose teachers described her as a 'very sweet child' and 'a dear little girl'. Her mother, Diane, was a music teacher at a primary school and her father, John, was in a local band and so, not surprisingly, Kimberley grew up in a musical household in which she was always encouraged to sing. Sometimes that backfired when she got into trouble at school for singing when she should have been working.

Her parents split up and divorced when she was four and, although her father was very much a part of their lives, her mother looked after Kimberley, her two sisters and her brother. Diane Walsh, like her Newcastle counterpart Joan Callaghan, always ensured her daughter made it every week to the extra lessons in a church hall, where she could become proficient in acting, dancing and singing at an early age. Kimberley started her professional career very young. She appeared in a TV series about reading called *The Book Tower* when she was five and also appeared in an advertisement for Asda.

Her elder sister, Sally Walsh, was already established as an actress playing the part of Lyn Hutchinson in *Emmerdale* during the latter part of the nineties, while Kimberley gained experience at the Stage 84 Theatre School in Bradford. She earned extra money working as a cleaner in a bakery from 7 a.m. to 1 p.m. every Saturday for the princely sum of £10. Later she worked as a waitress, which seems to have been de rigueur for the girls in the band.

Rather like Cheryl's teenage pop progress, Kimberley's acting career was always on the verge of a breakthrough. She had various small parts before reaching the final four auditioning for the role of kennel maid Maria Sutherland in *Coronation Street*. Suzanne Shaw of Hear'Say was also in the final four but they both lost out to Samia Smith, better known as Samia Ghadie before her marriage. Kimberley decided to go to college instead and was studying English and Media Studies in Leeds when she auditioned for *Popstars: The Rivals*. She fully intended to continue the course after she was, at first, rejected for the final ten.

Kimberley appeared one of the more level-headed of the band and she and Nadine were calmer than the other three. She always got on well with Cheryl and they had kept in touch when Kimberley thought she was out of the show. If there was an odd one out among the five, at least to start with, then it was Sarah Harding. She had to overcome the media storm over the voting scandal and about being chosen ahead of Javine. In the house, Cheryl roomed with Nicola while Kimberley shared with Nadine. Sarah, blonde and brassy, admits that she was worried she was not going to fit in.

Sarah is a force of nature. She plays hard, drives hard, drinks hard and lives her life with the throttle out. Her real name is Sarah Hardman but she changed it to Harding after a rift with her father. She comes across as a stereotypical loud Northerner but was born in the genteel surroundings of Ascot in Berkshire and has pop music roots, although low-key ones. Her father, John Hardman, was in a seventies pop band called Sunfighter, which managed one appearance on *Top of the Pops* with a song called 'Drag Race Queen' which, rarely for a record receiving TV exposure, failed to chart.

Her mother, Marie, was from Manchester and moved back up North when her marriage ran into difficulties in the late eighties. They settled in Stockport. Sarah had a tough time at school and, displaying her headstrong nature, left at fifteen before she had sat her GCSEs. She admits, 'I was a bit of a reprobate.' Her father's recollection of the causes of the family break-up is not the same as Sarah's, who is completely loyal to her church-going mother, whom she describes as a 'really good person'. She now has no contact with her father, although as a little girl he would take her to his recording studio and bought her first electric guitar when she was eight.

Sarah is the only member of Girls Aloud who nominates Madonna as her role model. The superstar, who inspired a whole generation of female performers, featured in Sarah's repertoire when she took to the karaoke circuit, performing at pubs and clubs around the North-West as well as a caravan park in north Wales. She earned extra money with a succession of low-paid jobs, including waitressing in Pizza Hut, driving a van, phone operating and even debt collecting.

Back home in Stockport she started a girl group called Project G and was planning to record some material when she applied to *Popstars: The Rivals*. She had already tried but failed to win a place on the 2002 series of the BBC alternative, *Fame Academy*.

Sarah has always had a one-dimensional image in the press. For the media she's a rollicking good-time girl and her image starts and ends there. She's a great deal more complex than that, admitting that she has always suffered from chronic insecurity. She had made some bad choices where men were concerned so she has had to suffer intrusive kiss-and-tells as a result. One, during the finals of the show, was a particularly graphic story about sex in the woods.

The girls had to get on to survive after being thrown together by circumstance. The method of selection meant that it would be impossible for five random girls to become the best of friends for ever but Cheryl and Nicola were already heading that way. Sarah, who says she was never a 'girl's girl', was perhaps the odd one out and was always a bit removed from the others. She never shared a room with any of them, always preferring her own space. Chris Park, who saw them every day, provides an interesting assessment of their differing personalities. He observed, 'Nicola was misunderstood because she is quite a sweet girl. She nicked my socks. Sarah was very bubbly and outgoing. She'd had a bit of a tough time and was quite brave, I thought. Nadine was a lovely girl but very young. She appeared younger than she was [seventeen]. Kimberley was very smart and very pretty. She was ready. If they started shooting the video tomorrow, she looked like she could walk straight into it. And Cheryl . . . she was stunning, outgoing and friendly. A lot of blokes will like a girl if the girl in question is nice to them.'

9

Sound of the Underground

Cheryl was so thunderstruck by what had happened to her that she sat on her bed and stared into space for an hour. That would be the last hour she would have to herself for the foreseeable future because, theoretically, she was only halfway through the competition. She and her four new bandmates still had to battle the boys for the Christmas number one. After the finals show on 7 December 2002, there were just fifteen days before the special edition when the winner would be revealed.

The music business likes to create interest in the Christmas number one because it encourages sales. Being Santa's favourite, however, does not guarantee prestige or an avalanche of future hits. The Spice Girls and Westlife cashed in but their names are among those of such pop luminaries as Bob the Builder and Mr Blobby. The recurring success of Cliff Richard's seasonal offerings had tended to devalue the position in the eyes of the music critics. This year, however, would be the first when the reality talent shows would field a contender.

The bookmakers were in no doubt. The boy band was going to walk it. Graham Sharp, spokesman for William Hill, said, 'The race to be Christmas number one is usually looking wide open at the beginning of December. But this year it looks all over bar the singing with almost every chart expert tipping One True Voice as a certainty.' The boy band were an odds-on favourite at 4/6 while the girls were not even second-favourites. They were 13/2 outsiders behind a record called 'Scorpio Rising' by Death In Vegas featuring Liam Gallagher. With these odds, one could question why the girls were bothering.

Nadine gamely said the girls would be very happy to make it to number two in the charts: 'I would be absolutely over the moon. I'm seventeen, I've just left school, and even to record a song, or shoot a video – I mean, that's an honour.'

A number of factors soon showed the betting odds to be ridiculous. First, One True Voice was a cheesy name for a group. Pete Waterman had wanted to call the new group The Boys, but that plan was scuppered when it was remembered that this was the nickname of Glasgow Celtic footballers, even though it was spelled differently (bhoys), and there would be copyright problems. The boys themselves came up with One True Voice so they only have themselves to blame for one of the worst names in pop music. The cheesiness became riper when it was revealed that their single would be a cover of the Bee Gees' song 'Sacred Trust'. Take That had enjoyed a number one record with the Bee Gees' classic 'How Deep Is Your Love' but that was a much better known track. Take That were also the premier boy band of a generation, not reality TV winners. As Neil Fox, DJ and *Pop Idol* judge, observed, 'Whoever chose that song, it was a diabolical decision.' Everybody seemed to hate the song but the schedule was so tight that there was no time to go away and choose a new one.

The first publicity shots were also very revealing. The girls looked fantastic together. Sarah, the tallest at 5 ft 7 in, tilted her head so she was in line with the shortest, Cheryl at 5 ft 3 in. Anton, the silky-voiced black singer with One True Voice, was so much taller than the others it looked as if a basketball player had gate-crashed a photo shoot for jockeys. The velvet jackets the boys wore looked as if they had come from their dads' wardrobes. One insider on the show observed, 'They looked ridiculous.' As one of the final group said, 'It was called *Popstars: The Rivals*, but the girls didn't really have any rivals.' One of the misguided assumptions was that young girls would always buy the boys' record ahead of the girls'. That might have been the case before the Spice Girls but 'Girl Power' changed all that. Girls now identified with female pop

Natural born talent: Cheryl always loved to perform and ballet was one of her first loves.

Cheryl won a Bonny Bairns competition when she was four, one of many victories for the 'little smasher'.

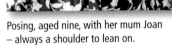

Posing, aged nine, with her mum Joan — always a shoulder to lean on.

When she was ten, she appeared on stage for the first time as one of the tots in Aladdin at the Whitley Bay Playhouse in January 1994.

Strike the pose – Cheryl has a talent for the theatrical element of dance. Above: with Garry Junior. Right: with her regular dance partner, James Richardson. The pair were Northern Counties Champions.

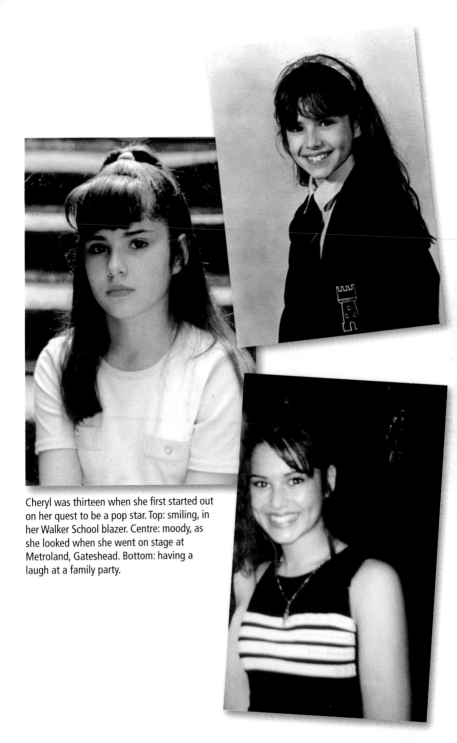

Cheryl was thirteen when she first started out on her quest to be a pop star. Top: smiling, in her Walker School blazer. Centre: moody, as she looked when she went on stage at Metroland, Gateshead. Bottom: having a laugh at a family party.

Popstars: The Rivals. Above: beaming, after singing 'You're Still The One' during week two of the live shows. Right: worried, her performance of 'Nothing Compares 2U' left her in the bottom two in the third round.

Manager Louis Walsh as he is seldom seen – surrounded by girls at a Westlife party during *Popstars: The Rivals*.

'Come On!' – Cheryl shouts for joy when she is the first chosen for Girls Aloud.

How to celebrate 'Sound Of The Underground' becoming the Christmas number one in December, 2002. Above: sweet and demure. Below: yay!

Hiding her emotions behind celebrity shades on her way in to South West Surrey Magistrates Court, Guildford.

At a Soho bar with Nicola Roberts. They were inseparable during the early days of Girls Aloud.

Natural beauty. Cheryl looks stunning in red at the London premiere of *Love Actually* at the Odeon, Leicester Square in November 2003.

stars. The Spice Girls had three consecutive Christmas number ones.

And then there was the song. Louis Walsh observes, 'It was all the song. You just need one song.' Even Pete Waterman, in charge of One True Voice, conceded, 'The first record was brilliant.' The first reports indicated that the girls were going to release a cover of the East 17 number one 'Stay Another Day' on a double A-side with an as yet unwritten song. That all sounded a bit safe and boring, although the East 17 hit was the first record Kimberley ever bought, just after her thirteenth birthday. The name of the second track, 'Sound of the Underground', was released to the press on 18 November while the live shows were still being aired. This, we were told, was a brand new specially written song – a promotional line that turned out to be a big fib as another girl band, called Orchid, had already recorded it.

The veracity of the assertion that this was a new song depends on whether it remained new because it had never been released. Had Orchid recorded it on the assumption that it would be their first single? Or were they merely laying down a demo that the song's writers could use to try to sell the song to an established recording artist? There were rumours that the song was turned down by Samantha Mumba, an exotic-looking Irish-born singer and actress who already had six top ten singles behind her and was being managed by Louis Walsh. This may have been the connection that brought the song to Girls Aloud, although Samantha was also signed to Polydor. Of much greater significance for the future were Xenomania, the writing and production team behind it.

Time was of the essence, so the song was recorded before the world knew which five girls would be in Girls Aloud. The spare girl, who turned out to be Javine, could be removed. Orchid's backing tracks and vocals were used because of time more than anything else and they were given a 'special thanks' on the track. One of the trio, Louise Griffiths, a leggy brunette, had her chance of pop glory when she made the final eight of *Fame Academy* in 2003, although this may have had more to do with her being the girl-friend of Formula 1 racing driver Jensen Button than her singing abilities. She now has a blossoming acting career.

The track's history turned out to be immaterial when it was played against 'Sacred Trust'. 'Sound of the Underground' had edge and was feisty. Music critic Alexis Petridis, writing in *The Guardian*, observed, 'Girls Aloud's debut single . . . proved a first: it was a reality pop record that didn't make you want to do physical harm to everyone involved in its manufacture. Sound of the Underground featured Fatboy Slim dynamics and an irresistible chorus.'

'Sacred Trust', by comparison, was dated and dull. Cheryl thought it was rubbish; the Bee Gees did not figure in her record collection. The competition between the two camps became suitably bitchy, which was good for sales. Pete Waterman waded in by revealing that 'Sound of the Underground' was not a new track and that Girls Aloud did not sing on it. He famously added that he would commit suicide if One True Voice made it only to number two. The great British public would not hold him to that promise.

While it was transparently obvious to everybody else that 'Sound of the Underground' would be a winner, the girls themselves, novices in the pop world, were less convinced. Kimberley commented, 'It sounded different, but a Christmas single? I think we all thought it was f***ing crazy.' The first time Nadine heard it, she said, 'What the f*** is this?' She had a point. The lyrics were pretty incomprehensible, all about water running in the wrong direction. It didn't matter because the overall feel of the song was undeniably fresh.

The girls' marketing and promotion of this song, masterminded by Polydor, was quite brilliant. They had a team assigned to them and everything showed flair and creativity from the very first promotional photos of them wearing tight white T-shirts emblazoned with the logo 'Buy Girls, Bye Boys'. The girls threw themselves into an exhausting two-week schedule. They were immediately assigned a Man Friday called John McMahon who had the title 'tour manager' but in effect had to wipe their noses, make sure they had clean knickers and get them out of bed in the morning – and buy them pizza! The girls loved him.

They barely had time to draw breath before they had to report for Monday morning duty to shoot the video. The director, Phil

Griffin, was one of the best in the business, with a track record dating back to Billie's debut 'Because We Want To' and including Westlife, Damage, Atomic Kitten and 'Round Round' by the Sugababes. Phil has a happy knack of bringing a chart song to life. For 'Sound of the Underground' he wanted to present a dark location that would draw attention to the menacing drum and bass of the song. They were dressed in a combination of black and pink and performed in an underground cage, five girls in a row with five individual mic stands – a pose that would become trademark Girls Aloud. It looked as if Cheryl and the girls had stumbled onto a cold, dark set of *CSI: New York*, performing a song while Mac and his team pored over some gruesome evidence. It was, in reality, a derelict warehouse in West London and was just as chilly as it looked, especially as filming began at five in the morning and ended at three o'clock in the middle of the night. Welcome to the glamorous world of show business.

They all looked a million dollars, although Cheryl probably looked two million in a pink cut-off top. This would be the first time an audience could see who sang what. Sarah started things off but then Cheryl sang the second and third lines of the verse and would later sing the second line of the second verse. Cheryl and Nadine had the most distinctive tone to their voices but with Girls Aloud it would always be tricky to work out which of them was singing at any time.

The two weeks of competition whizzed by. Even though they were all young, healthy girls, they found the schedule shattering. John McMahon tried to keep their spirits up as he woke them for yet another early start on *GMTV*, an appearance on *CD:UK* or *Top of the Pops*. An early bonus was support from Radio One DJ, Jo Whiley, which gave some legitimacy to a reality TV band. They also made the pages of *OK!* magazine for the first time, although Princess Diana's brother, Earl Spencer, was the main story.

The bitchiness between Girls Aloud and One True Voice escalated with Cheryl doing her bit to fan the flames. There is nothing like a good feud to drum up sales. The low point – or high point, depending on how you viewed these spats – came after both bands made their debuts at the popular London club G-A-Y. The fall-out was conducted in the pages of *The Sun* newspaper. One of the boys, Daniel Pearce, said, 'They sounded so flat. They just can't sing. They can't harmonize.' Cheryl wasn't having that and countered, 'The fans at G-A-Y were chanting "number one" to the girls and the boys weren't too happy. If they can't even sell themselves to gay men, well, it says it all, really.' Cheryl is not quite right on this occasion. Girls Aloud were tailor-made for a gay audience and would continue to build an important gay fanbase. Kylie Minogue represents the premier sound for the gay market and Girls Aloud could happily follow her example. One early critic even dubbed the girls a 'five-headed Kylie'.

The boys apparently suggested the girls looked 'tarty', a view that met with an angry response from Cheryl: 'To call us tarts is outrageous.' The boys were coming across as ungallant and sour, not a winning combination. Cheryl also had little time for Pete Waterman's suggestion that they didn't sing on the record, referring to it as 'the stupidest thing'. She told *The Observer*, 'How did he think he was going to get away with that when people heard us singing live on TV for ten weeks?' Cheryl was already revealing herself to be the sparkiest, most outspoken member of the group. Belatedly, the boys tried some rock 'n' roll behaviour by trashing their luxury house before they left, causing damage estimated at £15,000, which, as one record company man wryly commented, was 'probably half their wages'.

The records were released on Monday, 16 December and Girls Aloud immediately found an ally in Caroline Sullivan of *The Guardian*, who showed remarkable foresight. 'Girls Aloud could, in my view, be the first girl band to matter since the Spice Girls . . . It would be nice if what fans aspired to was not the dumbed down blonde Topshop fillies of Atomic Kitten but a female act with attitude and opinions . . . If the band can sing, and this lot can, it's a bonus.' An aspiring band could not ask for better than that, especially as it would have been much easier to jump on the bandwagon dismissing all reality groups after the demise of Hear'Say.

On the very first day of release it became obvious that the girls were going to win. They sold 60,000 more copies on the first day and cantered to victory. By the time they were in their dressing rooms for the special *Popstars* show, they knew they were the Christmas number one and could start celebrating before it was announced to the TV audience. In the end 'Sound of the Underground' sold 213,000 copies during the first week as opposed to 147,000 for 'Sacred Trust'. The Cheeky Girls made it a clean podium sweep for the reality show, taking third spot with 'The Cheeky Song (Touch My Bum)', perfectly illustrating the power of television in these matters. 'Scorpio Rising' made number fourteen.

Before we feel too sorry for Pete Waterman, it should be pointed out that One True Voice were signed to his own record label, Ebul, which was in partnership with Jive Records. So, thanks to the power of television, Pete had been a judge on a programme that paid him and, subsequently, reaped the commercial benefits of a hit record as well. It is the blueprint for Simon Cowell and *The X Factor* contestants, and great business – the phenomenally successful Leona Lewis, for example, is signed to Cowell's Syco Records.

Cheryl returned in triumph to Newcastle for a Christmas break during which she was fêted in the pub by her friends and family. It was a world away from the glitz and glamour of the *Smash Hits* Poll Winners Party, where she had rubbed shoulders with ever-smiling celebrities, but this was home. The irony of reality television is that it plunges the participants into a totally unreal world. Newcastle – that was real. And so was the news that their popular tour manager, John McMahon, had been killed on Christmas Day. He was behind the wheel of a Chrysler people carrier that had left the road and crashed into a telephone pole near his home in Stafford. He died at the scene.

The papers carried a grisly picture of the battered vehicle with Girls Aloud painted on the side. John, who was forty-three, was well liked in the music industry, having also worked with Craig David and Ms Dynamite. He had only been with the girls a short time – just a month – but it had been the most exciting time of their lives. The television programme had been nerve-racking but the whirring merry-go-round since then was a breathless adrenalin rush. They relied on John. A spokesman for Polydor had the thankless task of trying to strike the right chord: 'On behalf of the girls and Polydor, we are truly shocked and upset by the tragic loss of someone we all adored and loved. Our thoughts are with John's family.'

Louis Walsh said, 'He was a lovely bloke and very professional. I've just got off the phone to Nadine. She's totally shocked and upset.' John's death put a dampener on what should have been a very happy time. Cheryl joined the girls on 6 January for John's funeral in Stafford. The year 2003 was getting off to a bad start.

10

The Incident

Cheryl always refers to it as 'The Incident', making the whole saga
sound like a report from a policeman's notebook. It had all started
so well, just a girls' Friday night out with Nicola. In the early days
of Girls Aloud, the two girls had become inseparable. They were
nineteen and seventeen, and after a long day in the recording
studio near Guildford the last thing they wanted to do was put
their feet up with a mug of hot chocolate and a good book. 'Sound
of the Underground' was still number one in the charts and they
had become instant celebrities. Since the end of *Popstars: The
Rivals*, barely a day seemed to go by without a television appearance. Everywhere they went they would be recognized and,
because it was a new feeling in their lives, they were not yet fed up
with that kind of attention.

Being in a studio is not especially gruelling. Making pizzas or
burgers for ten hours is far more like hard work. Cheryl had spent
many hours in recording studios in Newcastle so she knew exactly
what to expect. It was boring, lounging around in a chair, reading
magazines, drinking coffee and chatting hour after hour waiting to
be summoned by the producer who was painstakingly assembling
a track. The vocals always seemed to be the last thing. Afterwards
everyone went out for dinner to discuss how it was going before
saying their goodbyes. The girls were staying in a local hotel in
Guildford but Cheryl and Nicola were not ready to turn in then.
They decided to adjourn to a bar and, from there, to a nightclub

in Onslow Street called, unfortunately, The Drink. And that is exactly what Cheryl did – she downed champagne, vodka, Red Bull and the lethal liqueur Aftershock. She was having a great time in the VIP area, being looked after by Phil White, head of security at the club, who cheekily told her she looked better on TV than she did in real life, which led to giggles all round. She was having fun and enjoying being chatted up by the eligible young men of Guildford.

Cheryl did not have a reputation for being a big drinker in Newcastle and her petite frame was not built for bingeing. She quickly became drunk or, as an eyewitness observed, 'completely paralytic'. Cheryl and Nicola adjourned to the ladies' where, according to university student Lauren Etheridge, 'She did not walk out of the cubicle, she fell out of it.' What exactly happened next, however, became the subject of allegation and counter-allegation, which threatened to ruin Cheryl's hard-earned success.

As she was leaving, Cheryl grabbed a handful of sweets and little lollies that were on the counter and then proceeded to get into an almighty row with the toilet attendant, a thirty-nine-year-old black woman called Sophie Amogbokpa, who thought she was leaving without having the good manners to give her a tip. In the subsequent uproar Nicola ran off to get Phil White, who walked in to watch Cheryl unload a right hook on Sophie that would have made Mike Tyson proud. The attendant certainly looked like she had gone a round or two with the ex-heavyweight champion.

Cheryl was boiling with anger and the police were called. Instead of being tucked up in her comfy hotel bed, she spent the rest of her Friday night in the police cells. She was locked up in Guildford police station for ten hours and used up her only phone call to ring her mum in Newcastle. She was given police bail and told to report back to the station in March. Cheryl was released just in time to be fetched by limo and taken to the ITV studios on the South Bank to rehearse for *Ant and Dec's Saturday Night Takeaway* on which Girls Aloud were scheduled to appear. When Cheryl arrived at the studios, it became clear that urgent repairs would be needed. She, too, was sporting a battle scar and overnight had developed an unsightly 'shiner'. The show's make-up artist, Richard Ardoff, was summoned to work his magic and the great British public who watched never knew the behind-the-scenes drama.

When the story broke in the *Sunday Mirror*, the morning after the morning after, it was clear that this was not something that was going to be shrugged off as youthful high spirits. The headline on the front page said it all: 'She punched me in the eye and screamed: "You f***ing black bitch ..."' It was not the violence that was a potential disaster for Cheryl, it was her alleged use of the word 'black', which immediately brought the element of race into the story. There was worse to come.

The newspaper laid it on with a trowel. Sophie Amogbokpa, we learned in the sixth line of the piece, was a 'church-going law student, who earns £25 a night to pay her way through college'. One detail was not in doubt – Cheryl had whacked her so hard she needed hospital treatment for an eye so badly swollen she could not open it. The picture of her face revealed the awful damage.

Sophie told the newspaper everything, saying she had no idea at the time that Cheryl was a pop star: 'I don't care how many number ones she's had. She shouldn't have said those things to me or hit me. I had done nothing to her and whoever gives me an eye like this should be punished.'

The trouble began, said the attendant, when Cheryl took a large quantity of sweets, not the one or two that clubbers usually wanted. When she asked her why she needed all those, Cheryl responded, oddly, that her father owned the place and she could do what she liked. Sophie grabbed her arm as Cheryl went to leave, causing her to drop the sweets into a sink.

The attendant claimed, 'The girl stood there screaming and shouting, saying, "You black bitch, you f***ing black bitch, I will deal with you."' She continued that, as the security guard came in, 'She punched me in the face. She broke the frame off my glasses and they fell off.'

Phil White then grabbed the struggling Cheryl while Nicola, it was claimed, was 'cowering in the corner'. The bad news for Cheryl was that, in the newspaper article, Phil completely backed up Sophie's allegations. He said that when he restrained Cheryl, she was shouting, 'Let me at that f***ing black bitch; I want to hit her', and subsequently bawled out, 'Bring that Caribbean nigger here; I want to hit her.' Phil said that after the police arrived Cheryl fell to pieces and started sobbing.

The club's manager, Giovanni, also confirmed the use of the phrase 'black bitch' and said the police were called because 'it was a hard punch and because of the racially aggressive nature of her comments'.

The article was highly damaging to Cheryl, and Polydor were quick to issue a statement: 'Cheryl categorically denies allegations of racist abuse. She is completely devastated by these allegations. She was involved in an incident at the club but fought back in self-defence.'

The story was a great scoop for the *Sunday Mirror*. The newspaper had, it seemed, completely sewn up the story and none of the protagonists involved featured in any of the follow-ups pursued by other papers. The club refused to comment, having already given chapter and verse to the tabloid. Clearly the exclusive deal had been fixed up with lightning speed. Cheryl's trial by tabloid was destined to be a key feature in the saga. The original story caused her enormous distress but, it could also be argued, provided her with a 'get out of jail' card.

Back in Newcastle, her friends did not realize the full extent of the seriousness of the allegations against Cheryl. Nupi Bedi, who had been celebrating Cheryl's success with her family at Christmas, recalls, 'We just had a laugh about it – typical Cheryl, having a go. Northerners just don't think about these sorts of things because everybody goes out for a drink and worse things happen. You see worse things in a pub, you know what I mean.'

Polydor's statement, however, is highly revealing. The most damaging aspect of the incident was the race element and Cheryl's career would stand or fall on that issue. When that became clear, her friends and family rallied around in the strongest fashion they could. After the *Sunday Mirror* had beaten their rivals with the first story, it was left to the *News of the World* to counter with Cheryl's version of events in which she said she acted only in self-defence, had called the attendant a bitch but categorically denied being a racist: 'I am distraught that people are accusing me of racism. It couldn't be further from the truth.'

Joan also robustly defended her daughter as a 'quiet, sensitive girl' who had always enjoyed the music of black artists and dated several boys from the 'ethnic communities' including Haydon Eshun from Ultimate Kaos. This was completely true. Cheryl had always enjoyed the company of black boys. Much was made of Cheryl's friendship with Javine Hylton during *Popstars: The Rivals* and also that she was involved with Jacob Thompson, who was of mixed race.

Nothing in Cheryl's life, past or present, suggested any element of racism. When allegations of this nature surface, the defence always seems to be that 'some of my best friends are black'. It's used so much that people might become slightly cynical about those claims. In Cheryl's case, they appear to be entirely genuine. Her cousin Andrea Bell was married to West Indian-born Jeffrey Blaize, and Cheryl adored their little baby. Nupi observes, 'She loved the little baby to bits. I never found Cheryl to be racist at all. I thought the press made a very big thing about it and it was very unfair.'

Polydor continued to be on her side: 'There is obviously a lot more to this incident than meets the eye and we will be getting to the bottom of it. Cheryl is with the rest of the band at the moment and they are all being completely supportive of her.' Louis Walsh also took a conciliatory line, acknowledging Cheryl made a mistake but also giving her the benefit of the doubt: 'There are two sides to every story. It's very easy to point the finger and accuse the famous person of being in the wrong. She knows what she did was wrong and I have spoken to her about it but I'm not giving her the boot from the band. I have told the girls that they have to be on their best behaviour from now on because they are in the spotlight.'

The most important words of that quote might appear to be the news that Cheryl was not getting the sack. But that only tells part of the story. Privately, Louis thought Girls Aloud were one-hit wonders and would speedily go the way of Hear'Say. There was little point in firing Cheryl if the band were not going to last. 'Sound of the Underground' was number one for four weeks and eventually sold more than 600,000 records. That, however, is a disappointing result for both a Christmas number one and a reality show chart-topper. The idea that this was some sort of fabulous result is wide of the mark.

They may have been the first girl band to debut at number one but so what? The music business is entirely driven by sales. The Spice Girls debut single 'Wannabe' may not have entered the charts at number one but it sold more than twice as many copies as 'Sound of the Underground'. The facts do not lie. Hear'Say's debut sold more than a million copies. Will Young, who had won *Pop Idol* nine months before *Popstars: The Rivals*, sold more than a million copies in the first week. The insipid 'Evergreen' went on to amass 1.7 million in sales – and it wasn't even Christmas.

The Spice Girls' first Christmas number one in 1996, '2 Become 1', sold more than a million copies. Their final seasonal hit, 'Goodbye', in 1998 sold 830,000 in the UK. Even the novelty record 'Can We Fix It', the Christmas number one for Bob the Builder in 2000, sold more than a million copies. 'Sound of the Underground' did quite well but not in any sort of way to guarantee future success. Louis Walsh now admits, 'I didn't expect them to serve their purpose much beyond the TV show and the Christmas record.'

Girls Aloud were effectively on trial, long before Cheryl would have to face a real one. The best thing Cheryl could have done at this time was to duck well beneath the parapet and not attract any attention whatsoever while the hurricane of publicity died down a little. That did not happen. Just a couple of weeks later, she was asked to leave a Newcastle nightclub, Baja Beachclub, after getting involved in a water pistol fight with footballer Titus Bramble and other Newcastle United players.

Cheryl would discover a painful truth over the coming months. When you have fallen by the roadside, the media do not offer a helping hand like the Good Samaritan. Nor do they studiously walk around you like the priest in that parable. Instead, they stop and administer a good kicking. Everything about her life was going to be subject to intense scrutiny from now on. Her family's antics were not helping. Her brother Andrew was treating the magistrates court in Newcastle like a second home. He was there at the end of January with his sister Gillian following their drunken brawl in November. They pleaded guilty to affray and were bound over to keep the peace for twelve months with a fixed penalty of £100 each to be paid if they got into further trouble. The court heard that they had been celebrating Cheryl's success on *Popstars: The Rivals* but the evening deteriorated and they ended up drunkenly fighting with each other before starting an all-out punch-up with a man and a woman outside the metro station in Byker. The woman, who suffered an asthma attack, needed treatment at Newcastle General Hospital for cuts – and a black eye.

Andrew was back a couple of weeks later pleading guilty to three charges of harassment. He had been arrested in November for screaming abuse in the street and sniffing from a blue carrier bag full of glue. He was charged at Byker police station and released but two hours later was caught again in a pub car park, sniffing glue and screaming 'f***' repeatedly. He told police officers to 'get off my glue'. A week later another similar incident saw him arrested yet again for screaming abuse and carrying a bag of solvent.

Andrew was in court again the following week, facing the more serious charge of interfering with a vehicle after he was caught breaking into a Ford Sierra. He was seen on CCTV rifling through the boot. His defence lawyer, Lewis Pearson, highlighted his problems with solvent abuse and said, 'What upsets him most is the fact that the press are here. She [Cheryl] is a member of a pop idol band and they wish to use his conduct to shame her.' The case was adjourned for sentencing until 7 March.

Cheryl would be facing her own D-Day that month. On 13 March, she reported to Staines police station to be told that she was being charged with racially aggravated actual bodily harm. She was again released on bail to appear before Surrey Magistrates Court in Guildford on 25 March. It was the worst possible outcome. Cheryl immediately issued a statement: 'I am totally devastated by the charge that has been brought against me. I have always maintained that I am entirely innocent of the accusations that have been made, and I am determined to fight to prove my innocence.'

At the second hearing the charge was amended to racially aggravated common assault. She arrived at the court in a people carrier with blacked-out windows, and wearing a long black coat and celebrity shades. But this was not a guest appearance on a frivolous TV show. She was again bailed to appear at a later date. At this rate she would be neck and neck with her brother to see who could appear most in court in 2003.

The newspapers continued to make unhappy reading for Cheryl. A couple of days after another nerve-racking court appearance, the *News of the World* carried a kiss-and-tell story from Jason Mack: 'I Had Rub-A-Dub In The Tub With Girls Aloud Cheryl'. The story was in the best traditions of Sunday tittle-tattle and was exclusively about sex, leaving the impression that Cheryl and Jason were at it like rabbits from dawn till dusk, giving no account to the laughter and the many tears the couple had shared.

Cheryl was mortified because she had cared so deeply for Jason. It was the usual knock-about fare of sex in the bath, sex in every position, sex while her mum was at the supermarket, sex while Joan was having a cuppa downstairs, sex to R&B tracks and ... more sex. The article also claimed that Jason had thought Cheryl had a fantastic backside when he first saw her, which, considering she was twelve, was completely untrue. Jason had tried to be nice about his former girlfriend, saying, 'I'm so proud of her', but that sentiment was lost in the trawl through their bedroom secrets.

At least Cheryl wasn't the only one mortified by the article. Jason, too, could not believe his eyes when he saw it in black and white: 'I told them, "I'm not saying any filth about her or things like that".' Jason was paid £10,000 for the story but was so ashamed of the result that he has never touched the money. He still has all of it lying in the bank even though he has had more than his fair share of hard times.

The irony was that he was finally pulling his life together. After he and Cheryl finally split, he went on a rapid downward spiral and started injecting heroin as well as smoking it. He recalls, 'It's a good job we split because I got worse and worse. I didn't get any better. I just went into self-destruct mode. I wasn't just taking heroin but everything I could get my hands on basically – valium and sleeping pills – anything to block it out.'

In the summer of 2002, while Cheryl was trying to get into *Popstars: The Rivals*, Jason was trying to get into a rehab programme. He realized he was trapped in a vicious cycle: 'I looked in the mirror one day and I thought to myself, "If you don't stop it now you won't be here in twelve months." I would have been six foot under.'

The wait for a rehab programme was eighteen months so Jason, not wanting to leave it that long, resorted to the desperate measure of getting arrested in the hope that he would be given a DTO (Drug Treatment Order) and sent to a centre for treatment. He started stealing jars of coffee but, with a dash of black humour, proved so adept that it took him ages to get arrested. Eventually the plan worked and Jason has been clean now for seven years.

Jason saw Cheryl and Joan in the Shields Road, early in 2003, when he was coming out of a pharmacy where he had collected his medication: 'We stood on the corner and spoke to each other and she could tell by looking at us that I was on the mend. I told her what I had been up to and she says, "I'm glad for you" and that was it. Then two or three weeks later I did that daft thing, selling the story. I never saw her again.'

Life for Girls Aloud was not getting any easier either. The inevitable rumours about Cheryl's position in the band were followed by the news that their first tour had been cancelled because of lack of ticket sales. They had been due to play a dozen dates in March with One True Voice and other performers from *Popstars: The Rivals*. By coincidence the day after she appeared in court for the first time, the girls had been scheduled to play Newcastle, which would have been highly embarrassing.

Interest in the tour had been disappointing but it would also have been completely hijacked by the furore surrounding Cheryl, so it was probably just as well that it was cancelled. Louis Walsh gamely blamed One True Voice: 'Being associated with One True Voice was not doing them any favours. It wasn't selling. Nobody was buying any tickets. Girls Aloud are doing brilliantly and they don't need to be supported by anyone else.'

Behind the scenes not everyone was convinced they were 'doing brilliantly'. Polydor were desperately trying to take the heat off the girls and banned them from turning up at the Brit Awards at the end of February. Louis Walsh explained that the directive came from the top of the company: 'They are not to go out to parties where they will be photographed. I had to ring them up on the afternoon of the Brits and tell them to stay away. It's a shame because they would have looked great.'

11

Xenomania

Despite the united front, it is not hard to imagine that Cheryl was not the most popular member of Girls Aloud at this time. Louis Walsh found that he was extremely busy with his managerial commitments to Westlife. The girls say that in two years under Walsh's management, they received only two phone calls from him. Their survival in the fickle world of music would be entirely down to the girls themselves – and the outcome of a notorious court case.

For the moment all they could do was carry on recording their first album and hope that the release of their second single would allow some breathing space. At least they were able to leave the soulless apartment block in Westminster. Polydor found them flats in a more exclusive building in Friern Barnet in North London, where it would be much more of a mission to go out and get into mischief. Princess Park Manor was a magnificent Victorian estate set in thirty acres of parkland with superb sporting and leisure facilities, including a huge swimming pool. It was paradise for a bachelor girl.

As in the original *Popstars* house, Kimberley shared with Nadine while Cheryl linked up with Nicola. Life was not glamorous at all. Nupi Bedi recalls going to visit Cheryl and finding the girls in a high state of excitement – the new telly was arriving. The girls were a long way from being rich; Polydor gave them an allowance of £800 each per week, which was a good deal more than waitressing paid but nowhere near a celebrity wage. At least they had a cleaner.

Recording was the only light in the darkness. The process would prove to be vital in the development of Girls Aloud because it brought them into close contact with a publicity-shy production guru called Brian Higgins. Originally from the Lake District, Brian had spent much of the nineties as a keyboard player with the excruciatingly named Motiv8. He wanted, however, to write and produce so he set up his own concern, Xenomania, and promptly wrote his first hit, 'All I Wanna Do' for Dannii Minogue, which reached number four in 1997. In the small world of pop celebrity, Dannii Minogue would connect with Cheryl Tweedy many times. Brian is vague about his odd choice of company name, only explaining that it's the opposite of xenophobia (hatred of foreigners or foreign things).

His second hit was the huge-selling 'Believe', which was number one in the UK and the US for Cher in 1998. In a classic pop story, he missed out on producing the track because he was too embarrassed to invite the famous pop diva to his grotty pad above a shop. He was not the man who decided to put the dreaded Vocoder on the record – that dubious accolade goes to Brian Rawling, who ended up as producer. It was all part of the learning process for Brian Higgins, who during a painful fifteen years realized he needed to be in control to produce the sound he wanted. He moved out of London to a village near Westerham in rural Kent and set about recruiting a like-minded posse of artists, writers, musicians – and accountants – all under one roof. He wanted to create Motown UK and Girls Aloud would be his Diana Ross and the Supremes.

Brian memorably summed up the philosophy of Xenomania to *The Observer* newspaper: 'What we stand for is everything about the interesting side of music but with tunes that the postman will whistle.' By the time of 'Sound of the Underground', the company had grown in stature, producing and writing 'Round Round', the debut number one for the Sugababes. But it was with the five girls of a manufactured pop band that everything Brian had been working for slotted into place. They responded to the respect he gave to their opinions and his single-minded approach in producing the very best sound for them. He could be honest to the point of being blunt with them but, after some initial teething problems with pop star egos, the girls realized that he was a godsend. Cheryl describes it as a chemistry between them.

The other key figure in the development of the Girls Aloud sound was Xenomania's chief songwriter, Miranda Cooper, a stunning, blonde ex-dancer who was able to pass on some advice about the advantages and disadvantages of being an attractive woman in a male-dominated business. Don't ever call her a dolly bird. Her father was a director of the royal jewellers Asprey's, and she was as upper crust as Girls Aloud were piecrust, far more likely to appear in the pages of *Tatler* than the *News of the World*. She did get on famously with the girls, however, perhaps because she, too, had paid her dues. She had been 'discovered' by Dannii Minogue at a dance studio, and until she met Brian, her biggest claim to fame was as one of the backing dancers on Gina G's Eurovision winner 'Ooh Aah . . . Just a Little Bit' in 1996. Brian admits that he is a strong believer in the development of long-lasting creative relationships and he has been working with Miranda since meeting her through Dannii in 1997.

He explained the Xenomania dynamic to *Music Week*: 'We are a very restless group of people. We rarely celebrate success, we just enormously enjoy working together. Invariably, when a record comes out and becomes a hit, we are too engrossed in the record we are currently making to really register anything but relief that the hit has been achieved.' Xenomania is not a pop factory. That suggests churning out hit after hit on a conveyor belt with little regard for the end product. The philosophy is simple – each song is special and different. They were not going to rest on the success of 'Sound of the Underground'.

The first thing was to find the important follow-up single. This was probably more important than their first record, which five cardboard cut-outs could have taken to number one. This time everybody was expecting them to fail. The song Miranda and Brian, with co-writers Nick Coler and Lisa Cowling, came up with was 'No Good Advice'. It already showed some of the touches that would become trademark Girls Aloud – a tight production with a singalong chorus – one, in fact, that the postman could whistle along to. And nobody did a Mel C, singing over the top of the tight melody line. Brian liked to keep things very much together, limiting the range of the harmonies so that nothing grated or seemed out of place. The girls were far more Bananarama than Spice Girls, all singing within their comfort zone. The song also had all the bolshie qualities of 'Sound of the Underground' with the girls not needing any good advice because they were 'already wasted'. The BBC online review described the track as displaying 'more brassy and in-your-face lyrics of defiance and determination'.

The song seemed tailor-made for Girls Aloud but was personal to Brian Higgins, who wrote it about a time when he felt a failure following the collapse of an earlier record deal. It was nothing to do with Girls Aloud at all. The girls, also, were not at all keen on the track when Brian first played it to them and the ensuing 'discussion' proved to be the crossroads in their relationship. Brian recalls, 'They said, "That's not our sound." I objected to the use of that phrase "our sound". I told them they had five minutes to talk about whether or not they wanted to continue with me. They went away and spoke about it and since then it's been fine. They come in expecting to work, and there's a trust there which, I think, dates back to that day.' The exchange typified Girls Aloud both collectively and individually – they were feisty enough to have their own opinion, but smart enough to change it.

The accompanying video was one for the boys and, arguably, not as successful as 'Sound of the Underground'. The girls, dressed in the tightest silver spray-on outfits, danced around a big red car for some unexplained reason. Cheryl hated the whole experience, especially when her trousers split. She came across as snarly and moody, which she probably was at the time. The girls may not have been happy with the video but it was voted the fifth sexiest video of all time in a 2006 poll. They did look hot enough to barbecue chicken. Cheryl had shorter hair at this time and seemed to be going through a phase of wearing crop tops all the time, showing off a shapely bust, toned stomach and, from the other side, Bing's kitchen table tattoo. She would later joke that she was going through one of her worry diets, where stress – this time the court case – would result in her weight plummeting.

Five months had passed since the end of *Popstars: The Rivals* and the glare of publicity surrounding the Christmas number one. The girls were still very newsworthy because of Cheryl's assault charge but, musically, it was a long time to disappear. Traditionally, a big-selling record is followed in rapid succession by son of big-selling record, an ill-conceived clone of the original. 'No Good Advice' was similar but different. The girls threw themselves into the promotion, seemingly on *CD:UK* every week. The single debuted at number two on the charts, beaten to the top by R Kelly's 'Ignition Remix'. It was a disappointing result but could have been much worse. One True Voice's second single only made number five. They would be kaput by July, surviving just seven months.

A week after the release of 'No Good Advice' came the debut album, unoriginally titled *Sound of the Underground*. In the sleeve notes Cheryl thanks two people who were helping to keep her sane during her impossible year. First, Nicola, to whom she says, 'You're all of it!' Life for the two girls in Friern Barnet was like an episode of a sitcom – *Girls Behaving Badly*. They were the female equivalent of slobs – slobettes. Cheryl did not need an excuse to be the world's messiest girl, and in Nicola she found an instant soulmate. They can laugh about it now. Cheryl admits in *Dreams That Glitter* that their flat was a 'filth pit', sporting the heady aroma of bacon and pizza. They never cooked. They never washed their clothes for the simple reason that they did not know how to work the washing machine. When Joan came to visit she would work her way through the pile of cruddy clothes.

The second important person Cheryl thanked was Drew, the girls' tour manager, Drew Lyall, who would keep her spirits up when the grim reality of her impending court case would infiltrate the heady pop world. Cheryl had opted for a proper trial in front of a jury so the whole process was going to drag on until the autumn. When it all threatened to become too much, Drew would drive her up to Newcastle to see her family and go to old haunts, eat Chinese food with her friends and watch soaps with her mum. Rumours surfaced that she and Drew were romantically involved for a time. He was merely being the best support to her, something she acknowledged at the time and since.

Cheryl was not being a complete hermit and still had time to date and be linked with a number of good-looking young men – most of whom, incidentally, seemed to be black. The best rumour, certainly in Newcastle, was that she was dating the well-known footballer Kieron Dyer. One of the urban myths about Cheryl was that she had been in the car with Kieron when he crashed his Ferrari into the Swing Bridge over the Tyne. She has always denied any involvement with the star winger, although she did go to a football match with him. She cheekily added: 'We didn't go out on a date but I wouldn't mind though. I think he's really nice.'

The rumours of a fling with Haydon Eshun also surfaced with reports that they had spent several days together at the K West Hotel in Kensington. Cheryl was simply a nineteen-year-old single girl who could pick and choose her men. She made it clear she was not interested in Duncan James of Blue but, for a few months, did go out with Adam Walsh, Kimberley's brother, whom she met when she had been invited up to Bradford. Cheryl really liked him: 'We just clicked and everything's going great. He's like a male version of me and everything and we're getting along just fine.' In the beginning they would double date with Kimberley and her boyfriend, Martin Pemberton. Kimberley was apprehensive at first, saying, 'If anything goes wrong, it's going to be awful.' Adam was in Yorkshire and Cheryl lived in Friern Barnet and lived a hectic, exhausting existence so, in the end, the romance barely got off the ground before it was over, although everyone was at pains to say it was completely amicable when they called it a day.

The album was a disappointment, although they tried their best to promote it. The girls, always their own harshest critics, were not especially pleased. All the best tunes seemed to be at the beginning, including the two hit singles and the one that was earmarked for their third release, 'Life Got Cold'. Not all the tracks came from Xenomania and the girls felt that counted against it. It was also too long. The critics, however, were mainly kind. Jacqueline Hodges, in her BBC review, said, 'Brian Higgins injects an element of instant-catchy-cool to the songs without going overboard in trying to shape uber-chic dance floor hits . . . their debut album is sure to shut up at least some of their cynics'. Alexis Petridis in the *Guardian* thought it 'jolly'.

Sound of the Underground was denied the top spot by Justin Timberlake's sublime album, *Justified*, which was no disgrace. The greater problem was that sales were disappointing. *Justified* sold seven million copies worldwide so they were never going to compete with that. But, despite their best efforts, only 100,000 copies had been shifted in the all-important first month. A couple of singles and an album might be all the record company were prepared to do for reality TV winners. Cheryl was faced with the horrible thought that the album was doing less well than everyone hoped it would because of her impending court case. Fortunately for Girls Aloud, Polydor liked them and intended to give them every chance to recoup the £1 million they had spent on the group so far.

Cheryl and the girls may not have realized at the time but the public also liked them. Anyone who saw them perform at Party in the Park in July would agree. The crowd on a midsummer's day in Hyde Park were totally involved in their performance, singing, or more accurately shouting, along to 'I don't need no good advice', giving it an enormous anthem quality as if they were leading the singsong at Wembley before a football match. Girls Aloud, manufactured by television, were cheered, not booed. They were ordinary (very pretty) girls and good fun. Cheryl danced away in white crop top and red trousers as if she didn't have a care in the world.

In August the cheerlessly titled 'Life Got Cold' became the third single from the album and did much less well than the other two. The track still managed number three in the charts but stayed a shorter time. The song was downbeat and bore a startling resemblance to the Oasis classic 'Wonderwall', which most of the critics immediately noticed. The *Sun* quoted an insider: 'They are all big Oasis fans so I'm sure they won't mind comparisons with their classic love song.' It was certainly moody enough to be a homage to the Gallagher brothers.

'Life Got Cold' was not a good career move. Girls Aloud were in danger of becoming miserable. They needed something good to happen.

12

On Trial

The trial of Cheryl Tweedy began on Thursday, 9 October 2003. Cheryl was subdued and looked worried when she arrived on the first morning wearing a white jacket and tailored pin-striped trousers. Her hair was in a demure ponytail. She was ushered past photographers by court security before denying the charges and listening to the opening remarks of the prosecution barrister, Ms Patricia Lees.

She heard an account that was broadly the same as the one that had originally appeared in the *Sunday Mirror* newspaper. Sophie Amogbokpa described the argument over the sweets and her version of Cheryl's behaviour, culminating in Cheryl punching her and her glasses falling off. This time, however, there was an important difference: Cheryl had someone in her corner, defence barrister Richard Matthews, who was able to cross-examine Sophie. Her original statement, the jury learned, had not contained the word 'black' and Mr Matthews asked her why that was. She was unable to explain this.

Mr Matthews also suggested that it was Sophie and not Cheryl who had been the original aggressor: 'You went on the attack because you thought Cheryl Tweedy had taken too many lollies. You punched Cheryl Tweedy.' Sophie denied the suggestion. She did agree, however, that she was 'reliant' on the money she made from the lollies, sweets, chewing gum, make-up and perfume that were available in the ladies' room. But she insisted it was not her 'habit' to become aggressive if she didn't get a tip and also denied grabbing Cheryl's bag to try to retrieve the sweets.

Cheryl would have her opportunity to tell her side of the story later. For the moment, the prosecution pressed on with student Lauren Etheridge, who described how drunk Cheryl was and that she had earlier seen her sitting on the floor 'swaying'. Crucially, under cross-examination, Lauren confirmed that she had said in her witness statement that she did not believe the attack was 'racially motivated'.

The trial proved to be the greatest ordeal of Cheryl's life to date. Day after day she and Joan were collected from the flat and driven to the court to relive the nightmare evening in The Drink. She had pleaded not guilty to two charges: racially aggravated assault and the alternative charge of assault occasioning actual bodily harm. The stark fact remained – she could be jailed for a maximum of two years if she was found guilty.

Another clubber, Bryony Gibbs, was called on Friday and confirmed that Cheryl was drunk and had fallen over while trying to text and dance at the same time. She said, 'When the toilet attendant leaned forward to take the lollies from Cheryl, Cheryl punched her.' The only good part of her testimony from Cheryl's point of view was that Ms Gibbs made no mention of racial name-calling.

That was not the case when Philip White, the nightclub's security head, took the stand. His evidence did not do Cheryl any favours. He described Cheryl's punch as a textbook right hook he identified from his days of boxing training. He then said he had picked Cheryl up, taken her to the other end of the lavatory and tried to calm her down. She was shouting towards Sophie, 'I am going to do you. You f***ing black bitch. I'm going to do you.' He told the court, 'She [Cheryl] was trying to get out of my grip. We have been told to be more gentle with females because of some of the allegations you get, but she was very strong, a very strong young lady.'

Mr White then made one of the more curious allegations regarding the incident. He said he took Cheryl to the VIP room to calm down whereupon she shouted, 'Get that jigaboo up here and I'll sort it out.' The word 'jigaboo' is a derogatory and offensive piece of American slang for a black person but not commonly used in the UK. On that note, the case was adjourned until the following Tuesday, when, after ten months of torment, Cheryl would finally have her say.

Cheryl was in tears and using a tissue to dab her eyes as, for the first time, she described how she had punched the attendant only in self-defence, after she herself had been hit. She said that when she came out of the cubicle she had taken five lollipops from a display by the sink. As she reached into her handbag to pay for them, she sensed there was a 'problem' with the attendant. She tried to calm her down and said, 'Hang on a minute', but, as she looked for the money, she saw Sophie leave her chair: 'I think she thought I was just going to take them without paying. The next thing I felt was a blow to my face. I was stunned. I wasn't expecting it. I was scared and angry.' She heard Nicola shout, 'Oh my God!' and run off to get help.

Cheryl continued, 'I didn't call her a f***ing black bitch. I was thinking, "How the hell do I get out of this one?" She's a big woman, quite scary-looking with quite broad shoulders. I felt scared of what she was going to do. I was in a strange area in a strange club. I wasn't sure of the situation. I whacked her back but I don't remember how hard. I was feeling scared, upset and angry. There's no way I'm going to stand there and let someone hit me when I can defend myself.'

On the central issue of racial abuse, Cheryl told the court that not only had she not used the word 'jigaboo', she had not even heard of it. She admitted swearing at Sophie but strenuously denied using any kind of racial abuse. She also said that her whole life had been under a cloud all these months: 'It's been sickening. Embarrassing. There's no way, no matter what state I'm in, that I would refer to anybody by their colour.'

Cheryl had to face barbed comments from the prosecuting counsel that fame had gone to her head but countered that her good fortune did not mean 'the way I was brought up and the person I am had changed'. She concluded, 'I know in my heart, Sophie knows in her heart and the Lord above knows that I am telling the truth. I defended myself and this is all that matters to me.'

At least she had told her side now. In a nutshell, she had punched Sophie but only in self-defence and she had never used any form of racial abuse. The next day it was Nicola's turn in the witness box. She confirmed that Cheryl did not strike the first blow, saying that Cheryl had, in fact, been hit twice before she retaliated: 'She just retaliated as anybody would if they had been punched in the face.' Nicola then had to face up to the prosecuting counsel suggesting she had made up the story to help her friend. Nicola said, 'At the end of the day, it's my life, my career and I am not going to lie for anybody.'

A second witness, Erin Connolly, alleged that Sophie had, in fact, assaulted her because she thought she had queue-jumped and 'had pulled me back hard enough to rip my collar'.

Much of the defence strategy rested on demonstrating that the racist allegations were a fiction devised to sell a good story to a newspaper. Giving evidence, the club's director at the time, Paul Endersby, admitted telephoning a public relations agent within an hour or so of the row between Cheryl and Sophie. He maintained that he wanted advice on 'how best the media could be handled'. The PR, it was claimed by the defence, arrived at the club to conduct a 'debriefing' session with staff.

It was alleged that only those who had attended this debriefing claimed that Cheryl had used racist language. No one else, including the other girls in the toilet, had heard Cheryl use racist language. And, the defence said, the allegations only emerged after Sophie had met with the agent and subsequently spoke exclusively to the *Sunday Mirror*. Mr Endersby said in court that he thought the agent had been paid for arranging the newspaper deal.

Philip White also confirmed that he had been told to speak only to the *Sunday Mirror*. Mr Endersby further revealed that the club had decided that a single publication was the best way of dealing with the story. Cheryl's barrister, Richard Matthews, said this was pointing towards 'a decision to put a certain story forward'. The defence was clearly implying that Cheryl had been stitched up.

At this point Nupi Bedi was called as a character witness.

Cheryl's solicitor had asked him and he was pleased to help. He had driven all the way from Newcastle that morning, leaving home at 4 a.m. to support Cheryl. He was happy to do it for a friend. He was just the man to confirm in strong terms that Cheryl was not and had never been a racist.

In the final speeches, Ms Lees continued to let Cheryl have it with both barrels. She declared that famous people sometimes behaved in a manner 'totally inappropriate to their status'. She continued, 'You just have to think about allegations of inebriated rock stars behaving as if nobody else is important and they can do what they like. These people are not above the law, nobody is.'

She concluded, 'Who do you think was behaving well or badly – the stone-cold sober lavatory attendant who might lose her job or the drunk Cheryl Tweedy who was, frankly, all over the place?'

In his summary, defence barrister Richard Matthews reminded the jury again of the entanglement between the club and the media. He highlighted that Cheryl had acted in self-defence and had not used any kind of racist terminology. And, with that, the judge promptly adjourned the case for the weekend, which was the worst possible outcome for Cheryl's nerves.

She spent a restless couple of days, unable to eat through worry. The case seemed to be going on for ever. On Monday morning, 20 October, Cheryl, head bowed, arrived at the court in a white suit. Friends say she was very quiet and subdued. Once again, just as she had been when Cheryl was growing up, Joan Callaghan was by her daughter's side. Cheryl acknowledged the debt she owed her mother: 'I couldn't have coped without her. She was my rock.' Friends confirmed that Cheryl was very worried and tired because of sleepless nights.

The jury found her not guilty of the charge of racially aggravated assault but guilty of the alternative charge of assault occasioning actual bodily harm by a majority verdict of 11 to 1. Cheryl gasped and covered her face with her hands. Judge Richard Hawarth said, 'This was an unpleasant piece of drunken violence which caused Sophie Amogbokpa pain and suffering. Her eye was painful for three to four weeks, there was bruising for three months and for a while she had blurred vision. You showed no remorse whatsoever.

'I take into account your age and good character and do not think you will re-offend.' He asked Cheryl if she understood the comments and she replied, 'Yes, I do.'

The judge sentenced Cheryl to 120 hours of community service and ordered her to pay Sophie £500 in compensation as well as £3,000 towards prosecution costs. The verdict and sentence was a good result for her career but she now has a criminal record. It was not a triviality. Nupi Bedi observes, 'Both Joan and Cheryl were upset. They weren't jumping for joy.'

Outside the court, Cheryl, supported by Joan and Drew Lyall, faced the cameras, while her solicitor, Paul Harris, read a statement on her behalf that focused on the dismissal of the race charge: 'I am thankful that the jury has accepted that this incident had nothing to do with race. I am not a racist and anyone who knows me knows I would not say anything racist.'

Polydor were quick to issue their statement: 'We are pleased Cheryl has been found not guilty of the main charge against her. In light of this decision, Cheryl's position in Girls Aloud is unaffected.'

The newspapers, as is their custom, decided to sit in judgement on Cheryl as well, but they were of the opinion that she was not of good character. *The Daily Telegraph* was unimpressed and ran a feature under the headline, 'You're not a racist, but a simple thug? How groovy, Cheryl'. The writer, Jenny McCartney, pointed out that to insult Sophie as a black woman would have been career suicide. She wrote, 'To punch Ms Amogbokpa simply because she was a human being trying to do a thankless job properly, however, appears to pose no public relations problem at all.'

The central argument of the article was that nobody cared about Cheryl being found guilty of assault and, therefore, having a criminal record. Cheryl's future had hung in the balance on the race charge and nothing else. Ms McCartney concluded: 'The loutishness of Cheryl Tweedy – and what the music industry's indifference to it says about the power of celebrity – should repel us.'

The *Daily Mail* chose to drag her family into the spotlight, bringing up her brother Andrew's glue-sniffing and his and Gillian's conviction for violence. Even Joan did not escape censure. And Cheryl was 'at times arrogant, foul mouthed and capable of callous behaviour'.

Even the *Journal* in Newcastle were unsympathetic to their city's favourite daughter, dwelling on the prosecution's argument that Cheryl was full of her own self-importance and posing the question of whether the overnight success provided by reality shows was too much for some, i.e. Cheryl, to handle.

The former *Top of the Pops* producer Chris Cowey, from Sunderland, told the paper: 'What has changed with the emergence of these shows is the way people sometimes do not have to work very hard to get this fame. If you serve some sort of apprenticeship – whether it is in the music industry, doing the clubs or in another profession – I think you get used to dealing with the public face to face.'

Chris, who obviously had no idea that Cheryl had spent years of her childhood working hard for a break, was also uncomplimentary about Girls Aloud: 'During my time at *Top of the Pops* you would come across some less talented [performers] who had definite potential to become brats. And I have to say Girls Aloud come under this banner. They weren't the most friendly of the hundreds of acts we had on the show.' Chris also advised Cheryl to learn from all that had happened to her.

Cheryl could deal with most of the newspapers having a go. It came with the territory. One article, however, rankled above all others. Cheryl was so angry at the opinions expressed in the *News of the World* by television personality Ulrika Jonsson that she still talks about it today and lists 'celebrity columnists' as her pet hate.

Ulrika wrote: 'Cheryl Tweedy from the pop group now more commonly known as "Girls A Lout" has got her just desserts. Her behaviour when she punched a toilet attendant showed she had let drink AND fame go to her head. She is an arrogant bully who, it goes without saying, sets an abysmal example to young women. However, I predict she will go solo and have a highly successful career. There's nothing like bad publicity for selling records.'

It was lucky for Ulrika that she did not live in the same street as Cheryl, who would have unloaded her Mike Tyson right hook for a second time that year if she had met the Swedish celebrity. Cheryl responded, 'I was furious by what she said. I just thought, "I've never met you, you don't know me, how would you know? How dare you say that about me!"

'She says I'm a bad role model but what kind of role model does she think she is? I've got news for her – she just needs to take a look at herself and watch out if she ever bumps into me or the girls.'

Five years later Cheryl repeated exactly the same 'How Dare She!' sentiment in *Dreams That Glitter.* She said Ulrika's comments were 'horrible' and that it drove her wild.

Hopefully, as far as Cheryl was concerned, her now notorious court case would soon become as newsworthy as cold mashed potato. Sophie Amogbokpa briefly fanned the flames, however, by engaging the renowned solicitor Imran Khan to pursue a civil action against Cheryl.

Mr Khan, who represented the parents of the murdered teenager Stephen Lawrence, sent a legal letter to Cheryl's solicitors outlining Sophie's claim for an apology and substantial damages. He explained, 'The only choice she has is to take this matter to the civil court so Ms Tweedy will finally acknowledge what she has done and the extent to which she has affected Ms Amogbokpa's life.'

The problem appeared to be that Cheryl had not apologized to Sophie for the assault but had said sorry to fans, friends and family. Sophie said, 'I want the world to see the way she really is. She is attempting to carry on with her life and ignore what I went through. When I heard what she told the media, it was as if I was being assaulted all over again.'

Having the whole ghastly experience dragging on was the last thing Cheryl needed. Fortunately, everything went quiet after this flurry of legal activity. Sophie Amogbokpa has never uttered another word on the subject. Cheryl is still cross-examined about it and remains unrepentant. Her justification has always been that her upbringing meant that she would always defend herself. She told *Vogue* magazine in February 2009 that she had never denied calling Sophie a 'f***ing bitch' nor hitting her and would have hit her again at the time: 'That's what we were taught on the estate – you have to defend yourself and that was what I was doing.'

The newspapers all had their say but the views of Cheryl's friends, people who actually know her, are of far more value when looking again at the case. Nupi Bedi observes, 'You see people getting away with this sort of thing. You see fights all the time and it's not like she did it with intent, it was just circumstances.

'I felt it was all because of what she was, which is very unfair. She's got a criminal record now, which is also unfair, you know. I was really disappointed about that.'

Chris Park, who is also from Newcastle, is sure the racism side of it was non-existent: 'I think history has proved that should never have been on the table. That was the annoying thing about it. Because, anybody can have a fight, but that was the ingredient that jeopardized her career. And that was what nearly got her thrown out of the band. And it would have been crap.'

Cheryl has admitted that the incident prompted her to watch her actions more carefully. But she also says, 'I'd rather avoid a fight than get into one. But I have my limits.'

Sophie Amogbokpa decided against pursuing a civil action. The trial was over for Cheryl. The jury, however, was still out on the future of Girls Aloud.

13

Jump

Everybody had said the right things after the case. Cheryl went on *GMTV*, sat on the sofa and declared, 'Without the support of the girls, I do not think I would have got through it as well as I did, to be honest.' Nadine, meanwhile, revealed, 'She got emotional a lot of the time but we all just tried to be there for her and help her through just as best as we could.' Kimberley said that the whole episode had brought them all closer together.

The oldest cliché in the entertainment manual is 'The show must go on.' They could not admit publicly that they were a band in crisis. Cheryl's acquittal on the racism charge had staved off the execution but they needed more than a temporary reprieve. Three days after her conviction, Cheryl joined the girls to perform their new single on *Top of the Pops*. It was quite simply a barnstorming performance oozing *joie de vivre* and a party atmosphere. The song was 'Jump' and was probably as important for Girls Aloud as their debut hit, 'Sound of the Underground'.

Cheryl was quite modestly dressed in combat trousers and top and seemed to take a small step away from centre stage, leaving Nadine to do most of the singing. It was time to remind everyone that there was more to Girls Aloud than punch-ups in nightclubs and that there were four other girls whom the world seemed to have forgotten about these past few months.

'Jump' was one of the great feel-good tracks of the 1980s, when it was a huge hit for the Pointer Sisters. More importantly, the song had longevity – one of those records guaranteed to get the party started. The Pointer Sisters, a group of black sisters from California, enjoyed huge popularity for a few years with hits including 'Automatic', 'Slowhand' and 'I'm So Excited'. They brought a more soulful sound to the territory previously occupied by Diana Ross and the Supremes. 'Jump (For My Love)', as it was originally titled, was such a classic, how could Girls Aloud do it justice?

The answer was that they gave the song joy, the defining quality for the future of Girls Aloud. The girls themselves recognized the change. Cheryl observed that the fans no longer wanted them to be snarly and moody; they wanted them to be fun. There were quite enough bad things going on in the world without having to listen to a bunch of stroppy women. The critics agreed. Paul Scott in *Stylus* magazine online said, 'It's like being surrounded by a drunken hen party and finding enchantment instead of repulsion.' Several years later Scott thought that 'Jump' was the most enduring of all the many hits of Girls Aloud.

As they always did, Cheryl and the girls threw themselves into non-stop promotion of the single. Barely a week after her conviction, Cheryl had to go on stage and face the world again at the National Music Awards night at the Carling Hammersmith Apollo in West London. This time Cheryl was not being modest and keeping out of the limelight. She joined the others on the red carpet for a round of smiles and poses for the cameras in a black mini-dress and shiny black thigh boots.

The usual suspects were on parade, including Simon Cowell, Declan Donnelly, Jordan and Amanda Holden, who was the host. The media pointed out that Girls Aloud walked away with no award, which was gleefully interpreted as a thumbs-down in response to the Cheryl incident. They had been nominated as Best Newcomer but lost out to Busted. That ceremony was only six years ago but it is a telling snapshot of the fickle world of pop and how quickly those in the spotlight can return to the shadows: Rachel Stevens was named favourite female singer, while Gareth Gates received two awards for favourite TV performance and favourite male singer.

The girls' performance of 'Jump' put everyone in a good mood.

The record also had another important advantage – it was part of the soundtrack for the new Richard Curtis blockbuster *Love Actually*, starring Hugh Grant and an all-star cast. Curtis and Grant had made a habit of popularizing songs by British performers in their movies – 'Love Is All Around' by Wet Wet Wet started the fashion in *Four Weddings and a Funeral*, followed by 'When You Say Nothing At All' by Ronan Keating in *Notting Hill*. The trick also worked for Geri Halliwell's uninspiring version of the Weather Girls' 'It's Raining Men', which was her last number one in 2001 when it featured in *Bridget Jones's Diary*.

The premiere of *Love Actually*, on 16 November 2003, promised to be one of the biggest cinematic events of the year and gave Girls Aloud the opportunity to dress up for the occasion and show a style to the world that transcended their usual 'girls out on the pull' look. They did not disappoint. Cheryl dazzled in an ankle-length scarlet ballgown in a wrap-around style crossed at the neck. The huge crowd showed that there was absolutely no hangover from the court case whatsoever in the minds of the fans as they shrieked out the girls' names.

Nobody seemed to mind that thanks to an unforeseen setback the girls had not featured in the film *Love Actually* at all. Originally their version of 'Jump' was the one playing when Hugh Grant, as the Prime Minister, does his impromptu dance in Number 10 Downing Street, one of the movie's most memorable scenes. The producers had taken the decision at the last minute that the original Pointers Sisters recording should be used in the film because Girls Aloud had yet to make any impact abroad, particularly in the US, which was the most important market for any film.

Everybody was naturally disappointed, although the publicity was the main thing and the girls received plenty. Most people thought they were featured in the film anyway – they were on the British soundtrack. The important thing was that Girls Aloud were mixing with A-list guests and looking the part. The red carpet at the Odeon, Leicester Square, was a considerable jump from The Drink nightclub. Cheryl was not feeling quite at her best because she had come straight from recording *The Frank Skinner Show*, then a leading national talk show. All Frank seemed to want to talk about was the court case, which did not thrill her, but that was soon forgotten when she had her first taste of this glamorous world of designer frocks.

'Jump' was released the week after the premiere and made number two in the charts, beaten to the top spot by 'Mandy', yet another Westlife ballad. The Irish boy band have such a loyal fanbase that they are almost impossible to beat in a chart battle. The success of 'Jump' was even more significant, however, when it sparked interest in the first album and, not surprisingly, was added to the track list when it was re-released for Christmas.

The year 2003 was ending so much better than it had begun. Girls Aloud started winning things. They won Hot New Talent at the prestigious *Smash Hits* Poll Winners Awards, 'No Good Advice' won the Popjustice.com £20 Music Prize, 'Sound of the Underground' was named Best Single in the Disney Channel Kids Awards, while the girls were Best *FHM* Cover of the Year at the marvellously named *FHM* Bloke Awards. The last two awards perfectly summed up the core fanbase of Girls Aloud – little girls and lusty lads, an unbeatable combination.

They also continued to be the darlings of the G-A-Y. aficionados. The audiences at the famous West End nightclub at the Astoria had taken Girls Aloud to their hearts right from the start. They were guaranteed an enthusiastic reception from the most loyal fans in the business. The guys copied their dance moves while the girls admired their favourites. Cheryl and Nicola added some spice to their New Year gig by sharing a kiss on the lips. Madonna and Britney were the first to try this particular publicity gambit but it still worked for the two friends. The kiss was more camp than erotic, coming at the end of their act when the girls were dressed as red fairies flashing their stockings at the audience.

Cheryl still had to finish her community service in Newcastle. She picked up litter from the streets and sandpapered benches at the Blue Star Football Club in Woolsington, just down the road from Newcastle airport. She also worked at a care home for people with the debilitating disease multiple sclerosis. She told *The Sun*, 'There was one old guy there and I had to dress him and give him cereal in the morning. He was just so sweet.'

The experience was a sobering one for Cheryl, who was not given any special treatment – nor did she expect any: 'It was really rewarding. The idea of community service sounds really grim but it made me realize just how lucky I was to lead the life I do.' At least she managed to get on with her sentence without the unwelcome attention of paparazzi hoping to catch a glimpse of a hot new star up to her neck in rubbish.

Her community service was completed by the time Girls Aloud appeared at Newcastle's premier gay venue, the Powerhouse Club, at the end of January 2004. Cheryl could see for herself that she was still the darling of her home town – or, at the very least, of the gay audience there. They performed their four hits to a wildly enthusiastic audience.

The most important news of the new year was that there was now no question of Polydor dropping Girls Aloud after just one album. The new fun-packed girl band was given the go-ahead to start work on a second album. Despite their fears about the future, they still had strong support from their team at the record company, especially Peter Lorraine, the marketing director, and Poppy Stanton, who had masterminded their first campaign with 'Sound of the Underground'. Cheryl also had particular reason to be grateful to their head of publicity, Sundraj Sreenivasan, who had more than earned his money looking after Miss Tweedy during the past year.

The one person they believed they were not getting enough help from was Louis Walsh, the man the public still believed was the guiding hand behind the band. In reality they were practically managing themselves, a state of affairs they resented at the time and would lead to a certain frisson between Cheryl and Louis some years later on *The X Factor*.

Girls Aloud, uniquely among female bands, have managed to keep any animosity between them firmly out of the public gaze. There were always rumours but nothing compared to the spats that used to occur between Mel B and Geri Halliwell, or between Mutya Bueno and the rest of the Sugababes. One of the top American managers would never work with girl groups because they harboured grudges – World War Three would break out over some borrowed nail varnish and then the Cold War would set in for ever.

Louis freely admits that he is much happier looking after a boy band. He was unable to tap into the girl bands' personalities in the way Brian Higgins could. Louis explains, 'Girls want to talk about hair, clothes, make-up, all the things that are important for their look on stage, and for me, life was too short for that. I couldn't handle five separate conversations with five different girls, all with their own problems and questions.'

Vitally, however, and despite their inexperience in the music business, Louis recognized that the girls understand the 'gang mentality' and the importance of sticking together. Any private feelings about Cheryl's assault case were never aired in the news-papers. The girls had no formal media training so they just muddled through, learning as they went along. Looking back, Cheryl will admit that Louis leaving them alone meant that they were responsible for their own futures. Cheryl observes, 'We learned a lot and we learned it fast.'

The decisions they made were good ones, none better than throwing their weight exclusively behind Xenomania for their musical future. They understood that the most successful of their songs were those with Brian Higgins at the helm. From now on his stamp would be on every single track. They started to work out how best to collaborate. This was a team effort. Brian and Miranda Cooper were able to tap into each girl's personality and experi-ence and, from there, craft a song that reflected who the girls were.

Kimberley explained, 'It infuriates Brian when people say bad things about us not writing our songs. He's like, "I couldn't have this kind of success without you and the whole team of people around us." The way we look, the way we are as people – all of that inspires Brian to write.' Before the second album started to take shape, Brian invited each girl in for a chat to find out what was happening in their life, their experiences and their ambitions. He must have booked a long appointment with Cheryl, although all the girls had a story to tell. Kimberley, for instance, had broken up with her steady boyfriend, footballer Martin Pemberton, while

Sarah, still independent of the other four, had moved in with Mikey Green, one of the members of the now defunct One True Voice.

In other words, Brian was able to get in tune with the girls in a way Louis Walsh could not. Brian certainly would have been infuriated with Spice Girl Melanie Chisholm having a go at his girls, describing them on TV as 'pop puppets' who would never be as big as the Spice Girls. She would repeat that sentiment in the newspapers: 'There's no doubt Girls Aloud are absolute babes, but to be honest they always look miserable. I'm not sure they enjoy the work as much as we did. They're good but they'll never be the next Spice Girls.'

Her comments are not exactly overly rude, although nobody trying to be taken seriously wants to be called a 'babe'. In musical terms, the Spice Girls were the previous generation and Mel C's remarks were a bit like a retired footballer saying that the current players were not a patch on those of his day. Cheryl began to channel her natural feisty nature into words rather than actions. Her putdown of Mel C was priceless: 'When we were at primary school, we were inspired by the Spice Girls. It is sad she has had to bitch about us to get publicity for her records.'

Mel C might have been more complimentary if she had known of Brian's plan for each of the girls to help write one of the songs for the new album. Not everybody was keen on the idea. Nadine did not fancy it at all: 'I needed to be pushed into it because I wasn't really interested.' Miranda Cooper and another writer, Lisa Cowling, tutored each of the girls. Cheryl had, of course, helped write plenty of songs back in Newcastle. She was always working on lyrics when she was going out with Jason Mack.

This time Brian wanted a contribution to the melody. He told *The Observer*, 'We don't let them out of the room till they've given every ounce of melodic instinct that they've got in them. Then we pile some more in. And when you listen back to the completed track at the end, you find they've contributed really well.'

Brian Higgins was bringing a supremely positive attitude to working with Girls Aloud and they thrived on that energy. Cheryl contributed to the track 'Big Brother', one of the coolest of all

Girls Aloud's songs with a very catchy chorus that was instantly memorable. It could have been a hit single, but perhaps not for Girls Aloud because it lacked the danceability of 'Jump'.The most successful Girls Aloud singles are all classic dance tracks. Brian knew he was under pressure to find the right formula for Girls Aloud singles time and again. They needed to sound good on the radio.

Nearly eight months passed between 'Jump' and the release of the first single from their second album. The girls had misgivings about such a gap. In their first year Girls Aloud had a single in the charts for thirty-five out of fifty-two weeks. In their second year they had vanished. Plans to release a holding single after 'Jump' were abandoned by Polydor, who shrewdly judged the girls needed a lower profile for a while.

Cheryl's major problem during this stage of her career was her fluctuating weight. It was the start of a continuing battle with the bathroom scales – believing herself to be either too fat or too thin. In the early days of Girls Aloud, she considered herself too fat after she saw a pair of designer jeans she wanted in Selfridges, took them into the changing room and found she couldn't do them up – a disaster that women everywhere could relate to. Cheryl burst into tears. She slightly spoiled the effect for 'women everywhere' when she revealed to *Vogue* magazine that she was crying because she had gone up to a size 29 waist and was nine and a half stone – not exactly obese.

For Cheryl, however, it was enough to prompt her to try the then fashionable Atkins Diet. She had read in a magazine that Jennifer Aniston was a devotee of the diet, which favoured protein and nothing much else. Cheryl survived on chicken for weeks, which was not her favourite but was a little better than the Big Macs and pizza she preferred at this time.

The girls were under constant pressure to lose weight, an occupational hazard for women in pop. The Spice Girls had suffered exactly the same pressure. According to *The Sun*, Louis Walsh reportedly told Girls Aloud they were looking too meaty. The newspaper quoted a 'source' who said that the problem for a couple of the girls was their love of junk food. As a result they signed up to fitness training at the Princess Park complex every morning. Louis may or may not have advised them to lose weight, although he barely had enough contact to be so outspoken. A more likely explanation is that the girls themselves decided they needed to be in better shape when it came to promoting the new record and there was talk of their first tour in the near future. Nicola never had any weight issues, Nadine loathed working out and Kimberley did the Atkins Diet with Cheryl.

Ironically, one of the tracks they were working on for the new album was called 'Deadlines and Diets', a nicely judged song about one-night stands and subsequent betrayal in newspapers. Cheryl observed with youthful candour, 'People have one-night stands and if people don't like the song, tough shit.' They wanted to release it as a single but, rather like 'Big Brother', it was not quite right for the radio. 'The Show', however, was pure radio. The first single from the yet-to-be-released album impressed the critics. Alexis Petridis wrote in *The Guardian*: 'The track is based around a frantically exciting electronic noise that seems to have escaped from an early 1990s rave record.' He thought it a perfect example of Xenomania's 'uniquely rousing approach to pop'. The single was released at the end of June and, frustratingly, just missed out on number one, which that week was Usher's 'Burn'. The video helped set the tone for this period of Girls Aloud, still fun but tongue-in-cheek as well. The girls all played characters in a beauty salon. Cheryl was 'Maxi Wax', tearing a strip off the chest hair of a hunky client. It was a laugh and light years away from the brooding cages of 'Sound of the Underground'.

As part of the promotional drive, the girls sang live on *Top of the Pops* for the first time. They had not endeared themselves to the programme's producers by refusing to do so before, preferring to concentrate more on their image and the performance. An important part of their job as Girls Aloud was selling the song. This was too good an opportunity to miss. They opened the first-ever outside edition of the long-running show, which was desperately trying to arrest a steady decline. Even better for Cheryl, it was filmed in Gateshead's Baltic Square. Cheryl surveyed the thousands of screaming youngsters and announced, 'Can I say it's so nice to be surrounded by so many Geordies.' Girls Aloud, however, did not receive the biggest cheer – that was reserved for boy band Busted, singing 'Thunderbirds Are Go'.

Cheryl was careful on this visit to her home town not to make any waves. She had kept a low profile all year with just a few tabloid stories about alleged shenanigans with various footballers. The next single from Girls Aloud was 'Love Machine', which would have given headline writers a heaven-sent opportunity if she was involved in more scandal.

Fortunately, the media were not up to date with Cheryl's private life. She was still living in Friern Barnet and, back from her trip to the North-East, was on her way to the shops one day when she passed a very famous footballer who would change her life.

14

Ash

Cheryl was never going to fall for a man with a silver spoon in his mouth. She has no time for privilege or spongers. She admires achievement and men who have pulled themselves up through talent, passion and the desire to improve their lives and those of their family – perhaps a man who understood what she had gone through to achieve her own measure of success. Of course, it would help if he were good-looking too.

Nadine and Kimberley had both been in steady relationships with footballers, while Cheryl was forever being linked with them. In the age of David and Victoria Beckham, football had become glamorous and exciting for a new generation of young people. Like pop music, the sport offered a means of escape, a fantasy world for millions struggling along in tower blocks and council estates.

England fullback Ashley Cole hates talking about his upbringing in the tough streets of Tower Hamlets in the East End of London. Even in his much maligned autobiography, *My Defence*, he avoids the subject of his Barbados-born father, Ron Callender, who left the family when Ashley was three and younger brother Matthew was two. His father now has a new life in a small town outside Melbourne in Australia. Ron explained, 'I'm not a bad dad. I didn't run away and desert them. I'm not hiding in Australia like Ned Kelly.'

Ashley also declines to share any memories of the unprepossessing block in Mostyn Drive that was home; or the local Bow

School, known locally as Bow Boys, a tough environment for any kid growing up, especially a diminutive child with a black father and a white mother. Ashley was brought up in a predominantly white household.

Cheryl could relate to a situation in which the best you could do was to keep your head down and pretend not to notice the drugs, the violence and the empty purses, and dream of getting out. Her family struggled to make ends meet. By coincidence Ashley's parents never married and split after having two children together – just like Cheryl's mum and dad.

Ashley's father struggled to get a job in the late seventies and early eighties. As a result the family was very poor. Ron added, 'Ashley is someone who is aware of not having much money. Times were hard for us back then.' Ron would later describe as 'heartbreaking' his split from Sue and his two boys. He lived near them at his parents' house and says he saw the boys as much as he could but that it wasn't easy, especially with the daily grind of trying to find a day's work. In the mid-nineties, Ron met and fell in love with an Australian barmaid and they decided on a fresh start in her homeland.

Ashley prefers to dwell on the positive side of his childhood, the fulfilment of his dream of playing for Arsenal and his love for his mother, Sue, a big football fan. His tribute to her in the book is quite moving: 'I don't know how to thank the one person I owe my life to – Mum – because thank you don't seem enough . . . I'd have been lost if she hadn't been behind me every step of the way.' Sue and Ashley have, it seems, a bond every bit as strong as Cheryl and Joan's. He credits her with instilling in him a belief that living in the world is not easy but you have to keep going and live the dream. And, just as Cheryl was single-minded in pursuing her ambitions in Newcastle, so Ashley focused on football, playing for Puma FC in the East London leagues, where other famous footballers, such as England captain John Terry and Ledley King of Spurs, also honed their skills.

Football clubs spot their talent young and Ashley signed an initial development contract with the Arsenal Soccer School of Excellence when he was nine. While his younger brother, Matthew, was 'out in nightclubs', the teenaged Ashley stayed focused. At fifteen he was established as one of the most promising youngsters on Arsenal's books. By nineteen he was in the first team. He has been a fixture in the national side since 2001, playing in the World Cup in South Korea in 2002 when England lost to Brazil in the quarter-finals. He arranged for his father to have a ticket and enlisted his mother's help to pass it on. Ron would later describe it as 'his proudest moment' when he watched the game.

Two years later, in Euro 2004, Ashley was named in the 'Team of the Tournament', despite England unluckily going out to Portugal, again in the quarter-finals. Ashley was still only twenty-three but already enjoying a stellar career, including two Premier League titles with Arsenal.

You might have expected Cheryl to have bumped into Ashley at one of the numerous VIP events she attended around town. By a freaky coincidence, however, he also lived in the Victorian splendour of Princess Park Manor. The luxury complex is so big that you might never meet another tenant. Ashley lived at number 19, while Cheryl and Nicola shared number 127, miles away. Ashley, known as Ash to his friends, did spot Cheryl walking by one day when he had popped in to see a former Arsenal player, Paolo Vernazza, who lived in another apartment. Cheryl described the encounter: 'I walked past the window and he shouted, "Hey, hot lips" and "Nice bum". I hate stuff like that so I rolled my eyes and was, like, "Piss off."' Cheryl had no idea then that Ashley and his mates would always make a beeline for the window when Girls Aloud were walking by. Rather like David Beckham, who said he would marry Victoria Adams the first time he saw her, Ashley Cole knew then and there that Cheryl Tweedy would become Mrs Cole.

The next time he saw her they chatted for a few minutes. It was a blisteringly hot August afternoon. Ashley was playing tennis with his Arsenal team-mate and friend, Jermaine Pennant, on one of the outdoor tennis courts when Kimberley and Cheryl drove by on their way to buy an electric fan. Kimberley had met 'Penno' before so they stopped when he waved and called them over. The boys were glad for an excuse to take a breather. She introduced Cheryl and they talked briefly through the fencing round the court before the boys resumed their game. Ashley revealed in *My Defence* that they were in tune from the very first chat. Cheryl was, for the moment, not interested.

On her way back from the shops, Cheryl spotted Ashley by the courts with the bonnet up on his car. It was an Aston Martin, always a vehicle to get the attention of a girl, however famous. Ashley had spent too long listening to the sound system while playing tennis and the battery had gone flat, which was a little embarrassing. At least he did not ask Cheryl for a jump start. He did, however, ask for her phone number, which she refused to give, saying, 'I can't. I'm sorry.' Cheryl thought Ashley was very handsome and was struck by his dark eyes.

Now was not a good time for Cheryl to start dating properly. During the last six months she had managed to keep a much lower profile and had repaired much of the damage of the nightclub incident. Girls Aloud were in the middle of a frantically busy time when singles, an album and a tour were all coming through fast. 'The Show' had been a success but that was only the beginning of the second instalment of Girls Aloud. Cheryl had always gone on plenty of dates but had only had one long-term relationship – Jason Mack – so perhaps she, also, had a sense of something special during her first conversations with Ashley Cole.

Not long afterwards Cheryl saw a picture spread about Ashley in *Zoo* magazine, so the next time he wandered by at Princess Park it was her turn to shout out, 'See yourself in the magazine? Looking good!' At least they were now on each other's radar. The following week Cheryl went home to Newcastle for a brief visit. Her mother had always been keen on clairvoyants and, on this occasion, Cheryl joined her on a visit to a local fortune-teller called Gareth Edwards. His words were startling. He told her she knew a footballer, had seen him in a magazine and that they were going to be together. She would be married before her twenty-fourth birthday. He even said she would give him her number. She decided to do just that – in a roundabout manner. Kimberley passed her number on to Penno and he gave it to Ashley.

Cheryl was too busy promoting the next single, 'Love Machine', to notice that Ashley was slow responding. At first, the girls loathed the track. They thought it excruciatingly cheesy and tried to block its release as a single until record company bosses persuaded them that they knew best. Brian Higgins described it as The Smiths meeting The Sweet. The girls knew when to listen to advice and 'Love Machine' proved one of their biggest hits, again just missing out on number one, this time to the instantly forgettable 'Call On Me' by Eric Prydz.

Despite their initial misgivings, the girls worked hard to promote the track. A fascinating glimpse into their lives was provided by one of their biggest journalist fans, Caroline Sullivan of *The Guardian*, who joined them for the promotion roller-coaster. She began by accompanying Cheryl and Nicola to the Annual Single of the Year Awards run by Popjustice.com. Girls Aloud had previously won the £20 Music Prize with 'Sound of the Underground', but this time they watched Rachel Stevens collect it for 'Some Girls'. Cheryl, wrote Caroline, was 'tiny, Geordie, puffing a Marlboro Light', which is something she never lets the cameras see her doing. Cheryl was also enjoying a drink, something else she is not keen on sharing with the rest of the world.

Cheryl obviously got on well with Caroline and happily chatted away about music critics, drugs and ex-boyfriends who sell their stories. She was peeved that so many people didn't give the band any credibility because they didn't write the songs on their first album. She also hated to hear other bands moaning. 'Get a grip and be f***ing grateful,' she exclaimed. 'I came from nothing. We lived on benefits. I could've been f***ed up on drugs.' It was all disarmingly honest from a girl who wears her heart on her sleeve.

The girls then went on MTV's popular show *TRL* where, to promote 'Love Machine', they were given a variety of sex toys and encouraged to guess what they do. Part of the group's appeal is that the rudeness of Girls Aloud lyrics contrasts with their emotion-free voices. They sing of a 'fistful of love coming your way' but they don't sound like Tina Turner or even Christina Aguilera when they do. There's nothing down and dirty about Girls Aloud – that's left to the imagination. It's all far more Graham Norton than Russell Brand.

About a week later Cheryl was in a hotel room in Scotland

where Girls Aloud had been promoting 'Love Machine', when her phone lit up with a text. It was one o'clock in the morning and she wondered who else was still up at that time. It was Ashley Cole with the simple message 'Fancy Meeting Up?' He had taken his time! It was over a week since she had offered her number but she didn't mind and texted back that she was awake and asked how he was. It was love at first text and the two exchanged messages into the night. And she did fancy meeting up.

Mindful that they did not want to be seen, they decided against a trip to the West End, settling instead for a relaxed, no-frills evening at Ashley's £750,000 pad. It was much tidier than Cheryl's. She did not have to dress up for the occasion, although Cheryl Tweedy in a pair of jeans and a baggy jumper is still going to look special. Ashley described it as simply 'a bite to eat and a few drinks'. In fact, when Cheryl arrived, Ashley was with a mate scoffing Kentucky Fried Chicken and she was mortified. Eventually the friend left and Ash was able to be more himself. Cheryl was impressed and they talked easily and openly over a glass or two of wine. They clicked.

The benefit of them both living in the gated luxury of Princess Park Manor was that they could take the initial steps in their romance away from prying eyes and, more importantly, prying lenses. Cheryl was determined that the relationship would be well established by the time the rest of the world knew about it. They used to cuddle up on the sofa and listen to their favourite R&B tunes. Ashley had become an instant fan of silky-voiced soul singer John Legend when he heard his first single, 'Used to Love U', and would play it on repeat. The song was released in August 2004 and marked the beginning of his romance with Cheryl – even though the sentiment was not exactly affectionate, ending with the line 'I used to love you.' On the contrary, Cheryl and Ashley were falling in love. She made sure that Ashley had an early copy of Legend's Grammy-winning album, *Get Lifted*, at Christmas time. The album contained the sublime ballad 'Ordinary People', which could almost have been an anthem for Ash and Chez – two ordinary people making their way in life.

The tabloids cottoned on to the new relationship in late

October when the couple were seen enjoying a night out at the Funky Buddha club in Mayfair. Cheryl joined Ashley after she had been photographed looking happy and smiling at the National Television Awards at the Royal Albert Hall. The couple cut a dash on the dance floor, which was quite brave of Ash considering that Cheryl is a fantastic dancer. From that night onwards their lives would be subject to close public scrutiny. Every outing would be photographed, every argument documented.

Cheryl's new boyfriend found himself the target of outrageous racism when the England team took on Spain at the Bernabéu Stadium in Madrid in November. At least his mother, Sue, had not travelled to the game to witness first-hand the disgraceful abuse her son was handed. The black players in the English team were subjected to obscene monkey gestures by a section of the Spanish crowd. Ashley spoke movingly about growing up with racism in the East End: 'At primary school you'd get kids who don't know what it means saying "You black bastard", "nigger". You don't condone it, but kids don't know what it means.'

His simple philosophy of life hit home: 'The main thing is, I'm human – like everyone else. Because I'm a different colour doesn't mean there is a difference.' Ashley's experiences make his view of his new girlfriend even more relevant. They had talked of her court case and the drunken incident that provoked it. He has no doubts whatsoever: 'I know she has never been a racist.'

November was proving to be a great month for Cheryl. Her relationship was progressing well. She took Ashley home to meet Joan, who gave the thumbs-up. Girls Aloud released the annual *Children in Need* record, a version of The Pretenders' love song 'I'll Stand By You'. The track was a big departure for them but any risk of alienating fans was offset by the charity aspect, with all proceeds going to the BBC's annual appeal. The public lapped it up and the girls had their second number one. The same week saw the release of *What Will the Neighbours Say?*. Their second album was not a sequel but a carefully crafted work that built from its first track, 'The Show', through to the more complex songs that followed. The difference was the carte blanche afforded to Xenomania. Brian Higgins had been thrilled when the girls asked him to produce every song, describing it as a 'fantastic musical opportunity'. One of the stand-out tracks, 'Graffiti My Soul', had originally been written by Xenomania for Britney Spears but she rejected it as not having enough of a chorus for her *In the Zone* album. Her loss was Girls Aloud's gain.

The album, whose title came from a line in 'Love Machine', only charted at number six, but this was the build-up to Christmas so sales in excess of 85,000 in the first week were a pleasing return. The album ended up selling more than half a million copies. On this occasion, the response of the critics was perhaps more important. They loved it, marvelling that Girls Aloud were making rousing pop records instead of spending Christmas working on the counter at Argos. The *Daily Telegraph* described it as a 'glorious piece of pop trash, with surprising hidden depths'. This newfound respectability was further endorsed when the girls appeared at the Royal Variety Show for the first time. They sang 'The Show', watched by Prince Charles, and joined Elton John and the other performers for a giggly rendition of the national anthem at the end.

Come December and the tabloids had a field day with Ashley and Cheryl when it was reported that they had had a huge row at his twenty-fourth birthday party at the fashionable Tantra nightclub in Soho. Cheryl had arrived with some friends, including Nicola Roberts, but had only been at the club for five minutes when it all went wrong. The *Daily Mirror* reported: 'It ended in disaster when the pair had a massive ruck in front of shocked partygoers after one of Ashley's pals made a nasty comment to the singer.' Cheryl, as she always will, gave as good as she got, and Ashley made the mistake of joining in, which sparked the argument. An 'insider' alleged that Cheryl was in tears, whereas Nicola told Ashley that her friend was furious: 'And if someone said something nasty about me, I would be too.'

Cheryl stormed off home. Ashley condemned the reports as 'rubbish'. The idea that Cheryl would stand up for herself was not exactly new; more interesting was the suggestion that Ashley acted differently when in the company of his male pals. 'When they're alone he's the sweetest guy in the world,' said the source, an observation that rang true. The other sensational aspect of the story was that Cheryl arrived sporting a large sparkler on her engagement finger, prompting all sorts of speculation that needed to be denied. The ring was a gift from Ashley but it was not for their engagement. Not a day would pass, however, without a journalist asking if the rumours were true. The downside of the media scrutiny was that their every move was being closely watched, so it did not help when Ashley was pictured with 'Penno' and two sexy blonde girls leaving a West End club. Cheryl would have to get used to pictures of Ashley out on the town. Meanwhile, she kept things bubbling away in a more positive fashion by confiding, 'We've spoken about marriage and are comfortable with it.'

Cheryl was about to be busier than ever with the first Girls Aloud tour set to start. Nearly eighteen months has passed since the formation of the group; they had survived a difficult first year and now could make some progress towards credibility. To do that, they had to tour. They were much more accomplished now and had gelled as a unit. At this time they also managed to trade in Louis Walsh for a manager who would perhaps suit them better. They asked Peter Lorraine, who had been so helpful in getting Girls Aloud off the ground, for a recommendation and he suggested an old friend, Hillary Shaw, who ran a respected agency called The Shaw Thing. Hillary had the right credentials for managing a girl group. She had guided Bananarama during their golden age when they had more chart successes than any other British girl group. She also managed Dannii Minogue.

Hillary was just what the doctor ordered. She seemed to understand instinctively that Girls Aloud consisted of five very different personalities and she needed to keep them all happy and moving forward together. Hillary was given a very simple brief: 'Make us some real money!' Here were five stunning girls, very much in the public eye, who were making zero in merchandising and endorsements. Her first job, however, was to organize the tour, *What Will the Neighbours Say?*, while the girls plunged themselves into four weeks of solid rehearsal.

The first date of the tour was scheduled for the Royal Concert Hall in Nottingham on 5 May 2005 but Hillary sneaked the girls into a couple of warm-up gigs in the Pavilion Theatre, Rhyl – not a venue that would be playing host to the Rolling Stones or U2 any time soon. The Welsh sojourn helped to calm some nerves so that they were better prepared for the official first night. The gig served as a blueprint for all future Girls Aloud concerts. They opened with 'The Show', which set the tone for a high-energy evening of dance routines and schoolgirl outfits. In his BBC review, Nigel Bell observed, 'Girls Aloud are *FHM* brought to life.' He continued an upbeat review: 'The best thing about this show was seeing a group finally realizing they were out on tour and growing in stage confidence.'

The Girls Aloud formula was disarmingly simple – enjoy yourself and everybody else will enjoy themselves too. The easy route for critics to take would have been to diss the girls and suggest they crawl back inside the television whence they came. Surely Girls Aloud were getting above themselves, especially when Cheryl was reported as saying they would go down as 'the band that changed everything'. That was stretching it a bit but Girls Aloud did have the chance to change how reality show creations were perceived. Despite Cheryl's well-publicized problems, they seemed to have a core of support – people wanting them to do well. The writer Julie Burchill loved them. Alexis Petridis of *The Guardian* wrote after attending the tour's first night: 'Girls Aloud are a unique and delightful phenomenon.' He also identified the importance of Girls Aloud being British. They did not 'travel' across the Atlantic, or even across the English Channel. Petridis observed, 'There is something shambolic and very British about Girls Aloud live, a whiff of *Seaside Special* adds to their idiosyncratic charm.'

Girls Aloud live was a hit. Disappointingly for Cheryl, Newcastle was not included among the eighteen official dates. On 21 May the girls played the NEC, Birmingham, which meant Cheryl could not attend the FA Cup Final at the Millennium Stadium in Cardiff. Ashley was playing for Arsenal against Manchester United. Cheryl wished him all the luck but had to watch the tense game on a hotel television. The game was decided on penalties. Ashley stepped up to take the fourth penalty and scored, leaving his captain, Patrick Viera, to net the fifth and win the Cup again for Arsenal.

After he had collected his third FA Cup winners' medal, Ashley planned to whisk Cheryl away to the desert resort of Dubai for their first proper holiday together. Her final concert was on 31 May, at the Waterfront Hall in Belfast. The timing was perfect because Cheryl was exhausted at the end of her first tour and was desperate for a holiday. Cheryl did not know it at the time but a very handsome £50,000 solitaire diamond ring was lurking in Ashley's hand luggage. He had bought it a few weeks earlier with the intention of finding the most romantic location he could to pop the question. Ashley's description of his proposal is the lightest and funniest part of his autobiography. He rang Garry Tweedy in Newcastle to formally ask for his daughter's hand and got off to a good start when Garry said yes. That was about the only thing to go right.

Ashley was planning a romantic ride on a camel – just the two of them plus the guide – stopping off at a little oasis in the desert, where he would get down on bended knee. The first part was ruined when it became clear that camel rides that day were popular and there would be at least another ten people acting as an audience. The day was sunstroke-hot and Cheryl, completely oblivious of his plans, was in a tetchy mood, not enjoying the heat and worried that the camels were suffering in the extreme temperature. They scrambled on their beast with Cheryl behind Ashley, clinging on for dear life as they began a very uncomfortable journey. Cheryl was moaning so much that Ashley ill-advisedly told her to shut up, which resulted in him getting the silent treatment for the duration of the ride.

When they stopped for champagne and strawberries and to watch the sunset, Ashley seized his chance. He did indeed go down on one knee to ask Cheryl Ann Tweedy to be his wife. Cheryl did not hesitate to answer yes. And then they both started crying. They were tears of joy. Cheryl described the moment: 'It was fantastic. He's a gentleman. It was all very romantic.'

Cheryl's new life was full of sunshine and optimism. Girls Aloud were on the crest of a wave and she was in love. Her old life in Newcastle, however, was a constant reminder of how things might have been. She admits that she would have been living an entirely different existence in the North-East if she had been thrown out of the group at the end of 2003. Twice, in 2005, reality bit back. Her brother Andrew was jailed for four years for a particularly brutal mugging. He and another man, Syd Rook, had targeted a teenager called Kian Brady after they spotted him walking home late at night from the city centre. Newcastle Crown Court heard the grim details. The pair had jumped on him from behind, knocking him over and pushing him to the ground. They then repeatedly punched him in the face and head, demanding his credit cards and pin numbers. They hit him again when they thought him too slow handing everything over. Eventually they ran off with his CD player, mobile phone and cash. The victim suffered such severe facial injuries that he needed hospital treatment. When Andrew was arrested, he still had Brady's blood on his hands. He went on the run for five weeks when due to face robbery charges and was given an additional three months' jail for jumping bail. And just for good measure, he was given another fourteen days at a later hearing for grabbing a police officer by the throat during a pub brawl.

When Cheryl returned to Newcastle to tell her friends and family the happy news about her engagement, her elder brother was behind bars. If Andrew was the bad news back home, then the sad news was the tragic death of her former close school friend John Courtney. Cheryl was devastated by the news that John had been another victim of heroin at the age of twenty-one. He was found dead in his uncle's flat, lying curled up on a grubby carpet next to the instrument of his untimely death, a syringe.

In an unselfish act of bravery, his grieving mother, Angie Courtney, agreed to let the Newcastle *Evening Chronicle* publish the harrowing picture of his corpse. It could have been Jason Mack or a hundred others who had succumbed to the hardest of drugs. John had been brought up in Losh Terrace, a street that Cheryl knew well, just a couple of minutes from Walker School. Bing Leighton, the father of her two brothers and sister, lived a few doors away.

Angie revealed, 'Cheryl was always a lovely girl and a good friend of John's while they were teenagers. She sent flowers and a card as soon as she heard the news.' Cheryl had tried to persuade John to give up the 'Devil's dust' before she left to embark on her *Popstars: The Rivals* adventure. She used to visit him and his sisters and was a welcome guest at family parties. She wrote him a heartfelt note pleading with him to get help to give up heroin. Angie recalled, 'He kept it on his wall to remind him he had to keep battling it.'

While John may never have reached the footballing heights of Ashley Cole, he was an extremely promising player for Newcastle Boys, earning the compliment that he was 'another Shearer'. The easy availability of drugs in his depressed neighbourhood proved too big a temptation for an impressionable boy and he drifted into a life of addiction and crime. Football was forgotten. Instead, he served time, which, for a while, seemed a blessing as he went into a rehabilitation programme. On his release, he was tempted once more, forgetting that his body could no longer tolerate the drug levels he was used to before treatment. He took an accidental overdose.

His death prompted a 'War on Drugs' campaign by the *Chronicle* and Angie and chief reporter Adam Jupp wrote movingly about John's death to increase awareness in the community of the perils of dabbling with drugs and where it might ultimately lead. Cheryl backed the campaign whole-heartedly: 'I am in total support of John Courtney's family in raising the awareness about the devastating effects of heroin addiction.'

John's death reinforced Cheryl's hatred of drugs and their effects. She had suffered because of her brother Andrew's addiction to glue and because of her boyfriend Jason's addiction to coke and crack – now a friend had lost his life.

15

A Spa Break in Baden-Baden

The Ryanair flight from London Stansted Airport to Baden-Baden had never had such a glamorous passenger list. This was WAG Flight No. 1 to Germany, taking the partners of the England football team to the World Cup. Never had the rule of one small piece of hand luggage been so flagrantly flouted as when the tabloid favourites set off to stand by their men. 'I didn't realize we were flying with Ryanair,' said Cheryl. 'I found it funny.' Frank Lampard's then girlfriend, Elen Rives, set the tone by reportedly making a scene when she was told her five pieces of hand luggage were too many. The Spanish-born model was not allowed to board and had to catch a later flight. Only the Queen WAG herself, Victoria Beckham, was missing from the expensively scented mayhem. She was stuck in the VIP area of Madrid airport waiting for the next available plane after her original flight was cancelled. It was all new to Cheryl, her first taste of tournament life – the FIFA WAG Cup.

WAG is an acronym for the 'wives and girlfriends' of footballers. When Ashley and Cheryl first started dating in the summer of 2004, the term was only just taking hold in the media. The television series *Footballers' Wives* had turned the spotlight on this group. Soon, however, the media realized that the real thing was even funnier, more outrageous and more glamorous than the fictional soap. From that time onwards, the pages of the tabloid press and the glossy magazines were obsessed with the shopping, clothes, beauty and drinking secrets of the WAGs. When the World Cup began in Germany in June 2006, WAGs were everywhere.

Their destination was Baden-Baden, a historic and beautiful spa town in the Black Forest area of south-west Germany. Before it was announced that the England team would be based near here, it was best known for its casino, a racecourse and, of course, a spa utilizing the famous hot springs. The word 'Baden' means bath and the springs had been used since Roman times to cure aches and pains. Former US President Bill Clinton is said to have been so enchanted by the town that he remarked, 'Baden-Baden – so good they named it twice.'

Cheryl had not been there before but she needed a holiday. She had just finished Girls Aloud's whirlwind second tour promoting their latest album, *Chemistry*. They literally had not stopped since the lead track 'Biology' had been released the previous November. The song was a well-received return to pure pop after the release of two less successful singles. 'Wake Me Up' had been the fourth release from *What Will the Neighbours Say?* and one single too many. It reached number four. The first from *Chemistry* was 'Long Hot Summer', which met with a disappointing response, making only number seven and selling less than 20,000 copies. The track would have longevity, however, and remains one of the girls' most popular live songs, perhaps due to its infectious Beach Boys-like guitar. Fortunately, everybody loved 'Biology', which has probably the finest intro of all the Girls Aloud songs – a thumping piano beat followed by Nadine giving it 110 per cent on lead vocal. Dom Passantino in *Stylus* magazine described the chorus as 'exactly how I imagine ascending into heaven to feel like – floating yet forceful'.

The *Chemistry* tour was billed as their first arena tour, beginning in Nottingham and ending at Wembley Arena ten days later, on 3 June. The highlight for Cheryl was her first Girls Aloud concert in Newcastle at the MetroCentre. The audience was packed with friends and family and she was given a special cheer every time she sang a line. It was like a football crowd, chanting, 'Cheryl! Cheryl!' The girl herself told the fans, 'I'm so overwhelmed I can't even talk. I told the girls you would be the best crowd and I wasn't wrong. I'm so proud to be a Geordie tonight.'

The Northern Echo disloyally suggested that Nadine was the real star of Girls Aloud. The newspaper also noted, 'They're a pretty attractive bunch, whose looks are very much part of the act. Where others would flounder, they pull off tutus and spray-on hot pants with great aplomb.'

The prim review failed to capture the sheer raunchiness of the performance in which the girls breathed sex in a variety of costumes – as scientists, beach babes and clubbers. They sang several covers, including a medley from the musical movies *Fame* and *Footloose* as well as a version of the aggressive 'I Predict A Riot' by the Kaiser Chiefs. In recognition of the tender age of much of their audience, the girls changed the lyric 'To borrow a pound for a condom' to 'To borrow a pound for the bus stop', which amused the reviewers. This was Cheryl's stand-out solo of the night, whipping up the crowd in a half-singing, half-shouting tour de force.

For many, the *Chemistry* album was the high point of the Girls Aloud recording career to date. Nadine described it as finding their sound. Once again, Xenomania were in charge. The album was an astonishing collection of rich and varied dance tracks embracing many rhythms and melodies. Not everyone agreed. Andy Gill in *The Independent* was less enthusiastic, noting the 'grim queasiness' of some of the tracks, although he did credit the girls with a 'sassy, assertive attitude'. Alexis Petridis in *The Guardian* was more positive: 'You could spend the rest of your life listening to critically acclaimed American artists and hear fewer ideas and less creative daring than you would in three minutes of *Chemistry*.' His final point is a telling one about attitudes to Girls Aloud: 'If snobbery keeps you from opening your ears, it's your loss.'

When 'See the Day' made the Christmas chart, Girls Aloud broke the record held by the Spice Girls for the most consecutive top ten hits by a girl group. The cover of the old Dee Cee Lee hit was their eleventh in a row. The enchanting ballad 'Whole Lotta History' made it twelve in March. Cheryl sang the opening verse and, in the video, looked wistful and ethereal as she gazed out the window pining for her lost love. She never looked so beautiful (or busty) and her voice had matured. Cheryl Tweedy was no longer chavtastic but had grown up into an elegant and classy young woman.

There was so much going on, Cheryl was not seeing as much of Ashley as she would have liked. The girls jetted off to Australia and New Zealand for the first time in February so the phone bills were astronomical. Ashley had his own problems to talk about. His popularity had suffered with the coverage of the tapping-up allegations involving Chelsea that had soured his position at Arsenal and made it likely that he would leave his childhood dream club.

Just after New Year, Cheryl was in New York with Joan when she had a call from the Girls Aloud office to say that the *News of the World* had rung for a comment about Ashley cheating on her with another woman in a hotel room. Cheryl immediately rang her fiancé to find out what on earth was going on. The story was completely untrue and Ashley's lawyer was able to prevent publication by tracking down CCTV evidence that he was enjoying a Chinese meal alone when he was supposed to be getting it on with his female accuser. Cheryl had not been confronted by such a story before and she did not care for it. As Ashley explained in *My Defence*, 'Cheryl trusts me but you can imagine her reaction when she's thousands of miles away and she gets news that some girl has gone to the papers.' It would not be the last time Cheryl would have to face a story about Ashley playing away.

And then she had to deal with an extraordinary whispering campaign suggesting that Ashley had been involved in a gay orgy – not the sort of allegation that the man engaged to Cheryl Tweedy would want on his CV. Ashley was boiling with rage at the insinuation and lost no time instructing solicitors even though the original stories had not named him. He wrote in *My Defence*, 'Me and Cheryl had to deal with the sickest load of crap ever invented at a time when we should have been planning our dream wedding.'

The stories in *The Sun* and the *News of the World* claimed that two Premiership players, one capped several times for England, were involved in some steamy action involving a mobile phone and a popular DJ. The papers might have expected to avoid any action because they did not name anyone, usually a safeguard against libel. But the Internet has moved the goalposts on such matters. The papers seemed to be treating it as some sort of music hall joke. Even Cheryl, said Ashley, thought it was hysterically funny. In the world of football, however, to be considered gay is like having leprosy. It's no coincidence that no footballers have come out since the ill-fated Justin Fashanu all those years ago. Ashley did not find the entirely false suggestions at all funny.

The campaign against him continued with the sort of innuendo that is only amusing after six pints down the pub. *The Sun* pictured Ashley and Cheryl after a romantic dinner on Valentine's Day with a picture caption saying that Ashley looked like he was waiting for a ring as he held his phone. It must have been on *vibrate.* All very jolly until Ashley's writ arrived at News Group Newspapers suing for harassment, breach of privacy and libel. Ashley won the case and received an estimated six-figure sum in damages.

The Sun ran an apology about the 'gay romp' story in which a mobile phone was used as a gay sex toy. 'We are happy to make clear that Mr Cole and DJ Masterstepz were not involved in any such activities. We apologize to them for any distress caused and we will be paying them each a sum by way of damage.'

Ashley had embarked on a high-risk strategy taking on the might of Murdoch but he had won. His problems were all ahead of him, however. The press is like an elephant – it never forgets. Ashley may have won two battles in a row but he was going to be involved in a long old war with Fleet Street. And he still had to play football for his country.

Cheryl had never been too bothered about football. She preferred to spend an evening with Ashley in front of the telly than turn up at a match. Her father, Garry, had been a big Newcastle United fan but she could take it or leave it. On the plane out to Baden-Baden she was more interested in her hotel brochure than in the programme for the World Cup. All the wives and girlfriends had been booked into the exclusive Brenner's Park Hotel, the Ritz of Baden-Baden. In the past it had played host to maharajahs and kings, including Edward VII. Now it was playing host to Cheryl, Coleen, Alex et al. Even Victoria had decided against a separate villa with her children so that she could join in, as did Nancy Dell' Olio, the long-suffering partner of England manager Sven-Göran Eriksson.

She could look forward to a pampering treatment called Body Torture, an all day long experience made up of fifteen South Pacific rituals designed to 'instil a sense of rebirth'. Among the ritual delights was an Arabian rough-cleansing massage with foaming olive oil and a treatment involving being smeared with Balinese yoghurt – the stick-thin WAGs would always prefer to have their food slapped on their skin rather than served on a plate.

Cheryl was much savvier these days where the media was concerned. She knew that her every move would be watched and that under no circumstances was she going to disgrace herself by drinking too much or by dancing on the tables. She was going to support Ashley and if she could gather some nice headlines in the process, then that would be a bonus. Her problem was that she did not know anyone. She needed to make friends but not to the extent of turning the trip into the hen night from hell. Fortunately, Victoria Beckham was there to add a touch of class to proceedings. One newspaper described Posh as bringing a little 'decorum' to the World Cup when most of the WAGs could not spell it.

The WAGs flew in on the Friday afternoon, the day before England's first game against Paraguay on 10 June. The first evening was a quiet night in, working out the all-important wardrobe, planning hair extensions and consulting the tan therapist. The £500-a-night rooms had been decorated with an arrangement of red and white roses topped with the flag of St George.

Saturday morning was an early wake-up call ready for the coach trip to the match at 10 a.m. Nobody had the full English, mindful of the skin-tight ordeal to come. Cheryl wore pink lipstick, a figure-hugging khaki top and a brown baseball cap that she kept on all day. Alex Curran (Steven Gerrard) chose white jeans and wedge heels. Coleen McLoughlin (Wayne Rooney) wore denim shorts, a white top with gold straps and very high heels. Abbey Clancy (Peter Crouch) had on a see-through blouse and beige cropped trousers. Last on the bus was Victoria Beckham, in skin-tight white jeans and top, hoop earrings and one of the sixty pairs of her own range of sunglasses that she was rumoured to have brought with her. Across the breast pocket of her blouse was a cross of St George – discreet but classy.

England won the game, a dull affair, by one goal to nil. Cheryl had the chance to chat to Victoria for the first time. At thirty-two, Victoria was ten years older but, of all the girls there, discovered she had most in common with Cheryl, a fellow pop star. Victoria was arguably the most famous woman in the world and was careful about her status. The paparazzi knew they would never find her in a compromising position. She was at the World Cup to support her husband, the England captain, and to promote the Beckham brand. Cheryl did not have a brand yet but she could do worse than attach herself to Victoria. It would guarantee maximum coverage for both of them.

Cheryl accepted Victoria's invitation to join her for a celebratory dinner in the Brenner's Wintergarten restaurant. The 'celebrations' were extremely dull at their table. They were joined by Sandra Beckham, David's mother, as well as his sister, Joanne, and the Beckhams' middle son, Romeo. They broke up at 9.45 and Cheryl went upstairs to her room to phone Ashley.

That was when the party started downstairs. The WAGs seated on the other side of the restaurant, Coleen, Alex, Abbey, Elen and Carly Zucker (Joe Cole) and another half-dozen or so girls were just getting into their stride with a round of pear bellinis to wash down the pizza and chips. Two more rounds followed before they launched into an impromptu and premature rendition of 'We Are The Champions'. Then it was time to adjourn to Garibaldi, an Italian restaurant and club that was one of Baden-Baden's few late-night spots. The girls sank a reported £450 worth of Moët & Chandon champagne, vodka and Red Bulls. Elen Rives got up on a bench to entertain everyone with some enthusiastic dancing. They staggered into taxis at 3 a.m., when Cheryl was already sound asleep. The *Daily Mirror* was suitably unimpressed: 'They swilled drink, smashed glasses, roared raucous chants and belted out bawdy sing-songs.'

Cheryl has stayed close to her family through the good times and the bad. Above: toasting her eldest brother Joe and his bride, Kerry, at their wedding reception. Bottom left: Sister Gillian is photographed leaving Newcastle Magistrates Court after being bound over to keep the peace following a brawl in Byker. Bottom centre: wayward brother Andrew, also pictured leaving court after one of his many appearances there. Bottom right: a rare picture of her younger brother, Garry Junior, who has always shunned the limelight.

Everybody knew Cheryl was in love by the time she and Ashley stepped out for a film screening in January 2005.

The look of love was undimmed when she and Ashley left her 26th birthday party at the Vanilla Club, London on 1 July 2009.

Triumph . . . Cheryl celebrates with Victoria Beckham at the England game against Portugal during the 2006 World Cup in Germany.

. . . And Despair. They are distraught after England go out on penalties.

Her least favourite Cheryl look: at London Fashion Week in September 2007.

Her favourite dress: she wore the Herve Leger design in April 2008 to cheer herself up during a rough patch in her marriage.

Cheryl on stage taking a breather during the *Tangled Up* tour at the Brighton Centre in May, 2008.

. . . Performing '3 Words' with will.i.am of Black Eyed Peas for her TV special *Cheryl Cole's Night In*.

. . . And putting her marriage problems aside for a rousing rendition of 'Fight For This Love' at the Brit Awards, Earl's Court, in February 2010.

The Cheryl Factor. Simon Cowell knew the TV public would warm to Cheryl's genuine emotions.

Cheryl and Dannii Minogue put their frock wars aside when Cheryl heard the happy news that her fellow judge was expecting.

All teeth and smiles – Joe McElderry gives Cheryl her second straight *X Factor* win.

Sad but still beautiful . . . the single girl.

The next night Cheryl again had dinner with Victoria, sitting well away from the other WAGs, this time in the Medici restaurant. Victoria had sea bass, Cheryl had sushi, which was her new favourite now that pizza was off the diet. They washed it down with Evian water and headed back to the hotel after an hour. The WAGs, however, spent more than 1,000 euros on pink champagne and cognac and left a very large tip.

This was just what the media wanted. WAGs providing raucous entertainment while Victoria and Cheryl did an impersonation of The Glums. The true picture was very different. Cheryl and Victoria were just being careful in front of the media. Victoria was in Germany with her three children while Cheryl wanted to be squeaky-clean. They did, however, enjoy each other's company. Cheryl discovered that Victoria was good fun and completely misrepresented by the press. She had suffered that fate over her court case but Victoria, it seemed, was forever being given a tough time by critics of her life and appearance. Cheryl observed, 'People don't realize that actually she's quite insecure. One night we went out for dinner and I was trying to make her laugh in front of the paparazzi just because they always say she's miserable. I was like, "Go on Victoria, just crack one smile!" And she was laughing but she was covering her mouth with her bag. And to me that's insecurity.'

Both ladies had, in fact, had a considerable amount of dental work to transform their less than perfect gnashers into Hollywood sparklers. Cheryl wore an invisible brace when she first made it into Girls Aloud.

As well as discussing girl bands and designer dresses, Victoria and Cheryl had another important topic to discuss – the possibility of Ashley joining David at Real Madrid. The move to Spain had not been a total success for the Beckhams, with negative headlines about the state of their marriage and the criticism of Victoria for not giving up her career and becoming a Spanish housewife. Cheryl had no intention of giving up her own career. She told Piers Morgan, 'I've worked hard to get where I am. I would either have had to move out there with him and commute or give up my career when we had finally been accepted as a band.' Cheryl is a tough girl and Ashley would have to find another football club. Victoria was already planning her family's new life in Los Angeles so she was not exactly singing Madrid's praises to Cheryl.

The picture painted in the press from the outset was that Victoria and Cheryl formed their own clique of two, suggesting they were in some way grander than the others. That was not the case. In particular, Cheryl found that she hit it off with Coleen, who is an extremely nice and popular girl. She explained, 'I loved Coleen. She is very down to earth.' The two girls would often lunch together away from the gaze of reporters. Coleen was equally complimentary about Cheryl. Coleen joined Victoria and Cheryl when they went on a shopping expedition during which they were said to have spent some 80,000 euros in an hour.

The day after a game, the England team were allowed a day off to spend time with their partners and families and get a taste of the bedlam that surrounded the WAGs. Ashley also managed to wangle permission from Sven-Göran to slip out of the hotel for an hour to wish his mother a happy fiftieth birthday. Sue thought she was having a joint birthday dinner with Cheryl, who would be twenty-three the following day, but when they arrived at the restaurant they found the other WAGs shouting, 'Surprise!' An even bigger surprise was when Ashley walked in carrying the birthday cake.

The ensuing party was the only time Cheryl let her hair down during her trip and the press, for once, never knew. England were knocked out by Portugal in the quarter-finals the day after Cheryl's birthday. They lost on penalties – the worst way to go out. It was all a bit of an anticlimax. Ashley flew off for a break in Marbella while Cheryl returned to England to resume preparations for the wedding. The WAGs had certainly made it much funnier for the watching public at home but Cheryl hated the label and what it stood for.

Ashley Cole, in *My Defence*, vigorously defended his wife's good name: 'Cheryl is not a WAG – she's a recording artist in her own right.' Cheryl did not want to be stuck with the tag 'Worthless WAG'. One writer, Lowri Turner in the *Western Mail*, was particularly scathing, describing the WAGs as modern-day Stepford Wives.

She wrote: 'How long before Cheryl Tweedy exits Girls Aloud in a cloud of expensive perfume and a *Hello!* wedding. The WAGs exist as over-primped trophies for their partners to parade as if they were another Aston Martin or Bentley. The thing is most of them are too busy shopping to notice their essential worthlessness.'

Clearly the WAG tag was something to be avoided at all costs. Cheryl was her usual outspoken self. She told *OK!*, the magazine which seemed to have her number on speed dial: 'Footballers' wives have no careers and live off their husbands' money. I was in Girls Aloud before I met Ashley and have my own successful career. I'm not going to quit the band and sit around in the sun all day or go shopping with Ashley's plastic. If I'm going shopping I'll pay with the money I've worked hard for. I would die of embarrassment if I had to resort to taking my boyfriend's cards.'

She added: 'It's like a comedy. Everyone's so flash. It's like, "Which wife is dressed the best? Which wife has got the best hair?" I'm like, "I've got my own career."'

Fortunately for Cheryl and all the other girls, the term WAG is probably past its sell-by date, although it will be interesting to see if it is dusted off again for use when England next play in the World Cup.

The Sunday Times published a survey on which WAG was receiving most press coverage at the World Cup. Cheryl came in first. It was not an accolade she would cherish.

16

For Fatter, For Thinner

Cheryl Tweedy became Cheryl Cole at a hotel called Sopwell House in St Albans on Friday, 14 July 2006. Sue Cole and Joan Callaghan gazed on proudly while two registrars sorted out the paperwork and called Ash and Cheryl man and wife for the first time. Cheryl had hit the aspirin in a big way after her hen party the night before. She had her big send-off at the Umbaba club in Soho, where pink champagne at £220 a bottle flowed through the night. One report said Kimberley had forked over £745 on her credit card when the booze looked to be drying up. Cheryl was helped home. For the ceremony she wore a little black dress and no make-up. The groom wore jeans and a T-shirt.

OK! magazine had paid £1 million for exclusive rights to the wedding of the year so it would have been a very poor return if this had been it. Fortunately, the newlyweds were just fulfilling a legal obligation before the following day's big event. They needed a venue with a licence to hold weddings. Sopwell House is a beautiful place for a wedding in its own right but Cheryl had grander plans. Every year seems to be the wedding of the millennium, all of them paid for by the glossy magazine. The Beckhams had set the bar very high when they were paid a million for their wedding at Luttrellstown Castle near Dublin in 1999. Jordan had lowered it considerably for her 2005 marriage to Peter Andre when the bride wore pink and the happy couple sat on pink thrones. They were married at Highclere Castle near Newbury, which had been

Cheryl's first choice for her own wedding until she discovered Jordan had thought of it first. She and Ashley were lazily watching TV one afternoon when a news report about Jordan's wedding was shown. Ashley recalls in *My Defence* that Cheryl shrieked, 'No way! Right, Ashley, we're changing venues.'

Amusingly, she did nothing to correct the impression in the media that she still intended to marry there and newspapers continued to write reports on her plans without realizing they had changed.

Her second choice was an inspired one. When she first drove through the gates of Wrotham Park in the Hertfordshire countryside north of Barnet, she knew it would be perfect. She instantly realized that the magnificent Palladian-style mansion would be a dream place to be married. The house was built in 1754 and, set in mature oak-filled parklands of 2,500 acres, it was just the place for a Jane Austen heroine to aspire to – or, in this case, a Heaton heroine. The house had featured in two recent movies, the Oscar-winning *Gosford Park* and the comedy *Bridget Jones's Diary*.

Cheryl had been determined to do much of the wedding planning herself, although she needed lots of encouragement from Joan to see it through: 'To be honest if it weren't for my family, I would have just run away and got married in Gretna Green.' The media are always a little peeved when *OK!* takes over proceedings and are willing the bride to take a fall so that they can ridicule her attempts at grandness and good taste. Tackiness is always in the eye of the beholder and usually says more about the class prejudices of the commentators than the quality of the occasion. Cheryl had set herself up for a kicking by declaring in 2005: 'We're not going to do a mag deal. We just want it to be a quiet affair with everyone we love there.' The small matter of a million pounds providing the funds for a dream wedding soon prompted a change of heart.

Ashley and Cheryl also did themselves no favours by releasing some pictures to promote the National Lottery's new draw the same week as the wedding. They were the height of camp, with Ash looking as if he had strolled in from the set of *Saturday Night Fever*. One critic suggested he looked like Lenny Henry's brilliant creation, the lothario Theophilus P Wildebeest. David Beckham can get away with all sorts of silliness – the male sarong, for instance – but poor Ashley has never enjoyed that level of public indulgence.

For their big day, Cheryl and Ashley had to preserve the exclusivity of their deal with *OK!* This secrecy always turns proceedings into something of a spy movie. In this case, guests were sent a secret code to reveal the date and a phone call to let them know where to rendezvous on the day. The guests were picked up at a secret location in central London and driven to Trinity Chapel on the edge of the Wrotham Park estate. They were asked not to bring cameras or mobile phones so that nobody other than the magazine had a pictorial record of the day. Guests were also requested to sign a confidentiality agreement not to talk about the day to any media.

Cheryl was determined to avoid any wild excesses, although some reports put the total cost of the day at £500,000. Her declared intention was to have a 'fairytale wedding'. She wanted a romantic wedding not a royal one, although she did decide to arrive at the big house in a carriage drawn by white horses. Cheryl could not indulge in a royal wave because the windows were blacked out so that no photographers could snap a picture of her wedding dress. On arrival, sheets were held up to hide her from the hordes of photographers who had gathered outside.

Cheryl was determined her friends and family would not be intimidated by the occasion. *OK!* reported that she wanted a young feel to the day. The understated theme was an angelic one, which perfectly complimented Cheryl's natural beauty. She explained, 'I wanted it to be angelic because it means everything is peaceful and beautiful and airy and light. Plus Ashley has always called me his angel.' The theme for the Cole wedding was simpler than the peculiar Robin Hood thread that ran through the Beckhams' ceremony. Cheryl chose a dress designed by Roberto Cavalli and rumoured to cost £100,000. Coincidentally, Cavalli is a friend of Victoria Beckham and designed the costumes for the Spice Girls' reunion tour, although Posh had chosen a Vera Wang dress for her wedding.

Victoria had worn a similar dress to Elton John's famous White Tie and Tiara Ball in 2005 but that did not bother Cheryl. They shared the same minuscule dress size so are probably the only two women in the country who could get away with wearing such a figure-hugging design. *OK!* neatly described it as a 'second skin'. Cheryl is very petite, something that is not always apparent when she fills the frame of a photograph. The image of Cheryl in her dazzling pale satin wedding dress dominated the issue of the magazine, which devoted nearly fifty pages to Ashley and his bride.

The bustier top featured a flurry of sequins, beads and diamanté and seemed to be struggling to contain Cheryl's breasts. The elegant train was trimmed with discreet bows. Critics might describe it as a little fussy but that would be unfair. There was certainly nothing of the meringue about it and it highlighted Cheryl's natural beauty. She decided against a veil covering her face, preferring a diamond tiara from Garrards. Ashley observed, 'She just looked so amazing, like a little princess.' He, too, was wearing a Cavalli creation – his tails were a vision of light beige silk, and he wore a glittering diamond earring. Whatever the cynics might say about such showpiece affairs, the wedding pictures showed Mr and Mrs Cole to be an extremely handsome couple who photographed well. They looked genuinely happy and gazed straight into each other's eyes when they said their vows. Cheryl had joked that she wanted to add 'For fatter, for thinner' into the traditional words, just to give everyone a laugh. Ashley did not find that idea so amusing and exercised his veto.

Garry Tweedy, in a designer chocolate brown suit, was grinning from ear to ear throughout, especially when he walked his daughter down the aisle to the sound of the gospel choir singing 'If I Ain't Got You', the exquisite Alicia Keys song. It might have been fun if Cheryl had chosen a Girls Aloud song but it's hard to think of an appropriate one. 'I don't need no good advice cos I'm already wasted' was definitely one for the hen night. Cheryl made sure her family were heavily involved. Her sister Gillian was her maid of honour and her younger brother, Garry junior, was the ring-bearer. Her three nephews were page boys. Sadly, Andrew was still in jail.

The wedding ceremony itself began at 5.20 in the late afternoon, lasted half an hour and featured the choir singing 'Ain't No

Mountain High Enough' and the appropriately titled 'Oh Happy Day'. Both Ashley and Cheryl were tearful as they exchanged rings from the celebrated London-based designer Stephen Webster. Cheryl's was a monster rock, an eight-carat single heart-shaped diamond with a cluster of smaller stones and a white gold band. The couple also made sure their mums played a part in the ceremony. Joan and Sue lit candles together and then Ashley and Cheryl used them to light another to symbolize the unity of their families. Joan told *OK!* that Ashley was a kind and gentle man.

Afterwards the guests were ferried half a mile to the main house for the reception drinks followed by the wedding breakfast in an adjoining marquee and, later, a party into the night. As always, the most fun for wedding watchers is finding out who was there and what they wore. The celebrity turnout was disappointing but merely a reflection of the company Cheryl and Ashley prefer to keep. They are not too bothered about shallow friendships and do not seek to air-kiss a dozen people at the Ivy restaurant on a Saturday night.

The girls were there, of course, looking sensational in their coral pink bridesmaid dresses that Cavalli had also designed. The knee-length dresses with leopard print trim around the hem would not have looked out of place as a Girls Aloud stage costume. They grinned happily for the photographs. Even Nicola Roberts managed a half-smile. They mixed happily with Cheryl's family and seemed genuinely pleased for their bandmate. Other well-known pop faces included the Sugababes and Jamelia.

Famous footballers were less apparent, with former England defender Sol Campbell the best known. This may or may not have had something to do with the ongoing controversy about Ashley's future with Arsenal. On the day of the wedding, *The Sun* carried extracts from his soon-to-be-published autobiography in which he claimed the Arsenal board had treated him like a 'scapegoat' over the previous year's tapping-up scandal with Chelsea. It seemed only a matter of time before Ashley joined the club in south-west London. Cheryl, meanwhile, had not endeared herself to the WAGs with her outspoken remarks after the World Cup.

Much had been made in the press beforehand about the

possible attendance of David and Victoria Beckham, the equivalent of footballing royalty. Some reports suggested they were clearing their schedules but in the end they did not attend. David was apparently recharging his batteries after the exhausting World Cup campaign. His mother Sandra, who already knew Sue Cole, 'represented' the couple. Victoria was there in spirit. Besides the link with dress designer Roberto Cavalli, Cheryl also chose the Beckhams' flower arranger, Simon Lycett, as well as using the Little Venice Cake Company that had baked David's thirtieth birthday cake. The potential problem of inviting the Beckhams was that their presence would overshadow the day and take some of the attention away from Ashley and Cheryl. From that point of view it was better that they did not turn up, although millions of magazine readers might have been disappointed.

The *Daily Mail*, which cruelly dubbed the occasion the 'C&A wedding' – a rather tiresome joke about the former Primark-style department store – snootily derided the dinner as being steak and chips. The food was prepared by Rhubarb Food Design, the society caterer responsible for the spread at Prince Edward's wedding to Sophie Rhys-Jones. The starter consisted of a prawn and crayfish cocktail, smoked salmon with watercress, a parmesan wafer and lemon wedges, accompanied by roasted and grilled vegetables with a pesto dressing. It was followed by fillet steak, chunky chips, grilled mushrooms, peas, grilled beef tomatoes, onion rings and a Madeira jus. It may have been steak and chips, but it was very posh.

Cheryl's father, Garry, was in jolly form. First, he paid tribute to his daughter: 'When Cheryl was born, I thought I was handed an angel. It was the proudest day of my life. She's independent, smart and stunning – perfect in every way. I couldn't ask for a better daughter. What I wanted for her was a smart, sensible, reliable partner and I'm delighted Ashley is all those things, and I'm delighted to welcome him to our family.' With that he whisked out a Newcastle United shirt, its famous black and white stripes emblazoned with the word 'Cole' across the back. 'Come on, Ashley, make my dream come true!' said Garry, to much laughter.

Ashley, although nervous, was the perfect gentleman in his speech, saying he was the luckiest man in the world and the proudest now that Cheryl was his wife. Cheryl, he said movingly, was his best friend, his greatest support and, now, his wife. He also remembered to present a bouquet each to the mums, Joan and Sue. Cheryl's mother looked petite and youthful in an ivory silk slip dress designed by Cavalli. In the wedding pictures, Cheryl towers over her. Even allowing for the bride wearing super-sized heels, Joan looked barely Kylie-size. The best man, Ashley's brother, Matthew Cole, continued the maternal praise: 'I'd like to thank our mum, who has brought us up properly.'

When it was time for the first dance, Cheryl had a surprise for her new husband. She had signed up his favourite artist, John Legend, to perform. He had flown in especially from the US just to appear in a tent in the Hertfordshire countryside. Amusingly, he did not have a clue who Cheryl and Ashley were. Girls Aloud were not known in the US nor were British soccer stars – only David Beckham has made any impact across the Atlantic. Cheryl's people had called Legend's people and fixed it up. The soul singer observed, 'It was a surprise she wanted to do for him. I thought that was really nice. It was cool. It was a nice vibe at the wedding and they were really sweet and they looked incredible. It was nice to be there.' John Legend does not come cheap and Cheryl could not have thought of a better wedding gift for her new husband.

After Legend had enchanted the guests with his set, accompanying himself on the piano, the stage turned into a club for the rest of the night with Ashley's friend DJ Masterstepz presiding. At 2 a.m. Cheryl slipped into her going-away outfit, a Cavalli cocktail dress, and she and Ashley were driven back to the hotel ready for their second night as man and wife, with the prospect the next day of jetting off for an idyllic honeymoon in the Seychelles.

Despite the many pictures of the happy couple on the day, *OK!* printed only one very small one of them kissing, although, apparently, they kissed three times during the ceremony alone. There are some things that are too personal even for the pages of a magazine.

17

The Gob

When Cheryl heard that Lily Allen had written a song called 'Cheryl Tweedy', she took it as a compliment and was happy to comment, 'I am very flattered Lily has written a track about me. I don't know why she wants to sing about wanting to be as pretty as me as she looks stunning. I'd like to look like her. It's about time we had a really cool British girl out there on the music scene.' The song was a B-side on Lily's first hit, 'Smile', and Tweedy rhymed nicely with seedy and greedy.

Cheryl was soon made to realize her mistake when singer-songwriter Lily said, 'I don't want to look like Cheryl. It's tongue-in-cheek; it's meant to be ironic. I don't have anything against her but I think the portrayal of her being the right thing for kids to look up to is wrong. It was a joke that not many people got. Of course nobody wants to look like Cheryl, they just think they do.'

A classic showbiz feud had begun. Cheryl replied, 'I thought Lily was being complimentary. But then she said, "I was being ironic. Nobody wants to look like that."' Lily also managed to call bandmates Nicola ugly and Sarah vile while referring to Ashley as horrendous. Cheryl described Lily's outburst as 'giving it Billy Big Bollocks'.

The next instalment came when Cheryl was a guest on Gordon Ramsay's television show *The F Word* and the chef called Lily a 'chick with a dick'. Cheryl, perhaps reluctantly, agreed, which made Lily even more outspoken in return: 'I may not be as pretty as you, but at least I write and sing my own songs without the aid of Auto-Tune. Taking your clothes off, doing sexy dance routines and marrying a rich footballer must be very gratifying. I'm sure your mother is very proud, stupid bitch.'

This was a war of words straight out of the Queen Vic in *EastEnders* – each girl giving as good as they could. Cheryl said, 'I have had enough of her and her big mouth. I can't stand people who give it but aren't prepared to take it. She should keep her mouth shut instead of feeling sorry for herself. I left school a long time ago and have no time for this.'

Nadine agreed that Lily was just 'so young and childish'. Cheryl's final word – for now: 'I don't play with little girls.'

Cheryl has never been reticent about saying what she thinks. She has arguably had more spats and verbal skirmishes than anyone else in pop. She is frequently called 'gobby'. A key quality that raises Cheryl's profile above the average is the unusual combination of looking like an angel while being outspoken. Cheryl is not a shy and demure little thing with a bland public image. She lives up to her 'feisty' label. Amusingly, she maintains, 'I don't hold grudges or stupid things like that.' Unsurprisingly, her best-known feuds are with other outspoken women. Besides Lily, her most public battle has been with the Welsh singer Charlotte Church.

The catalyst was Charlotte's first pop single, 'Crazy Chick'. Cheryl and the other girls were on a Radio 1 show when a listener rang in to say that it sounded like Girls Aloud. Cheryl cheekily said she'd let Charlotte get on 'with using their old sound'.

Charlotte is fiery herself. She took the comment as a personal slight. She said, 'Love, as soon as you can f***ing sing "Ave Maria", then you can have a go. That girl should piss off and go get a hobby.' Cheryl loved that and called Charlotte 'a nasty piece of work with a fat head', pointing out that her advert for Walker's crisps was very appropriate because it showed her 'stuffing her face'. All good knockabout fun, although perhaps Charlotte made the funniest remark on her own talk show when talking about the Queen's corgis: 'If I wanted five dogs without bollocks then I would have bought Girls Aloud.' In *Dreams That Glitter* Cheryl said that it was a shame that things had got out of hand with Charlotte. She may have decided to draw a line under the row, but Charlotte has since sounded off about Cheryl's performance on *The X Factor*, which suggests the feud is still simmering nicely.

Cheryl is quite happy to have a go if someone mouths off about her or Girls Aloud. Her hitlist includes Boy George – 'He's just furious we've got a better make-up artist'; *Never Mind the Buzzcocks* presenter Simon Amstell – 'I think he was one of those people who was bullied at school'; Mel C, One True Voice and the Pussycat Dolls. These were nothing more than a little push and shove.

But two people have really got under Cheryl's skin. They are not feuds because it's one-way traffic. The first is Ulrika Jonsson, whom, it seems, Cheryl will never forgive for her remarks after her assault conviction. The second is Pete Doherty, erstwhile boyfriend of Kate Moss. Doherty is the lead singer of Babyshambles and well known as a user of heroin. Cheryl hates everything about him because drug use hits a very raw nerve as a result of her past experiences. Cheryl has never taken drugs and maintains that she has no sympathy for addicts. She reportedly said, harshly, 'I really don't give a f*** how they feel. If they're in pain because of drugs, it's self-inflicted.'

Cheryl is breathtakingly honest about her old neighbourhood in Newcastle. She is not being the least overdramatic when she says, 'Heroin was there for the taking. I could easily have taken that route if I'd wanted to. But I always maintained my ambition and I'm proud of myself.'

Her antipathy towards Pete Doherty is fuelled by her belief that he is glamorizing drug-taking. She exploded in 2004, 'Pete Doherty is not a poet. He writes shit. He is a waste of fresh air. Why is he such a genius? Because he went out with Kate Moss? And he gets let off from jail. Kids think, "Oh, he doesn't even get locked up." More deserving people are on the waiting list for methadone every single day. It's not f***ing funny. Heroin is the latest trend. Teenagers think celebrities are having a wild time, living this amazing life.'

Cheryl's outburst is fuelled by real passion. She may be pleased to note that Pete Doherty's celebrity status seems diminished since his relationship with Kate Moss ended.

Two other verbal skirmishes are particularly pertinent to Cheryl's story. The first was with Dannii Minogue, whose path has criss-crossed with Girls Aloud since the early days of 2003. Dannii had a connection with Xenomania and shares Cheryl's manager, Hillary Shaw. The verbal skirmish began when Cheryl was quoted as saying, 'I think Dannii should get all her plastic surgery reduced. She doesn't look natural. I don't think men find her attractive.' Dannii countered by calling Girls Aloud the bitchiest in the business. 'I mean, the punch-ups, going to court . . . I don't want to get involved. I'm no chav.' The irony was that Cheryl now protests that she was not the member of Girls Aloud who made the original comments about Dannii.

Perhaps the most amusing barb aimed at Cheryl came from Simon Cowell, who was drumming up some interest in the new series of *Pop Idol* in 2003 and had some controversial opinions on Girls Aloud and Cheryl in particular: 'I think the Geordie girl, Cheryl, is terrible. I saw her last audition. She didn't sing a note in tune.' Simon was not too pleased when the girls were uncomplimentary about the contestants on *Pop Idol*. He suggested they sing live on his show to prove themselves. They were not keen. Dannii Minogue and Simon Cowell – two people Cheryl would want to avoid in the future . . .

Cheryl's outspokenness has helped to define her public image – the face of an angel and a big gob. The combination helped get her noticed. Music critics might suggest that Nadine Coyle is the member of Girls Aloud who can make it on her own but it doesn't always work out like that. On the evidence so far, Nadine does not have Cheryl's powerful personality. The comparison with Take That is interesting. Everybody thought Gary Barlow would have the brilliant solo career but it was Robbie Williams who had the looks and the big mouth.

Robbie had cheek, charm and charisma. Cheryl is quite similar. They also share a love of tattoos. Cheryl has them all over the place, including a discreet one on her bottom. The huge tattoo at the base of her back and the barbed wire design on her left thigh are her most visible and represent Cheryl's old chav style. Writer Tony Parsons hates them, especially the barbed wire and plant life design: 'Here is the woman with the face of an angel and the body of a goddess and she decides that what she really needs is a tattoo that belongs on a lobotomized biker.' Parsons memorably described it as like drawing a Hitler moustache on the *Mona Lisa*.

Cheryl also has 'Mrs C' tattooed on her neck. It was a surprise for Ashley and something she wanted to do for their wedding. The only problem with such a mark of affection arises if you split up and need to have the tattoo removed. Her most successful and stylish 'tatt', however, is the delicate tribal tattoo on her right hand, so much in evidence whenever she appears on television. Despite the misgivings of Tony Parsons and others, the tattoos are very much part of Cheryl's individual style, which is of paramount importance in creating a Cheryl Cole brand, her separate identity away from Girls Aloud.

Heat magazine traced Cheryl's path to becoming a stylish young woman. The steps included ditching tracksuits or 'trackies' as she called them, employing a stylist to do her hair – ditching blonde highlights – and make-up and wearing top designers. The most interesting step, however, was her marriage to Ashley. The magazine thought it gave her instant glamour and put her on A-lists, away from Girls Aloud world. One celebrity can achieve plenty of high-profile deals and publicity but a combination of two people, a double act, was even better.

Cheryl said she had no problem when she and Ashley were called the new Posh and Becks. She thought it sweet. It's not hard to see why. The Beckhams had a combined fortune of more than £100 million and were the best possible example of how a celebrity couple could achieve joint branding. Their marriage was a huge boost to their joint brand. Andy Milligan, in his fascinating study *Brand It Like Beckham*, puts it simply: 'Think of Posh and you think of Becks. Think of Becks and you think of Posh.'

Victoria Beckham is a very smart businesswoman who works tirelessly to promote the brand, aided by the Svengali figure of pop mogul Simon Fuller. Milligan describes her as 'savvy', a quality she inherited from her father, a self-made millionaire. Growing up, she would listen to her father on the phone while he struck another hard bargain. She listened to Fuller when he was managing the Spice Girls and turned to him to mastermind building the brand. When he took over their joint name, Fuller wanted to create the House of Beckham: 'With the Beckham name so renowned the world over for music, fashion and football, there are no boundaries to what we can achieve together.'

This mission statement appeared also to fit Cheryl and Ashley. Cheryl made the right first move by taking Ashley's name. They could not be a joint brand without a joint name. Once that had been sorted then everything achieved by one half of the partnership promotes the joint brand. Every time David Beckham scores a goal in sponsored boots or when Victoria is pictured in a Marc Jacobs dress, it promotes their joint brand. Cheryl had the music and was showing clear signs of improving her fashion sense from chav to classy. She might not yet be a possibility for the cover of *Vogue* but give it time. Ashley had football, was very good-looking and photogenic and looked a certainty to run out for his hundredth cap one day.

Everything started promisingly in 2006 when Cheryl secured a deal to be the face of a new Coca-Cola campaign. But then the couple's tongue-in-cheek National Lottery pictures were not so successful. And the prospects for the future were dealt a far greater blow when Ashley's book, *My Defence*, was published in September. He went from hero to zero. His actions over the Arsenal pay deal were interpreted as arrogant. The newspapers saw it as payback time and Ashley was called 'Cashley', a nickname he will never live down.

The notorious passage concerned the day Ashley was driving along the North Circular Road in his Aston Martin when his agent called to update him on the contract negotiations with Arsenal. Ashley had thought a deal had been agreed for £60,000 a week but his agent informed him that £55,000 was the best and final offer. Ashley revealed that he nearly swerved off the road. He yelled down the phone that it was taking 'the piss'. And, with that, Ashley lost all chance of ever following in David Beckham's footsteps. The

National Average Wage in the UK in 2005 was, according to *The Guardian*, estimated to be £22,411 – a sum Ashley would have earned in less than three days. David Beckham is rich beyond measure but he relentlessly presents the image of a modest, likeable family man to his adoring public. When he was accused of adultery in the national press, commentators amazingly turned on Victoria, declaring it to be her fault. Would it be the same for Ashley if similar stories ever circulated about him?

For the moment at least, Cheryl and Ashley were not looking like the new Posh and Becks. Instead she was ticking along with Girls Aloud, who released their *Greatest Hits* album in October 2006 followed by a tour of the same name. The problem was that everyone thought this retrospective after only five years together meant they were about to split up. Nadine now lived in Los Angeles and rumours persisted that she was not getting along with the rest of the band. At least Cheryl had started her 'break-out'. She was building up a public profile, an image more in keeping with an established star. She just needed something extra to become a leading brand, something that would give her the affection of the public. She had not bargained for what that might be.

18

Balloons and Flowers

Cheryl Cole does not have a 'private' life. She describes it as her 'personal life', understanding that she has unwittingly let the public into her world by allowing every aspect to be scrutinized. Somehow part of the deal for finding fame through reality television is to submit to intrusiveness far beyond the norm. If taken to the limit, the result is the macabre death in public of the *Big Brother* contestant Jade Goody. The breakdown of *I'm a Celebrity . . . Get Me Out of Here!* winner Kerry Katona is another example of where it becomes impossible to draw the line between good and bad taste. The private life of many of these young men and women is in public ownership.

Cheryl had always been free and easy with the media. None of Girls Aloud was given media training in the early days – perhaps nobody thought they would be around long enough to make it a worthwhile investment. Cheryl has a big gob and that has always been part of her personality and her charm. She was able to recover from the vilification of her notorious court case because she was always so straightforward and honest. She's one of those people that if you ask how she is, she tells you. When she and Ashley became engaged, she declared she would 'kill anyone' who cheated on her.

She was happy to tell the world she was feeling broody towards the end of 2007. She was so happy with Ashley that she wanted to share her feelings: 'We spend every minute together. He's not into showbiz parties or flashy restaurants. He just likes staying home with me. He's just an amazing, genuine man. I really want a baby and so does Ashley.' Here was a woman completely in love with her husband. She even dreamed of them having Christmas together, something that was proving impossible because of his football commitments. She announced on the radio, 'I can't wait to make Ashley Christmas dinner; that's a part of my life I'm really excited about.'

Work was neverending. Their fourth studio album, *Tangled Up*, had been released in November and reached a respectable number four in the charts at a time when the record-buying public were gearing up for Christmas. The first single from it, 'Sexy! No No No . . .' was partly written by the girls and made number five, but it was the opening track, 'Call The Shots', which was Cheryl's favourite. 'It gives me goosebumps,' she said of the Xenomania song which would become one of the most popular of all Girls Aloud tracks. The song won the 2008 popjustice.com £20 music prize with the site's writer, Peter Robinson, enthusing, 'It's the greatest pop song of the twenty-first century.

Cheryl started filming a TV series called *The Passions of Girls Aloud* in which the girls – minus Nadine, who did not want to be involved – had to set about a special challenge. Cheryl's was to learn street dancing so that she could be in the video for will.i.am's new song, 'Heartbreaker'. Hip hop had always been Cheryl's favourite form of music and of dancing – she wanted that feel all those years ago when performing at Metroland. Although street dancing at this level was new to her, she did have the advantage of hundreds of dance lessons. One of her teachers on *The Passions* said, 'I love it that you can pick up choreography.' Cheryl came across as very natural on camera, especially in her banter with mum Joan, whom she took to LA for part of the filming. 'You've got to look after me,' said Cheryl. 'No change there,' replied Joan.

Her mother was needed when *The Sun*'s story hit the news-stands on 25 January. It could scarcely have been more devastating. Certainly, it plumbed all the depths of sordidness. Ashley, it seemed, did not stay at home all the time. A blonde hairdresser from South London, Aimee Walton, was alleging that she had enjoyed a night of passion with Ashley – nothing too exciting about that, at first glance. Cheryl was used to receiving calls from her press agent announcing stories like this regularly. They were fraudulent and invariably dropped. Aimee's revelations were different.

Ashley had gone out drinking with his friends after Chelsea had beaten Sunderland on 8 December. They ended up at the CC Club in Piccadilly, planning to adjourn later to watch Ricky Hatton's world title fight on TV. The drink was flowing and one of the group spotted Aimee, a moderately attractive blonde, having a drink with a girlfriend. He sauntered over and invited them to join everyone in the VIP area. Aimee claimed Ashley was already drunk when she got there and could not keep his eyes off her and her little black dress with white stars on it. When it came to leave, one of Ashley's group told her that Ashley wanted her to go home with him. Home, in this case, was not the luxury mansion where Cheryl was watching TV with her mum, but, of all places, Princess Park Manor, where a mate still had a flat.

Aimee's friend drove. On the way, Ashley, it was claimed, threw up on the backseat of the car, covering his grey T-shirt with sick. When they arrived at the flat, the others stayed downstairs drinking while Ashley and Aimee retired to the bedroom.

Revenge, so the saying goes, is a dish best served cold. We will never know whether the meanness of this particular 'kiss and tell' was payback to Ashley for his successful legal action against the newspaper for their gay orgy stories. Aimee's revelations contrasted sharply with those of Rebecca Loos, who had been so complimentary about David Beckham's stamina while making allegations about the England captain. Some of the quotes from Aimee were far from complimentary and do not warrant repetition.

One question the paper did not ask Aimee was 'Why?' If her claims were completely true, what on earth possessed her to have sex with a man who was sick all over the place and with whom she had barely exchanged two words all night?

Cheryl faced a dilemma: how do you react when such intimate details about the man you love are aired in public? She could come out fighting, carry on with her frantic Girls Aloud schedule or retreat, shut herself away and hope everything would blow over. She chose the former strategy and gave a highly personal interview to the *News of the World* that was published the following Sunday. In it we learned that Cheryl had known for weeks that something had happened on that December night but had chosen to believe Ashley's account. Apparently he had arrived home the following morning, his clothes covered in sick. He looked awful and tearfully explained to Cheryl what had happened the night before. He told her about the club, meeting a hairdresser, drinking vodka and ending up back at their old building where he was so drunk the girl had to put him to bed. He said that he could not remember anything of what happened next. He was adopting the amnesia defence.

Cheryl told the *News of the World* that she immediately banished Ashley to the spare bedroom while she had heartfelt chats with Joan, who was living with them at the time. She could have thrown him out then and there but, with a hint of how she would act in the future, she chose to believe that nothing more sinister had happened than a night on the drink had ended badly. She also told the paper that she knew her husband had not had sex with Aimee: 'I know Ashley intimately. When he's under the influence he isn't capable. When I heard what this girl had said I realized she made part of the story up. And, to be honest, that has helped me get through this.'

Cheryl told the newspaper that she and Ashley were in love and that she adored him and that she did not intend to leave him – not the advice she was being freely given in the media. She said, 'I'm still hurt and angry but we've been working things through since December and we're now hoping to move forward and rebuild our relationship.'

If Cheryl was hoping that her full and frank interview would draw any line under the story, then she would be cruelly disappointed. Two more girls appeared to say they, too, had slept with Ashley. Cheryl's candid interview with the *News of the World* was made to look silly when Aimee entered the fray again to allege that Ashley's people had offered her money to have an abortion when she feared she might be pregnant. She described what Cheryl had said as 'infuriating and ridiculous'.

This was too much for Cheryl. She promptly packed a suitcase and left the family mansion in Oxshott for a rented flat in North London.

She needed time to think about the future. Did she leave Ashley or give him another chance? It was too early to decide and, in the meantime, she still had work commitments. She had to film the video for the next single, 'Can't Speak French', one of the best, most upbeat Girls Aloud tracks. Cheryl found the day extremely difficult, although it was better to be busy than moping around in a lonely flat even though Joan and the girls had been trying their best to keep her cheerful. You would never guess from the £100,000 video, for which the girls wore saucy 'Oh-la-la' satin corsets, that there was anything wrong. Cheryl described it in *Dreams That Glitter* as finding your 'inner performer', although she also admitted that it would have been a lot harder if she had been going through it on her own.

She persuaded Nicola and Kimberley to go on holiday with her to Thailand. She loved it there and has described it, along with Newcastle, as her favourite place in the world. The girls spent ten days on the sun-kissed beaches of the aptly named Phuket Island. They rented a £2,000-a-night villa, ate spicy Thai food and topped up their tans – and did not read any newspapers! The long-lens brigade followed her to take a series of pictures of Cheryl in her favourite straw cowboy hat and stunning beachwear, including a tiny red and white striped bikini. The obvious implication was 'Look what Ashley's missing'.

From there the girls continued on to Los Angeles, where Cheryl was scheduled to film the climax of her *Passion* with will.i.am. The title of the track 'Heartbreaker' had now taken on a grim significance with will.i.am apologizing and declaring that he didn't mean to break your heart. Cheryl went about it professionally and excelled on the video, although it would have been more of a surprise if she had been terrible.

The girls did their best to cheer up Cheryl by taking her out clubbing. She was photographed in a vivid pink dress at the Villa nightclub. She looked fit and well, although thinner than usual, after her holiday but, more interestingly, she had left her £150,000 wedding ring on the shelf for the night. It was a symbolic gesture and one that the whole world was quick to spot. She would later tell Jonathan Ross that taking off the ring was a meaningful gesture: 'You know you're in shit.'

During her night out in LA, Cheryl found time to indulge in some mild flirtation with an up-and-coming black US television star called Will Luke. There was much less to it than met the eye because Will was filming for a programme called *Parking Lot Pimps* in which he and a buddy try to charm phone numbers from unsuspecting young women. It was a fun night out and the girls, Will and his friends ended up in a hotel room at the Mondrian partying, singing and swapping stories until 4 a.m. Will explained, 'We just thought they were very cute girls who were very drunk.'

A video later surfaced showing Cheryl having a little weep with her arms round Will and giving him a couple of smackers on his shaven head. He said all the right things afterwards and was very complimentary about Cheryl: 'She kept saying to me, "You make me feel so good. You made me feel much better." She said she loved my bald head and kissed it twice. I felt the luckiest man alive. That was as far as it went but Cheryl was drop dead gorgeous. Her husband must be mad to cheat on a girl like that.' The whole world, of course, was thinking the same thing.

Luke also had a message for Ashley: 'If I could say one thing it would be, "Tighten up your game because you've got one hell of a great girl who will not be hanging round for you long."'

The newspapers took the opportunity to call the night 'Cheryl's Revenge', which was much too strong. She was just having some much needed fun and demonstrating to the world and Ashley that she could do that without indulging in any over-the-top bad behaviour.

Back in London, Cheryl honoured a commitment to appear at the Brit Awards. This was a huge night for Girls Aloud, who were nominated for the first time in the Best Group category. They lost out to the Arctic Monkeys, who, coincidentally, were big fans and had performed 'Love Machine' on tour. Cheryl monopolized attention with a canary yellow minidress and the hair extensions that have become an essential part of her look. She was not wearing her wedding ring. Everybody was looking for a sign that she was still upset and that her smiles were all for show. She said, 'The holiday was fantastic – just what I needed.'

The world, it seemed, was advising Cheryl to finish with Ashley. She, however, is a woman who makes up her own mind. A look at the way she has stuck by her brother Andrew or the two years she spent with Jason Mack indicates that she does not give up easily. So many celebrities seem to treat marriage as an accessory to be cast off almost as a whim. One row and they're off because 'it's just not working'. Cheryl has an old-fashioned attitude, never better illustrated than when she said, 'When I married Ashley I made my vows and promised we'd be together for better or worse. This has got to be the worst it gets.'

Cheryl and Ashley eventually met for a heart-to-heart at a neutral venue in West London. It took a while for the news to filter through but Cheryl had decided not to end her marriage. She may not have forgiven Ashley immediately but she was open to persuasion. She apparently laid out some strong ground rules for the relationship to continue, including him dropping friends she considered a bad influence and letting her know what he was up to every day. Some reports suggested she had insisted they move house so that they could make a fresh start. She later admitted that she had been tempted not to put her wedding ring back on at all, signalling how close they had come to a permanent split. She also told Jonathan Ross, probably tongue-in-cheek, 'I was tempted to put it back on – but in his head!'

Meanwhile, there was a tour to rehearse and two singles to promote. 'Can't Speak French' came out at the beginning of March and reached number four, the same position as 'Heartbreaker' the following month. Will.i.am came over to the UK and Cheryl joined him to perform the track on *The Graham Norton Experience*. Cheryl did not really do much but did put plenty of feeling into the line 'F***ing jerk!'

The *Tangled Up* tour opened in Belfast on 3 May and included two sell-out nights at the O2 in London. The critics could find little to criticize Girls Aloud about any more. David Pollock in *The Independent* newspaper described it glowingly as 'the only pop show in town'. The girls arrived on stage, wearing a mixture of superhero costumes and black spandex bondage gear, lowered by wires and striking crucifixion poses at which, Pollock noted, 'loud support for Cheryl Cole suggests her tabloid martyrdom has only increased her iconic status for young women'. Cheryl interacted with the crowd by letting them know that Kimberley was not feeling too well: 'She's been vomiting all morning,' she volunteered, helpfully.

The girls apparently get in the mood to be bootylicious on stage by listening to Beyoncé's 'Crazy In Love' in the dressing room. Rock bands on the road would have marvelled at some of the equipment required to keep the Girls Aloud juggernaut moving during the thirty-four-date tour: fifteen tubes of mascara, 145 sets of fake eyelashes, fifty cans of hairspray, 250 fake nails and 150 pairs of fishnets. The rock chicks would relax on the tour bus between gigs watching films. Their favourite was *The Little Mermaid*.

Ashley turned up with Joan to the concert at the Birmingham National Arena on 23 May and shared a tender embrace with his wife backstage. He was clearly trying hard to make amends. He sent Cheryl a gigantic bouquet of flowers and balloons and a bottle of Bollinger champagne. The gesture would have been smoother if he had not ruined the surprise by sending a text to ask if they had arrived. 'No!' came the reply. Cheryl laughed, 'He didn't really think that through, did he? Still, they are really beautiful.'

Unusually, there seems to be no reluctance in the media about describing Ashley's behaviour as adultery. Often the press are careful about such matters and include the word 'alleged', as if that makes everything all right legally. When Cheryl gave her famous interview to *Vogue* in February 2009, the headline on the article read: 'She tells Christa D'Souza about her meteoric rise, racism – and surviving her husband's adultery.'

In the media, Ashley was portrayed as the bad guy. Cheryl was the Princess Diana figure, gathering a huge amount of public sympathy by being the victim. If Ashley was such a rotten guy, however, why was Cheryl staying with him? Nobody seemed interested in the qualities she loved.

One side issue to the Ashley saga was the apparent threat it posed to Cheryl's friendship with Victoria Beckham. Reports suggested that Cheryl was upset that Victoria did not pick up the phone to find out how her young friend was coping. Victoria had, after all, gone through much the same with allegations against David. She, of all people, should understand what Cheryl was going through and be able to offer some sympathetic advice. Poor

Posh gets the blame when her husband allegedly plays away. Now she manages to get the flak when Cheryl's husband does the same. She can't win.

Cheryl and Victoria are not particularly close friends. They enjoyed each other's company during the World Cup in Baden-Baden but were thrown together by circumstance. Since then, Victoria missed Cheryl's wedding and the pair are not part of the same social circle. They are that modern phenomenon, text friends – friends that stay in touch through texting on their mobile phone. Even *OK!* magazine admitted that Victoria and Cheryl are not 'bosom buddies'. A well-placed source said that Cheryl wasn't upset at all and that there was no feud. Cheryl did, however, have the last word on the matter when she made a throwaway comment about Victoria's new clothing range. She announced that she thought it too old for her, which was deliciously bitchy, even if unintentionally so.

When the dust had settled on the home front, Cheryl was able to talk properly to *Vogue* about the whole 'horrendous' thing. She was outraged that Aimee had declared that she felt sorry for Cheryl: 'Saying all that stuff about a married man in that state? How he was vomiting on her and couldn't stand up straight? And then saying she felt sorry for me! For *me*. I feel sorry for *her*.' She also praised her husband. 'He has a beautiful soul,' she said. 'He's a very nice guy, and I'm not stupid. I know what I'm doing.'

One of the aspects of the affair that Cheryl did not bring up was the role of football. The beautiful game has a sleazy, macho culture in which young men from poor backgrounds are seduced by untold wealth and prestige at an age when they may not be mature enough to appreciate their good fortune. The trouble Ashley had was that the media, which perceived him to be another spoiled young footballer, were unlikely to be as forgiving as his wife. Any bad behaviour would be front-page news. Her popularity would continue to grow; his would not.

19

The Cheryl Factor

Simon Cowell is, on the surface, an unlikely figure to become friend and mentor of a down-to-earth Geordie from a rough council estate in Newcastle. He is a soft Southerner, privately educated and brought up in the genteel surroundings of Elstree in Hertfordshire. His family's next-door neighbour ran a film studio and young Simon would gaze enviously over the fence at the famous guests visiting next door. He recalls spotting Richard Burton and Elizabeth Taylor, Bette Davis and Gregory Peck arriving for parties. It made a huge impression on him: 'I thought, "This is very glamorous. I'd love to live in a house like that and have a party like that."'

Sometimes ambition can burn very brightly in a child. Cheryl wanted to be a performer; her husband, Ashley, was driven to become a professional footballer for Arsenal. Young Simon Cowell dreamt of rubbing shoulders with the rich and famous. He wanted to belong to the world which, for the great majority, would always seem just a fantasy. From an early age, Simon was always prepared to have a go and take a risk to achieve his goal. He left school at sixteen with an undistinguished academic record and began work as a runner at Elstree Studios, close to his home, where he perfected the art of making the teas. He went up in the world when his father, Eric, found him a job in the postroom at EMI. Here, the teenage Cowell quickly found his feet and demonstrated a natural flair for the record business. He moved rapidly upwards and worked in A&R before, at twenty-three, setting up his own small independent label, Fanfare Records.

His initial breakthrough came when he met and subsequently dated a vivacious black American dancer and singer called Sinitta. Simon found a song for her, 'So Macho', and set about making it a hit. He borrowed £5,000 to back his judgement and, through his perseverance, the track sold nearly a million copies and reached number two in the charts in the summer of 1986. He subsequently teamed up with Pete Waterman, and the hit factory of Stock, Aitken and Waterman produced several subsequent hits for Sinitta, including 'Toy Boy'. Simon is happy to acknowledge he learned a lot working with Pete. 'If I'm ever cruel,' he says, 'it's because show business is cruel.' He likes to tell the story of when Waterman called him 'bloody useless' and that he would value his opinion when he had a hit.

The cruel side of the business bit Cowell when his label ran into difficulties and he had to move back home with his parents. He joined Sony-BMG as a senior A&R consultant and famously signed up the actors Robson and Jerome. Robson Green and Jerome Flynn were two of the stars of *Soldier Soldier* and performed a limp version of 'Unchained Melody' in one episode, with no intention of becoming pop stars. Simon had other ideas and persuaded them to release the track on S Records. He enlisted Stock and Aitken to produce it. It was number one for seven weeks and sold more than one million copies, making it the best-selling record of 1995. More importantly, it was the first example of Simon recognizing the power of television.

When *Pop Idol* began in 2001, it had been arranged that the winning act would release their first record on S Records, and Simon, keen to protect that investment, was persuaded to become a judge. By the end of the first series, he was on his way to becoming a television institution. His famous clash with eventual winner Will Young was television gold. Simon Cowell is primarily a businessman not a TV personality. The success of the original series left him seeking further projects where television could be used to enhance his business portfolio.

Simon is not especially witty or clever in his famous putdowns of wannabes. He is blunt. He prefaces his rudeness with the catch-phrase 'I don't mean to be rude . . .' The viewing audience loves something they can depend on, which is why catchphrase-heavy comedies like *Little Britain* and *The Fast Show* have proved so pop-ular. We expect Simon Cowell to be rude and are genuinely pleased when he is. Kevin O'Sullivan, television critic of the *Sunday Mirror*, explains, 'People like this circus show and they love the ringmaster who brings it to them and they do not see beyond that silly white grin. It's an array of five faces – the eye rolling, the fed-up, the "oh, you're better than I thought", and so on. I know that Cowell is not keen on the idea of scripting the comments but, if you watch the shows carefully, you might think he could do with getting some writers in.'

After a couple of series of *Pop Idol*, Simon was able to introduce his own series, *The X Factor*, to British TV. A complicated legal case involving the mastermind behind *Pop Idol*, Simon Fuller, ended with a financial settlement that allowed Cowell to pursue *The X Factor* in the UK while working for Fuller in the US on *American Idol*. These shows have arguably led to Simon Cowell being the leading television personality on both sides of the Atlantic, as well as one of the wealthiest.

Kevin O'Sullivan recalls a lovely exchange when he was chatting to Simon during the second series of *The X Factor*. The important thing to remember is that Simon Cowell is one of the most charm-ing men in the business. O'Sullivan recalls, 'He was smoking his usual Marlboro Lights as if there was no tomorrow. He is great company and he kind of loves you, that's his charm. You are sucked in. We were pissing ourselves laughing over some of the bad acts when Louis Walsh knocks on the door. He bounds in, all neat with his shoulder bag and announces, "Simon, I've got a great idea for next week's theme. Westlife week!" And Simon rolls his eyes and says, "What a surprise." But sure enough, next week it was Westlife week.'

Simon Cowell, known behind the scenes as The Dark Lord, wants his shows to have credibility. Television insiders know he was 'incredibly pissed off' at the untrue suggestion that he had manip-ulated the result of *Pop Idol* so that viewers would vote for the overweight Scottish singer Michelle McManus. Conspiracy theorists may think he has the power but he would never show off to that extent. O'Sullivan explains, 'I don't think it's too controversial to say that Cowell doesn't do anything unless it's to his own financial advantage. He would never adopt a "I'll get you to vote for whoever I want you to vote for" policy.'

With a series as successful and as popular as *The X Factor*, it's always important to keep it fresh. The idea is dead when the public become bored with the format or the look of the show. There are always obvious ways to freshen things up. Simon has changed presenters, temporarily sacked Louis Walsh and introduced a fourth judge in order to spice things up. For the fourth series in 2007 he was looking for a new younger woman to spark things up a bit, especially with Sharon Osbourne. There were rumours that it might be Victoria Beckham, who certainly would have gained plenty of publicity for the show.

Simon, however, had Cheryl Cole in mind. Cowell was rumoured to be worried that Sharon was turning *The X Factor* into too much of a comedy show and he wanted it to be more serious than that. The show's mission statement is to create a pop star and it's vital to the programme's success that it does that. It had struck gold in the third series when Leona Lewis proved herself to be a superstar in the making. She probably saved the show.

Simon recognized that Cheryl was the member of Girls Aloud who could break out. She had shown herself to be a natural on television in some of the girls' own projects, such as *The Passions of Girls Aloud* and *Ghosthunting with Girls Aloud*. She had been fun on *Comic Relief Does The Apprentice* in 2007. She was also married to an England footballer and, because of that, liable to gather more headlines and publicity than the others – even if she and Ashley were not Posh and Becks. Cheryl may have hated being labelled a WAG but it had given her more media coverage than all the other girls put together. When he first approached her in early 2007, Simon could not have possibly realized just how many headlines she and Ashley would be gaining a few months later when their marriage hit a sticky patch, or how much public support she would have as a result.

Cheryl, it was clear, would be perfect – but she turned him down. She was too nervous; she was worried that she wasn't articulate enough, that she would not be understood and that the public would not like her. Disappointed, Cowell turned to Dannii Minogue but he had not forgotten Cheryl and, after the show limped through another series won by one-hit wonder Leon Jackson, he was still keen to persuade Cheryl to join them. He tried again. When Cheryl told him that she did not think she was articulate enough, he laughed and allegedly replied, 'Have you heard Louis?'

Kevin O'Sullivan observed, 'Cowell does have a serious talent for spotting what the masses will love. He saw something in Cheryl that would appeal to the kind of people who watch *The X Factor*. He persuaded her that the show was not about being articulate.

'I think Cowell is attracted to the Svengali element of all of this. He is attracted to having the ability to spot potential superstardom and developing it and making it happen. He saw in Cheryl someone he could turn into a superstar. I think one of the things Cowell persuaded Cheryl with was "This is how you become a star. Look at me, I can't sing, I can't dance but I've become the biggest star in the world because of television."'

Cheryl's *X Factor* adventure began in August 2008, when she appraised auditions up and down the country, just as she herself had been judged six years earlier. Had it all begun such a short time ago? From Cheryl's point of view, her fellow judges were very nearly the panel from hell. She had reasons to be wary of all three. But Louis Walsh bustled into her dressing room and was very welcoming. Simon denied ever saying 'the Geordie girl is terrible' five years before and, anyway, he loved her dog Buster and made a big fuss of the chihuahua when she brought him in. The original bust-up with Dannii was never mentioned. The papers made much of their mutual dislike but Dannii said, 'She was really scared at the beginning, so I said to her, "Anything you need, I'm here."'

The public had the chance to see Cheryl in action for the first time on 16 August 2008. She was an immediate hit, bringing an utterly believable compassion to the audition process. She explained to Jonathan Ross that she had been just like the rest of us when she had watched it at home, howling with derision at the losers who thought they could impress. She felt differently once she was on the show. 'It's this close,' she said, holding her hand up to her face. 'I thought, "This is wrong. I shouldn't be laughing in your face."' One of the first things to happen at the auditions in Manchester was that she was confronted by Nikk Mager, who had done so well in *Popstars: The Rivals*. Nikk had made the final ten and, although he had missed out on One True Voice, he subsequently enjoyed a measure of success with Phixx. He was not the first boy from the series to try his luck on *The X Factor* – Anton, who had been a member of One True Voice, had tried and failed to win through in a previous series.

Cheryl was clearly shocked to see Nikk and immediately said, 'I can't do this' and declined to judge someone who had been through it all with her just a few years before. His audition was not a success and he did not go through. Cheryl was obviously upset and gave him a hug. Nikk said, 'Cheryl came over and looked really upset. It's nice to know that she still cares and didn't want me to go through that.' Cheryl was in tears afterwards, declaring, 'That was awful.' Nikk managed to squeeze another five minutes of fame from his attempt and was interviewed on television and by the papers before he disappeared once more.

Cheryl behaved in an entirely natural fashion, exactly what Simon Cowell was banking on. It was almost as though she were sitting on the sofa in the viewer's lounge. She thought one contestant, Joseph Chukukere, was very fanciable and exclaimed, 'Oh, my God, you are gorgeous.' She sobbed when Daniel Evans told how his wife had died the year before giving birth to their daughter. She cried again when another contestant, Amy Connelly, revealed that she was brought up by her dad after her mum had died when she was a child. And then, when some of the more hopeless contestants auditioned, she would desperately try not to laugh but, in the end, would dissolve into a helpless fit of giggles. She also stood up to Simon, which greatly endeared her to the watching millions. On one occasion, she was obviously getting ratty and Simon commented that the show did that to you. 'No, it's you,' said Cheryl, and one could almost hear the cheering in living rooms up and down the country.

Simon Cowell had struck gold with Cheryl. Some critics carped that she was a sucker for sob stories. But writer Tony Parsons put it into perspective when he said that these were not 'sob' stories but true stories of sadness: 'Beyond the glamour and the glitz, Cheryl's brought some honesty and unashamed emotion to Saturday night TV. That is why she is suddenly the nation's sweetheart.'

Sue Carroll, columnist in the *Daily Mirror*, observed: 'It's precisely because she doesn't manufacture the tears and sympathy that we love Cheryl. There isn't a cynical bone in her beautiful body.'

Kevin O'Sullivan agrees: 'Cheryl is genuinely blown away by the moment, emotionally overcome and that's what makes *The X Factor* great. She has also been there and understands. She may not phrase it very well but, out of the four judges, she is the one who will make you think she knows what she is talking about. She does understand how to make harmonies, to sound good on stage. She does understand whether or not somebody is a good performer or whether they have star quality.

'And she is a Geordie. It's the received English of reality television. As soon as anybody speaks in that accent everybody thinks salt of the earth, working class, she is one of us sort of thing. It immediately registers.'

Cheryl's position was helped by Cowell promoting her, telling the world he 'loved this girl'. In return she was impressed at how easy he was to get along with and how he totally appreciated her Northern sense of humour. She called him a 'pussycat'. She laughed when she had a conversation with him 'through his mirror'. He never took his eyes off his image in the mirror despite the fact that one of the most beautiful women in the world was standing next to him. Louis mischievously says that Simon has more mirrors in his dressing room than a carnival funfair.

By the time the judges were awarded their categories to 'mentor', everybody wanted to be in Cheryl's group because it was blindingly obvious that her popularity was going to sway the voting public. In the end, she was given the girls, seemingly by far the strongest category anyway. Kimberley helped Cheryl choose her final three at a luxury villa in Cannes, although she looked bemused at being cast in the role of little helper, perhaps the first indication that there might be a Girls Aloud pecking order.

Cheryl took her mentoring role extremely seriously. Only a few years before, Girls Aloud had complained bitterly about the lack of help and guidance they received from Louis Walsh. She was determined that her girls received as much care and attention as she could provide. She said, 'I think I've got the best three', and she was right. She invited her three girls over for dinner at her palatial mansion in Oxshott. They ate pizza and talked of ambitions, make-up and hair. She was always available at the end of the phone to talk to them about any problems and even texted one, Alexandra Burke, at 2 a.m. to find out if she had sorted her hair problem.

Cheryl always made sure that from Thursday onwards she would be at the studios, helping her acts rehearse, advising and giving them confidence. She was very nervous before the start of each live show, recalling the anxiety she had experienced on *Popstars: The Rivals.* Louis Walsh observed that she could be seen to shake with nerves but 'once she is on screen, she is fabulous'. Louis thought she was 'fantastic' on the show, which was a warm compliment from the man who thought Girls Aloud would be one-hit wonders.

The judges' comments are not at all rehearsed, which may have been one of the reasons for Cheryl's nerves. At one point during the series, Simon called them all together and told them they had to cut out the tired old talent show clichés. Perhaps he was thinking of Louis, who always seemed to start his comments with 'You remind me of a young . . .'

Cheryl took it all very seriously and was genuinely outraged when one of her girls, Laura White, was voted off the show. When another, Diana Vickers, missed out, Cheryl invited her to share a Sunday roast at her house.

Alexandra Burke was the early favourite and in the end she proved a runaway winner. Like Cheryl, Alexandra had a dance background before seizing her chance as a singer. She was also Cheryl's number one fan and did not take umbrage when sternly advised by Cheryl not to have anything to do with boys on the show – advice Cheryl had failed to follow herself when she dated

Jacob Thompson during *Popstars: The Rivals*. Alexandra told her, 'Over the last six months our relationship has become more than an act and a mentor. You're an inspiration to me. You've become a friend.' Cheryl gave Alexandra a necklace as a memento of their success and told her always to be herself and to be honest – the two qualities that probably best sum up Cheryl herself.

Cheryl was so delighted at her success that she hugged 'The Dark Lord' and put her head on his shoulder. The only negative was that Cheryl looked amazingly thin. On finals night, her ribs were sticking out unattractively from the Julien Macdonald designer gown, with some observers suggesting her weight was down to seven stone. She looked like a size minus zero. Speculation surfaced that she was still suffering from Ashley's indiscretion, although a more likely explanation was that she was overworking.

As the weeks had gone by, you could almost see Cheryl gaining in maturity, her confidence growing and a subtle change from girl to woman going on. There is something eternally teenage about Girls Aloud but here was Cheryl carving out a bright, mature future for herself. Some things did not change and she still had to cope with her brother Andrew's ongoing problems. He had been arrested for spraying pepper into a man's face and was looking at yet another prison term. He had also sold his story to the *Sunday Mirror*, which had involved him meeting a reporter in the car park of the Chillingham Arms in Heaton, where a cheque for £25,000 was handed over in return for an interview about his famous sister.

Andrew revealed that Cheryl had come to visit him the previous Christmas in Acklington Prison in Northumberland, where he was serving a four-year sentence for armed robbery. Her hair was scraped back in a ponytail and she was wearing a hoodie. She cried as she tried to persuade him to go into rehab. He said, 'Cheryl wants to help me but I'm too far gone.'

Andrew had last seen Cheryl when she drove up from London after the birth of their sister Gillian's new baby, Keric: 'She told me she loved me and I told her I was proud of her on *X Factor*.'

Everyone, it seemed, was impressed with Cheryl on *The X Factor*. People seemed to recognize the Cheryl they saw on the television as the Cheryl they knew. Chris Park explains it well: 'I think this is a Godsend for her because she started off in *Popstars*, where everyone saw how she was so it would only work against her if she tried to be different now. She is herself. It's in her nature. She was great to some of the contestants because she can understand it from a totally different level. I think it has opened *The X Factor* up on a whole different scale.'

Simon Cowell evidently agreed. The first thing he did after the show had wrapped was to give Cheryl a pay rise for the next series to an estimated £1.5 million. She did not even ask for a rise – he just wanted to reward her for making that series the most successful so far. Contrary to popular opinion, Dannii Minogue's position was not in any serious doubt. As a programme insider explained, 'Simon does not want to bring anyone in and risk them upstaging Cheryl. She is very much the Queen Bee now and he has big plans for her.'

Professionally, Cheryl was already reaping the rewards from appearing on television. After Girls Aloud performed their new single, 'The Promise', on *The X Factor*, the song stormed to number one, their fourth chart topper. Simon Cowell was clearly delighted, his polar white teeth flashing brilliantly as the girls shimmied in Hollywood gowns that oozed glamour. Girls Aloud were getting the benefit of Cheryl's TV fame. That was even more apparent when the new album, *Out of Control*, was their first to go to number one. The album, their fifth with Xenomania, had a more mature feel to it than the previous four. While 'The Promise' was undoubtedly a great dance track, the girls chose not to perform it in the jeans and little tops of old. Talia Kaines, in her BBC review, described it as 'pop music at its finest'. She noted that the girls still seemed to be searching for the perfect pop song. Andy Gill of *The Independent,* who has never jumped on the Girls Aloud bandwagon, offered the opposing view: '*Out of Control* seems a singularly inapt title for an album of such meekly conformist pop.'

'The Promise' was clearly a stand-out track and the girls' great supporter Caroline Sullivan said it was the best four minutes on the album. Duncan James of Blue slightly spoiled things by saying that it reminded him of the theme tune to the TV series *Blankety Blank*. Perhaps the most interesting song on the album was their first collaboration with the Pet Shop Boys, who had been crafting superb pop songs for twenty years. Priya Elam in *The Times* noted that 'The Loving Kind' harked back to the famous duo's heyday of the eighties and could be 'one of the girls' best songs yet'. Rach Read wrote on the online site *Teen Today*, which probably better represented the Girls Aloud audience than the heavyweight newspapers: 'They have set such high standards for themselves in the past six years that they were bound to disappoint at some stage, and it has finally happened with *Out of Control.*' She did, however, love the 'stunning melancholy' of 'The Loving Kind'.

The impression the critics were giving was that Girls Aloud had reached a plateau. Even Caroline Sullivan thought it 'pushed the envelope a bit'.

The group featured in a Christmas special, *The Girls Aloud Party*, where they sang many of their best-known hits. Cheryl was also gathering personal rewards. *Glamour* magazine placed her at number one in their prestigious 50 Best Dressed Women in the world – one of several similar awards she won. The magazine's editor, Jo Elvin, said, 'In the past year Cheryl has become everyone's style crush. She's ridiculously gorgeous, beautifully groomed and always glossy, glossy, glossy.' She beat Kate Moss into second and Victoria Beckham into third in the poll voted for by readers of the magazine. From being one of the princesses of chav just a few years before, Cheryl had been transformed into a style queen. Designers wanted her to wear their clothes.

The Best Dressed Woman award was one of three that came Cheryl's way in a short space of time and demonstrated the position of regard and affection in which she is now held by the British public. The second was to be named as *FHM*'s World's Sexiest Woman. The citation read: 'With her flawless skin, high cheekbones, wafer-thin waist, perfect pins and criminally underexposed cleavage, it's like God himself decided her native Newcastle was looking a bit dowdy, and needed a beacon of angellike beauty at its centre.'

The third award probably mattered most. Girls Aloud hankered after a Brit Award as final recognition that the band could rightly claim a place among music's elite. There will always be some who cannot forgive or forget their origins in reality television, but in February 2009 they won their first Brit when 'The Promise' was named Best British Single. The girls were deliriously happy when they strode on stage. Sarah Harding yelled, 'It's about time!' Cheryl said, 'This is the cherry on the cake.' Ashley was there to lend his support and Cheryl dazzled in a white minidress designed by Georges Chakra. All three of these awards were voted for by members of the public. That is the true mark of popularity. Everybody, it seems, loves Cheryl Cole.

Cheryl was not standing still. She had a tour to rehearse for late spring and before that, in March, she and Kimberley were among a group of celebrities led by Gary Barlow of Take That who were climbing Mount Kilimanjaro for *Comic Relief*. While she was away, Ashley went for a night out with his mates. He ended up getting himself arrested.

While Cheryl was battling the elements and altitude sickness, 16,000 feet up a mountain in Tanzania, Ashley was arrested outside the exclusive Collection Club in South West London. Ashley had apparently taken exception to being photographed in the club chatting to a blonde girl. Ashley's lawyers prevented *The Sun* newspaper from publishing the pictures, claiming it breached his privacy under the Human Rights Act. The newspaper had a lot of fun with it, however, quoting a source who said that Ashley and the girl had been engaged in an 'intellectual conversation'.

Outside the club, Ashley appeared to lose his temper with both photographers and the police before being arrested for being drunk and disorderly and taken to a central London police station. After accepting a fixed penalty of £80, he was allowed to leave for his Surrey home at 5 a.m.

The timing of the incident could not have been worse for Ashley. Many reports said that he had promised not to go out drinking with his mates while Cheryl was away. The columnists had a field day at his expense. Lorraine Kelly spoke for the nation: 'Why does he persist in behaving as a single bloke when he is married to one of the most beautiful, desirable and popular women on the planet?' Lorraine also advised Cheryl to kick her 'buffoon of a husband' into touch.

Sue Carroll called Ashley a 'lickspittle of a man' and argued, 'He not only betrayed Cheryl by going out against her express wishes but humiliated her into the bargain.' Fiona McIntosh called him 'a plonker of a husband' and a 'whingeing, foot-stomping toddler who needs to grow up'. Ashley's unpopularity, it seems, is almost a mirror image of his wife's popularity. Fiona wondered how much more she would take. Within a year, she would have her answer.

20

3 Words

Cheryl had little time to worry about Ashley on her return to the UK from Africa. The *Out of Control* tour was about to start. The first date at the Manchester Evening News Arena was only a few weeks away, on 28 April. It would be the first of thirty-five concerts in bigger venues around the country in a whirlwind six weeks.

These days the true stature of an artist can be measured by The O2 arena in London – only the very biggest acts can fill it. The spring of 2009 brought Tina Turner, Britney Spears and Girls Aloud to the arena in Docklands. Fans of Girls Aloud come in all shapes and sizes, and they poured out of the North Greenwich underground station for a night of uncomplicated fun. As journalist Caroline Sullivan observed, 'I don't know anyone apart from the most pompous people who don't love Girls Aloud.'

The opening night did not start well for Cheryl. As the initial bars of 'The Promise' blasted out, the five girls, hair extensions blowing in the wind, came up from below the stage and burst into song. They looked like five Helens of Troy wearing white Grecian-style gowns. Cheryl, unfortunately, suffered an equipment malfunction and her platform stopped, leaving her stuck with just her head poking out. The audience did not mind and Cheryl carried on as if it were the most natural thing in the world to have happened. Gillian Orr wrote in *The Independent*: 'It only makes the crowd love Cheryl more.' Gillian also pointed out that the huge arena was 'in danger of descending into one giant, hellish hen party.'

By their second round of concerts at The O2, Cheryl had developed a nasty cough and Kimberley told the crowd on 23 May that her friend was not feeling too well. Cheryl spent her time between songs coughing and gulping down water at the side of the stage, but kept going even though she found her vocals challenging. Again, the crowd didn't care and reserved their biggest cheers for her, confirming that, inevitably after the success of *The X Factor*, she was now the star of Girls Aloud.

Perhaps just as inevitably it was first rumoured, then announced, that after the tour finished the girls would take a break to pursue various solo projects. Cheryl would have the chance to fulfil an ambition that she had dreamed about during her wannabe years at Metroland: she would record an album with an emphasis on R&B.

Performers seldom do as well solo as they did within the band. Gary Barlow, Ronan Keating and Tony Hadley are just three high-profile singers who failed to match the success of their groups, Take That, Boyzone and Spandau Ballet, which, of course, explains why they reformed to such acclaim. When you leave the band, you leave the brand – something all five Spice Girls discovered within a couple of years when they'd lost their individual recording contracts. The success of Robbie Williams post-Take That and Beyoncé after Destiny's Child is the exception rather than the rule. Would Cheryl follow Beyoncé's lead or stall like Victoria Beckham?

The first thing she needed was a good holiday. When the tour ended triumphantly in Newcastle on 6 June, she and Ashley, who had just won his fifth FA Cup winners' medal, went for a break to the south of France. They were joined on their holiday by Ashley's former Chelsea team-mate, Wayne Bridge, and his then fiancée, Vanessa Perroncel. Nobody knew it then but in just over six months all four would feature in front-page stories for all the wrong reasons.

Ashley and Cheryl looked very happy together as they were pictured soaking up the sun. Cheryl was photographed at the beach wearing a loud, lime green swimsuit studded with crystals. Physically, the tour appeared to have done her good. She was fit and toned, although there was some speculation that this was due to a state-of-the-art wind tunnel exercise machine she had installed at their new £4 million home in Oxshott, Surrey. The moment they started looking happy in each other's company again stories began to circulate in the media that they would be trying for a baby when the next series of *The X Factor* ended in December 2009.

The work schedule for the year meant there would be very little time even to think about getting pregnant. There was an album to conceive, however, and Cheryl was soon on a plane to Los Angeles to start recording at Record Plant Studios. In R&B guru will.i.am she already had one of the biggest talents in music in her corner. He gave her instant credibility as a serious artist. Cheryl was understandably jubilant when he agreed to be the executive producer on the album as well as writing many of the songs.

Will.i.am was born William Adams, the name he still uses on his songwriting credits. He was brought up by his mother, Debra, in the poor area of East Los Angeles. She encouraged his promise and ambition for a musical career as a young teenager. He joined up with a close school friend, apl.de.ap (Allan Lindo), and together they started to make a name for themselves around the LA club scene in the early nineties, rapping and dancing and building up a stage act. They became the Black Eyed Peas in 1995, when they were joined by Taboo (Jaime Gomez), who had been part of Grassroots, a collective of rappers, poets and actors that used to perform on the LA club circuit. Taboo later revealed that he was a poor Mexican kid, also from East Los Angeles, who had never had the money to attend a concert until he performed in one as a member of Black Eyed Peas. Together, the group sought to expand the audience's perceptions of hip hop, refusing to cash in or overstate their tough upbringings in the LA ghettos.

Will once told journalist Billy Johnson Jr, 'Half of my friends are dead, in jail, pregnant or on drugs.' Perhaps this simple statement holds the key to why he and Cheryl hit it off so well when they recorded 'Heartbreaker'. They both understood what it means to break out of an unpromising environment. Cheryl knew all about the untimely death of friends – John Courtney was one. She had lived through the detrimental effect of drugs during her time with Jason Mack. She had despaired at the continuing prison time served by her brother Andrew and she needed to look no further than her own mother, Joan, to see how easy it was to be pregnant and a mum at seventeen in her neighbourhood. She and will.i.am are kindred spirits. Her tribute to him in the sleeve notes to the album summed up that bond: 'You inspire me and your belief in me has given me the confidence to make this record and step out on my own. I luv you!!x'

The Black Eyed Peas became one of the most commercially successful acts in the world after they took on the beautiful singer Fergie (Stacy Ferguson) in 2003. While Will was helping Cheryl put the finishing touches on her first album, the Peas were number one in both the US album and singles charts. Cheryl's favourite track, which she helped to write, was '3 Words'. The song revealed the R&B influence and melodic chorus that she was aiming to achieve. Not surprisingly, it would become the title of the album as well as the opening track. From the beginning, *3 Words* was unmistakably Cheryl Cole and not an album cloned from Girls Aloud.

Will.i.am may have ensured musical credibility but Cheryl would soon have to face a potential hindrance to being taken seriously as a solo artist. Her amazing success as an *X Factor* judge might ultimately undermine her musical career. That would be in the future. For the moment, it remained to be seen whether Cheryl, in her second stint on *The X Factor*, was going to duplicate the success of 2008.

Cheryl was surprisingly low key to start with, leaving much of the show's pre-publicity to Dannii Minogue and Louis Walsh. She was too busy with the album anyway, but it also made sense to wait until the release of her first solo single in late October before doing the publicity rounds to guarantee maximum exposure at the right time. She was interviewed by acclaimed writer Chrissy Iley in Los Angeles in July but the agreement was that the feature would not run in *The Sunday Times* until just before the record came out.

Simon Cowell decided on a new approach for the sixth series of *The X Factor*: all the auditions would take place in front of a live audience. The more intimate surroundings of the judges' room, where Cheryl had first forged her bond with the British public, were going to be replaced by a noisy mob atmosphere. Could Cheryl emulate the amazing success of her first series in this environment?

Cheryl, it turned out, was still Cheryl. She engaged in some light Geordie banter with a smiley lad from South Shields called Joe McElderry. She went onstage in a very short checked dress to help a local girl, a personal trainer called Amie Buck, struggle through the Girls Aloud single 'I'll Stand By You'. Amie stumbled over the words to the song but, with Cheryl alongside her, she made it through to boot camp. 'I hope I can follow in her footsteps,' said Amie. This did not look likely when shy Amie was revealed in the press to be a £500-a-week lap dancer, although she did attract the interest of various 'lads' mags'. She did not make it through to the later rounds.

Cheryl stopped the show to give a young Welsh singer, Lloyd Daniels, a second chance after he murdered the Jason Mraz song 'I'm Yours'. 'I think he could be good,' she told Simon. 'But that was terrible,' she added quietly, echoing the views of millions of viewers. He proceeded to sing the R Kelly ballad 'If I Could Turn Back The Hands Of Time' a cappella and sailed through.

After her triumph of the previous year, Cheryl needed to be careful about becoming too emotional. Her tears are genuine and part of her personality but she realized they shouldn't become a trademark. She couldn't help herself, however, when a couple who had recently broken off their engagement sang a duet together. 'I think she still loves you,' sniffled Cheryl. And the world sniffled with her.

Perhaps the most poignant moment was when Daniel Pearce auditioned. He had been arguably the best singer in the ill-fated One True Voice, who had lost out so completely to Girls Aloud after *Popstars: The Rivals*. He could still sing – he cantered soulfully through Seal's 'Kiss From A Rose' – but now he sported a dated Mohican haircut and talked about his new family. He almost made it to the live shows but it seemed a little sad that he was trying again seven years after being a winner. He had trodden a very different path from Cheryl's and his fortunes are another example, if one is needed, of how fickle the whole music business is.

For most of her second series of *The X Factor*, Cheryl was quite spiky, blowing raspberries at Simon Cowell, standing up to Louis Walsh and supporting her three acts for the live shows. She again had a very strong category – the boys. 'Joe, you are a little star,' she seemed to say every week of her main hope, Joe McElderry.

She did have one major confrontation with Simon after Lloyd Daniels sang a lacklustre version of the Leona Lewis number one 'Bleeding Love'. The Dark Lord was unimpressed and blamed Cheryl: 'It's like a mouse trying to climb a mountain. I'm going to put the blame for that solely on the girl on my right, who's not working with you properly.' Cheryl was in tears when she admitted getting it wrong, prompting Lloyd to leap off the stage and put his arm around her protectively. That spontaneous gesture of gallantry almost certainly got him through to the following week. Cheryl admitted, 'It gets quite heated backstage. I don't feel like a competitive person but Simon is so competitive and rude sometimes that I find myself getting caught up in it.'

When the new series of *The X Factor* began, Cheryl already knew that her first solo single was going to be 'Fight For This Love', a very catchy pop tune and one of the tracks not written by will.i.am. Disappointingly, perhaps, it is probably the one song on *3 Words* that could have been a Girls Aloud single. It was written by Steve Kipner, Wayne Wilkins and Andre Merritt. Kipner, in particular, had written several big number one records over the years, including the debut hit for Christina Aguilera, 'Genie In A Bottle', and 'These Words' for Natasha Bedingfield.

The executives at Fascination Records (Polydor) showed commendable commercial awareness in choosing the track as the single even though Cheryl would have preferred '3 Words'. The title itself would get everybody talking about 'Fight For This Love'. Instantly, it became the anthem for Cheryl's marriage to Ashley Cole and for thousands of other troubled relationships. The song was a very safe bet in that all the Girls Aloud fans would accept it. It really was the song that would launch a thousand headlines.

In these days of modern marketing, a guest spot on *The X Factor* is like an oil strike. The good and the great of the music world now have no problem appearing on a reality show. The biggest television audience of the week will watch and listen to a five-minute plug for a new record. The 2009 series of Simon Cowell's baby produced week after week of number one hits – both singles and albums. Cheryl could probably have taken to the stage and sung 'Bob the Builder' and it would have been top of the charts the following week. That did not make her first appearance as a solo star any less anticipated or any less nerve-racking for her. 'My biggest fear is that the microphone will start shaking uncontrollably.'

Cheryl was scheduled to appear on 20 October, on the same show as the legendary Whitney Houston, who was making a comeback performing her new single 'Million Dollar Bill', which turned out to be rather dull. Her performance was anything but, however, with her dress strap breaking. The brief interview she exchanged with host Dermot O'Leary was embarrassing and a stark contrast to Cheryl's earlier super-slick appearance. Louis Walsh described Whitney's performance as 'pure car crash television . . . but it is live TV and she kept going. Everyone loves it when that happens.'

Much fuss had been made beforehand about whether Cheryl would mime or not. The suggestion was that it would be hypocritical to mime on a show that judged live singing. In the end, she part sang, part mimed. The debate is always a pointless one because it's physically impossible to perform any sort of energetic dancing and try to sing while you are desperate to take in a great gulp of air. Britney Spears always faces this barrage of criticism but the fans never mind as much as the critics because it is the show's overall effect that's important. And Cheryl looked stunning, dressed in a scarlet military tunic, matching army hat and harem-style leggings split to the crotch. The whole thing was beautifully choreographed, although Cheryl did not overextend herself in order to be able to manage the promised live bits – and the microphone did not shake. Nearly fifteen million watched on television, the biggest ever *X Factor* audience to that point.

Afterwards, Simon Cowell commented, 'This is really going to pain me but that was incredible. Unfortunately, you are going to be number one next week.' Part of Simon's torment was that Cheryl was the one '*X Factor* act' who was not signed to his Syco label. A jubilant Cheryl whooped, 'I feel fantastic', and went off to her dressing room to drink champagne with Kimberley, Nicola and Sarah, who had turned up to support her. Simon was right and 'Fight For This Love' sold 292,000 copies in its first week, making it the fastest selling single of the year. It sold more in the first seven days than 'Sound of the Underground' had. The track would give Cheryl her fifth number one of the decade. When all the counting up had finished, Cheryl's first solo single had sold 808,000 copies – more than any Girls Aloud record. She was placed at number twenty-nine in the best-selling songs of the decade. The online music magazine *popjustice* said, 'It's one of those songs you can have on repeat for an hour and a half without getting bored.' Cheryl, it added, sounded 'like a proper pop singer.'

Just a week later the album *3 Words* was also number one and Cheryl was top of the singles and album charts at the same time. Like the single, it managed two weeks at the top. The praise for the album, however, was not as universal as for the single. It was not exactly a backlash but Andy Gill in *The Independent* wrote: '*3 Words* is utterly bereft of imagination and risk.' More interestingly, he noted a thread of paranoia about relationships running through the songs, which he described as a 'fear that others are bent on destroying her relationship.' 'Love is brutal' seemed to be a constant theme. Tom Ewing in *The Guardian* thought Cheryl an 'expressive performer' shown to best effect when the production was stripped back. As a solo performer she wouldn't showcase well in the densely produced world of Girls Aloud but she could shine on the title track, '3 Words'. 'It's as brave and novel a song as anything Cole's group have released and shows how good she can be given a more imaginative setting.'

Cheryl continued to promote 'Fight For This Love', changing from scarlet to white for her appearance on *BBC Children in Need* in November. She recorded an emotional appeal for donations to help the four million children in the UK living in poverty and then demonstrated a growing confidence by returning in a Hollywood-style white gown to sing a duet with Snow Patrol, one of the most popular bands in the world. Cheryl Cole and Snow Patrol? It could have been a match made in hell but lead singer Gary Lightbody, who has one of the most distinctive and melodic voices in music, embraced the duet with unconcealed enthusiasm. He introduced Cheryl graciously as the 'very beautiful and wonderful Cheryl Cole'. They sang the haunting 'Set The Fire To The Third Bar' and when it was over you wished they would sing another. There was no miming; it was just a simple no-frills performance. This duet would be an enormous hit if it were ever released. Cheryl surpassed herself. Sir Terry Wogan, the perennial host of the evening, described Cheryl as the 'nation's sweetheart, so she is.'

TV executives were quick to cash in on Cheryl's popularity and she was paid a six-figure sum to star in *Cheryl Cole's Night In*, which allowed her to sing some songs from her album and reveal how much she loved her two Chihuahuas, Buster and Coco. Will.i.am joined her to duet on '3 Words' and guests included Rihanna, Alexandra Burke and Will Young. It could almost have been an *X Factor* show.

The X Factor juggernaut rumbled on, giving everyone associated with it fantastic publicity. Much was made of the style battle between Cheryl and fellow judge Dannii Minogue. Dannii, who is twelve years older than Cheryl, has never looked better than she did in that series. They both looked a million dollars every week, although GMTV's style expert, Mark Heyes, thought one of Cheryl's creations was 'one of the worst dresses I have ever seen. I've seen panto horses look better.' The black fan-styled dress, which cost £1,500 and featured metal piping snaking across the bodice, was designed by David Koma – although he may not want to admit to it now. Cheryl wore it for the rock 'n' roll-themed show and had to suffer Simon Cowell telling her she'd better sit up, implying that she was going to fall out of it if she didn't. Afterwards it became known as the 'dustbin lid' dress, although that did not stop copies of it from selling out online. The power of Cheryl, it seemed, could sell anything.

Cheryl spends a reported £100,000 looking good on *The X Factor*, although she earns far more as the face of the L'Oreal hair range. Dannii also spends liberally. They have to. Louis and Simon can wear the same old white shirt and suit but part of the appeal of the programme is seeing what the girls are wearing every week.

Despite the best efforts of the media, Dannii and Cheryl are not really in competition because of the age gap. Dannii looks better when she dresses as if she were on the red carpet at the Oscars. Cheryl wears a variety of minuscule numbers that only a young girl on a serious diet could get into. Some of them don't work. She did win the 'final', however, when she wore a silver and black frock that Mark Heyes described as a cross between 'a bejewelled mermaid and Jessica Rabbit'. She could not actually walk in it, however.

On the show, the momentum had been swinging in favour of Joe McElderry. By the time of the final, just before Christmas, he was odds-on favourite to win. Louis Walsh observed, 'He's gonna walk it.' He was right. His duet with George Michael on 'Don't Let The Sun Go Down On Me' was outstanding. After his victory he gushed about Cheryl's role: 'She is really caring and helpful all the way through.' He also went endearingly red when he was asked in an interview if he fancied Cheryl: 'I can't say that now because I know her.' Some of Cheryl's own secret formula had rubbed off on Geordie Joe – he was natural and nice throughout the competition.

Cheryl had now 'won' two *X Factors* in a row. Alexandra Burke and Joe McElderry were very different contestants and the suspicion remains that Cheryl would have carried any of the leading acts to victory. She had been emotional and close to tears when, during the final, she praised Joe and paid tribute to his family. An *X Factor* insider admitted, 'People have been voting as much for her as they have been for Joe.'

One of the things Cheryl could not do for Joe was make people buy his record, 'The Climb', and, surprisingly, it was not the Christmas number one. It was beaten by Rage Against The Machine's 'Killing In The Name', which had been promoted by an enterprising Internet campaign against *The X Factor* single. Joe was number one the following week and probably sold more records as a result of the 'battle'. Cheryl's second solo single, '3 Words', the title track from her album, was also released in time for Christmas and reached number four in the chart, which is quite respectable for a second single from an album, especially at the most competitive time of year.

Jim Shelley, the television critic of the *Daily Mirror*, summed up the sixth series of *The X Factor*: 'Joe's victory was an amazing climax to what has been an incredible series of *The X Factor*, not least because the quality of the contestants has been so dire.' He could have added that the judges, particularly Cheryl and Simon, were much more important to the show than the contestants.

Official viewing figures for the final of *The X Factor* were 19.1 million. The critics never fully appreciate how or why the rest of the country loves *The X Factor*. It gives us all something to talk and text about. It feeds our desire to gossip and argue just as much as the prospect of snow or the latest Manchester United game. 'Who do you think is going to win *The X Factor*?' must have been the most asked question of 2009 – a reflection of the importance of television in modern life. It may loosely be called a 'reality' show but it is the very lack of reality that gives the show its universal appeal. It is the stuff of fantasy and dreams.

21

Love Is Brutal

Cheryl began 2010 by being named *Hello!* magazine's Most Elegant Woman of 2009. Cheryl was pictured in a variety of outfits from the previous twelve months. Only one, a pale yellow Greek goddess gown designed by Atelier Versace, could truthfully be described as elegant, although at least the infamous dustbin-lid dress was nowhere to be seen. The accolade was voted for by readers, which is always a little more satisfying than those decided by executives who think giving Cheryl an award will guarantee extra readers. The magazine said, 'As years go, 2009 will take some topping for the 26-year-old woman who has fast become the nation's sweetheart.'

The magazine also, perhaps unwittingly, revealed that in a year of unrelenting triumph there were still some areas of Cheryl's life that could improve. For the millionth time she was asked about children and if she was feeling broody. 'Always', she replied. 'Maybe not yet, but definitely I would like a brood.' That sounded very different from the newspaper stories a few weeks earlier, which had shouted Cheryl's desire to quit *The X Factor* to have a baby. According to one source, 'Cheryl wanted to have a baby with Ashley in 2009 but put it off because of pressure of work.'

Baby speculation is just one of the irritations that female celebrities have to put up with. They have to accept it along with the constant analysing of every small change in their body shape and expert comment about what they are wearing when they pop out to the local store for a packet of cigarettes. Jennifer Aniston and Kylie Minogue probably hold the world record for having to answer the baby question, especially when they embark on a new relationship. Both ladies have passed forty now but, year after year, they have graciously said that they want children. Cheryl is not far behind. *Star* magazine, in its appraisal of her stellar year, had sections on *The X Factor*, her solo career, Girls Aloud and breaking the US – and babies. 'I can't wait,' admitted Cheryl.

Hello!, however, moved on from babies to highlight the potentially more interesting saga of Cheryl's wedding ring. The ring had assumed great significance when Cheryl had removed it during the Aimee Walton scandal. When she put it back on, it was an indication that she and Ashley had made up. She had told Jonathan Ross that taking off the ring had been a meaningful gesture, so everybody sat up and took notice when she now appeared on *The X Factor* without the ring. To counter the rumour mill, Cheryl agreed to release an image on Twitter of her holding up her left hand in front of her face and flashing the heart-shaped diamond monster. Underneath, it said, '3 Words: Diamonds Are Forever.'

The gesture was clearly aimed at squashing rumours that all was not well at Cole Towers or Hurtmore House, as their grand home was ironically called. A series of stories appeared in the press quoting sources proclaiming they had 'never been happier' and that, according to Cheryl, 'Everything is fine and I feel really, really content right now.' The whole thing appeared to be part of a charm offensive that included Cheryl's first public appearance at Stamford Bridge for months to watch Chelsea beat Portsmouth. It was a shame it was such an unglamorous fixture but Cheryl was beaming when Ashley drove them home in his Bentley. They were also happy to be photographed together going to a joint birthday party for Kimberley Walsh and Sarah Harding at the Kanaloa, the club near St Paul's that Sarah had launched with her DJ boyfriend Tom Crane. An eyewitness reported that Cheryl and Ashley sat together holding hands the whole night: 'When they thought no one was looking, they had a romantic smooch. It was just so sweet.' The problem for Cheryl was that these gestures did not completely end the speculation about the state of their relationship. It didn't help that Cheryl flew off with her mother to Cape Town for the New Year, leaving Ashley behind in the snowy UK. Instead of spending New Year's Eve with her husband, she was at a glamorous party hosted by a prominent American businessman, Preston Haskell. Joan and Cheryl spent a week sunbathing and socializing while Ashley began the year by losing a court case. He was found guilty at Kingston Magistrates Court of driving his black Lamborghini at more than 100 m.p.h. in a 50-m.p.h. zone. He claimed in his defence that he was being chased by paparazzi but was eventually banned from driving for four months.

Cheryl returned home to the news that Dannii Minogue was pregnant. All the baby speculation had been right but the media had the wrong judge. That did not stop the flow of stories about Cheryl wanting to quit *The X Factor* and follow suit.

Simon Cowell, meanwhile, signed a deal estimated to be worth £100 million to launch a US version of *The X Factor*. Would he take Cheryl? He observed, 'I think she'd be great over here. Cheryl's a star.' Cheryl could not be in two places at once and have a baby for good measure. Something would have to give.

One of the laws of news is the bus principle: you wait ages for the number nineteen bus into town and then three arrive at once. The same is true of news. It could be anything – something tragic like a cot death, amusing like a drunken sportsman or infuriating like a race attack occurs and the next day the media are reporting another one and the day after that yet another one. The agenda is set by the first news bus to arrive at the stop. In 2010 John Terry, the England captain, was on board and the sensational nature of his alleged extramarital shenanigans would set the mood for the second bus to arrive containing Ashley Cole.

The John Terry scandal burst into life on 29 January when an injunction was lifted that had prevented newspapers from revealing an extramarital affair with a former lingerie model. The England captain had obtained an interim so-called 'super' injunction to prevent the *News of the World* not only from publishing the story but also from even mentioning that an injunction had been obtained. Lawyers from the paper managed to overturn the order.

Over the following days a feeding frenzy in the press revealed that the story concerned an alleged affair that the defender had been having with Vanessa Perroncel, the former girlfriend of his best friend, Wayne Bridge, and also the mother of Bridge's three-year-old son. Lurid details and speculation mounted on a daily basis, culminating in Terry being sacked as England captain by manager Fabio Capello on 5 February. In the very small world of top-flight football, John Terry and his wife, Toni, Wayne and Vanessa, and Ashley and Cheryl had all lived within a short drive from one another in the golden football triangle of Oxshott.

Footballers, particularly England and Chelsea ones, were subject to immense scrutiny as a result. The news bus containing Ashley Cole, nursing a broken foot after he was injured in the game against Everton, arrived courtesy of *The Sun* exactly a week later. The story was a bizarre one. It really was a case of 'you couldn't make it up'. A busty blonde topless model called Sonia Wild claimed that she had received raunchy and graphic photos of Ashley posing in front of a bathroom mirror. Sonia, from Hull, said she received the photographs the night before the World Cup qualifier against Andorra in June. Sonia claimed they had enjoyed the new phenomenon of text sex. She had sent him sexy videos, including one of herself in the bath, and had seen, in return, Ashley 'in all his glory'. Sonia, a 28-year-old single mother of two, said the texting and picture messaging 'got hotter and hotter' and went on for hours throughout the night.

The sorry saga would have been quite funny if it hadn't been so embarrassing for Cheryl. Ashley admitted taking the pictures 'larking about' in front of the bathroom mirror while staying at the England team hotel in Hertfordshire. He denied sending the shots to Sonia and, instead, offered a tortuous explanation, which *The Sun* described as 'an amazing chain of events.' He claimed he had given the unregistered phone to a friend because it still had some credit on it, without realizing he hadn't deleted the risqué images. He explained, 'I can't believe I gave a phone away that still had stuff in its memory. I thought I had deleted it. It seems I was wrong as someone has used it to pretend to be me. I would laugh if my foot didn't hurt so much.'

The revelations were made while Ashley was receiving hospital treatment. Cheryl spent the afternoon with him before they both left in the early evening, looking particularly grim, in a chauffeur-driven Mercedes. A spokesman for them said that Cheryl knew Ashley had a pay-as-you-go mobile while he was 'between phones' and accepted his explanation. She was probably the only one who did. Columnist Polly Hudson trowelled on the irony in the *Daily Mirror*. 'I just hope he can stay strong. But when you have truth on your side, you have nothing to fear, so I'm sure he'll be fine.'

At a time when Cheryl would have preferred to slip away from the unforgiving public gaze, she was facing one of the biggest nights of her professional career – a solo performance at the Brit Awards. She had to go and rehearse on Valentine's Day, a circumstance made even more poignant by the number she was singing, 'Fight For This Love'. Cheryl could be forgiven for wishing she had never come across the tune. The very best spin that could be put on the story was that it was embarrassing. The problem for Ashley was that he had little public sympathy to fall back on after the Aimee Walton furore.

The embarrassments continued to pile up for Cheryl. She had given an interview to *Hello!* magazine before the texting story broke in which she declared, 'If it's worth fighting for, then fight. And in the case of me and my husband it's worth it. We love each other.' She also said, 'I love it when he surprises me.'

The surprises for Cheryl were far from over. Just like the John Terry epic, the headlines refused to go away and Ashley and his team-mate seemed to be in competition for who could occupy the most front pages. Ashley was soon winning. The day before the Brits, *The Sun* found a 'pretty secretary' who had received very similar pictures and more than 300 texts from the same telephone. The images contained a now famous one of Ashley sporting a pair of unflatteringly large white underpants. They were definitely not Armani as advertised by David Beckham. The problem for Ashley was that the messages and images were sent nine months before the ones to Sonia, yet were from the same phone he claimed he had given to a friend. The newspaper gleefully proclaimed that Ashley's explanation about the texts to Sonia was 'exposed as a lie'.

Sue Carroll, the strident *Mirror* columnist, asked, on the day of the Brits: 'Is parading naked and taking mobile phone pictures what young married men do of an evening these days?' For the second time in little more than a year, Sue had occasion to call Ashley a 'lickspittle' footballer.

The Sun cranked the temperature of the story up by many degrees the same day when the secretary, still not named, alleged that she had met Cole twice for sex. 'Ashley Bedded Sex Txt Girl' was the headline. They had met at a hotel the night before Chelsea were due to play Hull. It was in late October 2008, when Cheryl was busy in London as the new star of *The X Factor*. The elegant blonde, aged thirty, said she had a crush on Ashley. She told how she'd smuggled in some rosé wine and they watched films in bed before getting down to it. Perhaps the cruellest and most hurtful aspect of it all from Cheryl's point of view was the secretary's observation, 'It wasn't raunchy stuff, more like relationship sex.' Two weeks later she claimed that Ashley went back for seconds before a game against West Brom.

Most newspapers were quick to call the fling 'alleged' but *The Sun* was far bolder, describing Ashley as 'cheating' and Cheryl as 'betrayed'. At this stage *The Sun* did not name the girl involved, perhaps safe in the knowledge that her identity would not remain a secret for long in the modern world of Internet tittle-tattle. Within a day or two she had been named as Vicki Gough, a secretary at Liverpool Football Club.

The Brits at Earls Court were a triumph for Cheryl. She didn't win the award for Best Single of 2009 – she was beaten by JLS with 'Beat Again' – but she did turn up. And she produced a rousing rendition of 'Fight For This Love', hiding her emotions behind aviator sunglasses. Even the host, Peter Kay, was moved to comment: 'You've got to fight for this love – never a truer word said.' Cheryl had delivered a professional performance at a difficult time when the whole world was watching for a sign of emotional meltdown. The only sign on offer was that, yet again, her wedding ring was missing.

The ring was still absent the following day when she flew out of London to honour commitments in Los Angeles. At least it would give her time to come to her own decision about what to do, away from the influence of public opinion, however well-meaning. She could be forgiven for believing things could not get any worse. At least she was away when a third busty young woman, an American, claimed she'd had sex with Ashley in a Seattle hotel during Chelsea's pre-season tour of the US.

Ann Corbitt, aged twenty-eight, lost little time in revealing all the steamy details. Apparently they made love for three or four hours and she was complimentary about Cheryl's husband. But, echoing the observations of Vicki Gough, she said it was like having sex with a boyfriend, someone who loves you. The full story was in the *News of the World* and included alleged gems, such as the sex was unprotected and once again he'd sent a girl a picture of himself in white pants. She said he was distraught that he might 'lose his wife' over his indiscretion. Did Cheryl recognize anything from her account – for instance, his desire to hold hands when they went to sleep? Aimee Walton's descriptions of a drunken encounter must have seemed a lifetime away from these tales of relationship and boyfriend-style sex.

It looked as if Ashley was competing against the philandering Tiger Woods when the same day yet another girl recalled a bed-time romp. This tryst put the knife firmly into Cheryl because it allegedly occurred on a night when she and Ashley had been photographed as a couple for the first time after her appearance at the National Television Awards in October 2004. The account of Blackpool glamour model Alexandra Taylor was more similar to the Aimee Walton tale in that she alleged Ashley was thoroughly drunk. 'It was really lousy,' she declared.

Cheryl was still in Los Angeles while everyone waited patiently to find out what she was going to do. She was photographed with a young dancer called Derek Hough, a star of the US TV series *Dancing with the Stars*. The pictures carefully excluded the burly bodyguards who accompanied Cheryl everywhere. Derek is young, blond and good-looking and a picture of them together spared Cheryl a flurry of captions proclaiming how miserable she looked. Instead, there was much speculation that she was getting her own back on Ashley, as if she were honestly going to flirt and more with a relative stranger during one of the biggest personal crises of her life.

Derek had met Cheryl when he danced in the video for her third single from the *3 Words* album, 'Parachute', which was due for release in March. He had also danced with her on *Cheryl Cole's Night In* but nobody really noticed him then. At the very least his friendship would mean some extra publicity for the song.

While Cheryl was away, some enterprising burglars tried to break into her Surrey mansion, not realizing that Ashley was there. He called the police but the robbers had made their escape before help arrived. One theory was that they were after her wedding ring, which the whole world knew she was not wearing.

The story was moving so fast there was barely time to draw breath. Ashley was portrayed as so horrid he became like a pantomime villain. A poll voted him the most hated man in Britain, pipping John Terry to the top spot. The Muslim preacher Abu Hamza was third. Even Ashley's father, Ron Callender, was unimpressed, saying that Cheryl had been 'shamed' by his son's behaviour. Piers Morgan spoke for the nation when he described Ashley as 'the single most stupid cretin in the history of Planet Earth.'

Fiona McIntosh in the *Sunday Mirror* wrote of Ashley: 'Even by footballers' standards, he's a premiership sleazebag.' Fiona made a fascinating observation about Cheryl's feelings alone in her suite at the ultra-fashionable Chateau Marmont hotel in Hollywood. She was grieving not only the death of her marriage but also her unborn babies – the children she had imagined having with Ashley Cole.

All the gossip and speculation finally ended when Cheryl returned to England on 23 February. Ashley had been driven away from the family home in a silver Mercedes at 7.30 in the morning. Cheryl arrived there, in the back of a different silver Mercedes, just after midday. Ashley was already on his way to a clinic in the south of France when the following announcement appeared on Twitter: 'Cheryl Cole is separating from her husband Ashley Cole. Cheryl asks the media to respect her privacy during this difficult time.'

*

Cheryl clearly loves Ashley Cole. I remember seeing a picture of them together at her twenty-sixth birthday party in July 2009. She is clutching his hand and resting her head on his shoulder with a grin on her face. She oozes happiness. It is rare that a celebrity is captured in a moment of such naturalness and beauty.

The whole world seemed to cheer when she announced their separation. A short while before, Cheryl had said, 'Anyone who throws in the towel ends up achieving nothing.' She was talking about her decision to stay with Ashley after the first round of stories about his infidelity in January 2008. Celebrity marriages seem to end in the blink of an eye but nobody could accuse Cheryl of not giving her own every chance. In the end it took just nine days to go from heaven to hell.

For the first edition of this book, published in September 2009, I wrote: 'I don't know if she will stay with Ashley but she has shown exceptional strength in not following the media's suggestions that she should ditch her philandering husband. Cheryl is refreshingly stubborn in doing her own thing.' I had expected to end this edition on a note of triumph by reviewing Cheryl's performance at the Brits.

I would love her to announce that she has performed 'Fight For This Love' for the last time. She had the sympathy cheer, of course, but nobody wants that. Cheryl is not a victim but a successful, independent young woman who is facing the same emotional trauma many face every day in their lives. She has the misfortune to be swimming in a goldfish bowl while her personal life, as she knows it, disintegrates.

Her professional life continues to flourish. She is the support act for Black Eyed Peas on their sold-out late spring tour. After that it won't be long before we know what her *X Factor* plans are. She can expect a big pay increase. If she continues to progress under Simon Cowell's patronage, there will be no stopping her. She won't need Girls Aloud, although they are due to record a new album in 2010. Cowell may launch Cheryl in the US, although I hope she stays in the UK and doesn't end up living the high life in Beverly Hills. Cheryl is as British as fish and chips, a pint of bitter, *Dad's Army*, Wembley and complaining about the weather.

All the platitudes and clichés about Cheryl becoming a national treasure are correct, I think. She is beautiful but has her flaws. She makes mistakes but faces up to them. She loves her family, especially her mother Joan, who will be her rock during a difficult time. Her appeal in our modern impersonal world is that she does more than simply put a smile on our faces. When she weeps, we look for a hankie; when she blasts Simon or Louis, we cheer; when she thanks a contestant for his or her performance, we nod in agreement; when she is mistreated, we are furious and want to protect her; when she is happy, we catch that exuberance. She makes a connection.

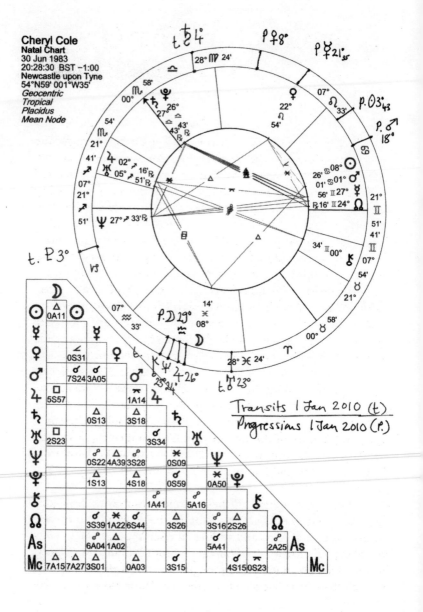

The Cheryl Cole Birth Chart

The birth chart of Cheryl Cole suggests she has the strength and depth of personality to be far more than a one-generation success. Moreover, anyone swayed by that beautiful face into a relaxed acceptance of her sweetness will be missing the main game – like all class acts, this woman is far more than her frocks and lip gloss. Her chart reveals a number of contradictions in her personality. These differences are blended in and held together to produce a character that is never quite predictable, or easy to pin down, but is one highly likely to make others sit up and think.

At the heart of Cheryl's chart lies a grouping of planets straddling the signs of Cancer and Gemini – signs that together have little in common. The most important of this group is the Sun, the planet associated with individuality, creativity and vitality. Sun Cancer people are known to have great sensitivity and respond to situations with their emotions rather than reason. They approach life in a gentle and indirect, yet persistent, manner. Joined to the Sun is the mighty warrior, Mars, planet of initiative and daring. Together they make a formidable pairing: the imaginative and protective nature of this Sun given a feisty and courageous twist by Mars. People with this combination almost always know what they want in life and have no doubts about their chances of getting it.

At best, the energy of these planets can work brilliantly together – Cancerian caution putting the brakes on the crazy impetuousness of Mars and adding another key ingredient, emotional intelligence, to what is already a heady intuitive mix. Cheryl will be able to read people as though they were a glossy magazine with all their heartfelt secrets on display. Those close to her will respond to her genuine empathy, although nobody should misread her kindness and think she is a pushover. Their comeuppance could be painful.

Cheryl may have softness and the ability to nurture but she also needs to lead, conquer and win, and will do so with the beguiling, quirky humour of a Sun Cancer and the focus of the relentless fighter, Mars. Quite simply, she has enormous personality.

Cheryl is also able to read her public, easily tapping into the mood of her supporters. This is evident from the links between the Sun and the Moon in her chart. She will experience certain issues and concerns in such a way that her public will feel she is one of them – someone who understands their lives and has something relevant to say. She will always ride the crest of her generation's wave, having earned their respect as well as their affection. At least once in her lifetime, she is likely to front a campaign – the Sun linked to Mars reveals she needs a cause to pursue.

The pull of the family is likely to be strong for Cheryl. She would have benefited in her early life from some degree of domestic stability, resulting from a certain unity between her parents. Importantly, this would contribute to a basic confidence that will help her through times of pressure. This parental security will not have been without its tensions. Her parents may have had much in common, including love, but perhaps they were unable to give themselves the time and space needed to nurture their own partnership. Such circumstances in childhood invariably mould the adult, although not necessarily in a negative way. Cheryl is likely to have experienced enough contentment to support her creativity and growth but not such amounts as would smother the desire to set her own compass and achieve in her own way. She would value independence.

Her father is likely to have been the more traditional parent and one whose directness and ability to precipitate events will have been absorbed by Cheryl. She may have appreciated his imagination, ability to tell a good story and tenacious memory. She may not have always found him easy to read – expecting a certain sharpness of response on occasion and then discovering he could be good at making allowances and had a very soft heart.

The relationship Cheryl has with her mother may be more complex. The Moon, which represents mother in the birth chart, makes strong links to both Uranus and Jupiter, planets associated with a need for freedom and growth. Uranus values honesty and the chances are her mother could surprise, even shock, by her straight talking. These are indications of a sympathetic, strong-willed, restless and larger-than-life individual. Her mother would have the vision to appreciate her daughter's need for musical creativity and the sense to allow her to develop her skills, providing much encouragement and protective support. Cheryl may see her mother as someone who, alongside experiencing the achievements of family life, perhaps inevitably had her own ideals and dreams sidetracked. From an early age, this is likely, quite unconsciously, to have strengthened Cheryl's desire to achieve the personal completeness that even a modest degree of independent worldly success brings and move beyond a conventional family set-up.

A very tight, positive link between Mercury, the planet that symbolizes siblings, and Saturn and Pluto reveals the importance to Cheryl of her sister and brothers. These planetary combinations suggest the nature of these relationships will be enduring, although more likely to be kept harmonious if there is an element of space in the mix. Most importantly, the contact with Pluto, Lord of the Underworld, indicates that Cheryl will benefit from the real-life education she received from family members. They will be linked – for ever really – by intense background experiences that no amount of classroom time could hope to replicate. Cheryl's formal schooling, in fact, may have been painful to her, sometimes experienced as alienating. She is likely to have felt shut out from a bigger world, with her need to express herself in her own manner invalidated. More positively, school would have provided boundaries and systems of discipline to which Cheryl would have been highly sensitive and appreciative. In the main, what is clearly spelled out in this birth chart is that what Cheryl has learned the hard way will be of immeasurable value to her.

Despite the strength of love for her family, this birth chart indicates a very strong need to break away from the past – at least until she has formed a strong sense of her own individuality and identity. Where some might feel lost without a highly responsive, closely enmeshed family, Cheryl, in the early part of her life at least, is more likely to experience such intimacy as suffocation.

Cheryl's Sun in Cancer emphasizes the point that she has a genuine need to remember and honour her roots and her birth family. But here there is a contradiction – the wealth of planets in Air and Fire signs make her objective, rather than lovey-dovey. So, she is more likely to be rational than emotional, distant rather than hands-on, but, nevertheless, her support will be real. The link between Saturn, known as the Great Teacher, and Mercury underlines her role as someone who sets an example and expects her lead to be followed. Thus, she may have blazoned a trail in her youth and hoped this would influence those she loved. This pattern will operate whenever Cheryl is part of a group – professionally or socially; she will set the pace and lead, but her influence may initially be invisible until her success is too obvious to miss.

Cheryl's tenacious and determined approach to life will be evident within her relationships. She will value those who are creative and able to balance an instinct for fun with an element of dignity and these are the qualities she will look for in her long-lasting friendships. Even in more passionate partnerships, friendship is the key word here, with its connotations of equality and a meeting of minds. There are many indications within the birth chart that despite Cheryl's compassionate nature and her enjoyment of intimacy, this is someone who needs room to breathe.

The awkwardness of dealing with divergent instincts – the Cancerian desire to mother and the Air and Fire signs' need to be free – will pose dilemmas for Cheryl. These are obviously not insurmountable: the positive link between Saturn and Mercury indicates abundant common sense, a well-placed Jupiter suggests both wisdom and an expansionist approach to wealth. But despite these positives, building her own family will present challenges, such as a child's need for emotional consistency versus a mother's need to fully explore and develop her marked creativity and difficult-to-rein-in desire to learn.

In January 2010, Cheryl should experience a successful culmination to a project first started in late May of the previous year and progressed that September. Then, Jupiter, the planet of good fortune, links to Pluto and Saturn. At a very simple level this will provide the chance to sort out situations that had previously been problematic either in personal relationships or group ventures. It is part of Cheryl's nature to yearn for an element of power and control but, at the same time, to be fearful of attaining this. It is this anxiety that is partially the cause of the driven perfectionist streak that is such a marked feature of her character. This transit should see her confidently stepping up to the line, impelled both by the natural born survivor's instinct to regenerate and her love for taking on new, inspiring ventures. It is worth remembering the power of Cheryl's Mercury in its own sign of Gemini. Beyond her undoubted musicality (signified by the almost exact opposition to Neptune, planet of imagination and all that helps us escape – for example, music) she is also a lucid, if somewhat impulsive and scattered communicator. It seems inevitable that at some point, given the number and strength of planets in the sign of Jupiter, she will become an increasingly authoritative and gifted speaker for a cause.

What she learns through this scenario may be of pertinent use to her two years or so later when, between December 2011 and January 2012, a series of tense contacts occur to her birth chart, signifying deeper changes. The first of these is when Saturn completes its twenty-nine-year cycle around the zodiac and returns to the same position it occupied at the moment of birth – known by many as the Saturn return. It marks a turning point when Cheryl will assess her life's progress and realistically review the balance sheet. This is coupled with an opposition of Pluto to her Sun, indicating a period when she will be forced to prioritize. This lasts on and off until September 2013 and is a non-negotiable transit: it will happen; it will leave its mark. Most commonly, this is associated with power struggles and Cheryl may either find that someone is attempting to dominate her or, conversely, that she, no matter for what good reasons, is trying to control someone else.

Cheryl's chart, with its powerful Jupiterian feel, suggests that some of the major issues she must face will be those associated with perfectionism. While obviously a desire to aim idealistically high can be beneficial, the refusal to acknowledge human limitations can be dangerous. Cheryl will need to watch her health. At best, excess perfectionism can cause true discomfort both to the individual and to those around them. The resulting profound disappointment when standards aren't met frequently leads to anger and distress. Cheryl will need her expectations of herself and others to be goals and not demands. Further, it is important to remember that being right all the time can sabotage the desire to be happy. Cheryl's gentle Sun in Cancer forms a slightly awkward link to Venus, suggesting that her need for popularity or to be loved means she is occasionally unable to confront unpleasant issues. If someone close to her reads this as weakness and tries to take advantage, she must find the power within herself to turn around such unhealthy manipulation. Positively, this will be a most ambitious time for this talented and multifaceted woman and one most likely to be successful if her personal vision manages somehow to support the well-being of others.

Madeleine Moore

Life and Times

30 June 1983 Cheryl Ann Tweedy is born in Newcastle General Hospital, the fourth child of 24-year-old Joan Callaghan. The family lives in a terraced council house in Cresswell Street, Walker.

Sept 1987 Garry Tweedy is born. He is named after Cheryl's father, Garry senior. Cheryl starts at St Lawrence's RC Primary School in Byker. Aged four, she enrols at the Noreen Campbell Dance School on the Shields Road.

May 1990 As a child model, Cheryl takes part in the prestigious National Garden Festival in Gateshead. Her agent, Pat Morgan, says Cheryl showed incredible professionalism for somebody so young.

Nov 1990 Wins the 'Star of the Future' competition sponsored by the *Evening Chronicle* in Newcastle. The judge describes Cheryl as a 'little smasher'.

July 1993 Attends the summer school of the Royal Ballet at the White Lodge in Richmond Park. She hates it and gives up ballet.

Jan 1994 Appears on stage for the first time as one of the 'tots' in *Aladdin* at the Whitley Bay Playhouse. She performs a dance solo in a jazz style.

Sept 1994 Begins an undistinguished senior school career at

Walker School. She sums up her time there: 'I was awful'. She had moved to Langhorn Close, Heaton, with her mother after her parents split.

May 1995 Competes with partner James Richardson in the UK National Dancing Championships in Blackpool. They reach the last sixteen. The youngsters are already Northern Counties Champions.

Oct 1996 At thirteen, starts performing regularly on stage at the Metroland entertainment complex in Gateshead. Cheryl is signed to AIM, a management company run by Drew Falconer. He arranges gigs for her in the North-East and London.

July 1999 Leaves school and begins working at JJ's café, just across the road from her house. The owner, Nupi Bedi, says Cheryl is 'very cheeky and funny'. She makes teas and coffees but is not keen on waiting tables.

Dec 1999 Starts dating Jason Mack, who runs a local furniture store and is eleven years older than Cheryl. They stay together for more than two years but the relationship is blighted by his drug-taking.

Aug 2002 Auditions in London for a new series called *Popstars: The Rivals*. She is number L786. She sings the S Club 7 ballad 'Have You Ever'. Judge Pete Waterman says, 'You would need to be dead if you didn't think she was stunning.'

Sept 2002 Called back for the second set of auditions at Imperial College, London. Starts dating another contestant, Jacob Thompson, a carpet-fitter from Leicester. He fails to make the final ten boys.

Oct 2002 Joins the nine other girl finalists living in a luxury house in St George's Hill, Weybridge. Subject of first kiss-and-tell feature when a teenage boyfriend, plumber Steve

Thornton, tells all to the *News of the World*. He says she served him jumbo bacon butties in the café where she worked.

Nov 2002 Is in the bottom two after performing 'Nothing Compares 2 U', but friend Aimee Kearsley is voted off. Her brother Andrew and sister Gillian are arrested in Byker after a drunken brawl; they had been out celebrating Cheryl's success. In a separate incident, Andrew was arrested for screaming abuse in the street and sniffing from a blue carrier bag full of glue. Cheryl sings the Richard Marx hit 'Right Here Waiting' in the final and is the first girl chosen for the new group called Girls Aloud. The others, in order, are: Nicola Roberts, Nadine Coyle, Kimberley Walsh and Sarah Harding.

Dec 2002 The girls beat the boys, One True Voice, in the battle for the Christmas number one. 'Sound of the Underground' sells 213,000 copies during the first week. Their first tour manager, John McMahon, is killed in a car crash.

Jan 2003 Cheryl is arrested following a fight with a toilet attendant, Sophie Amogbokpa, at The Drink nightclub in Guildford. She denies allegations of racial abuse.

March 2003 Attends Staines police station where she is formally charged with racially aggravated actual bodily harm.

April 2003 Jason Mack sells the story of their relationship to the *News of the World*.

May 2003 Girls Aloud's second single, 'No Good Advice', reaches number two. First album, *Sound of the Underground*, also reaches number two but sales are disappointing.

Oct 2003 On trial at Guildford Crown Court. Found not guilty of racially aggravated assault but guilty of assault occasioning actual bodily harm. Judge calls it an 'unpleasant piece of drunken violence' and sentences Cheryl to 120 hours of community service.

Nov 2003 Attends the premiere of *Love Actually* at the Odeon Leicester Square. Cheryl dazzles in a scarlet ballgown.

July 2004 After an eight-month gap, a new single, 'The Show', reaches number two in the charts and marks the beginning of the girls exclusively recording with the songwriting and production team Xenomania, who would be responsible for every one of Girls Aloud's twenty-one hit singles.

Aug 2004 Chats to footballer Ashley Cole, who is playing tennis in the grounds of the luxury North London apartment complex where they both live. Declines to give him her phone number.

Oct 2004 The world knows she and Ashley are an item when they dance the night away at the Funky Buddha club in Mayfair after Cheryl appears at the National Television Awards.

Nov 2004 Girls Aloud have a second number one, 'I'll Stand By You', in aid of *Children in Need*. Appear at the Royal Variety Show in front of Prince Charles.

April 2005 Cheryl's childhood friend John Courtney is found dead from a heroin overdose at a flat in Newcastle. Cheryl later backs the *Evening Chronicle*'s 'War on Drugs' campaign, which began as a result of John's death.

May 2005 Girls Aloud play their first official live gig at the Royal Concert Hall in Nottingham. They had warmed up with two nights in Rhyl and play eighteen dates in all.

June 2005 Ashley proposes after a camel ride in Dubai. Andrew, her brother, is jailed for four years for a brutal mugging.

June 2006 First Girls Aloud concert in Newcastle, at the

MetroCentre. Cheryl says she is 'proud to be a Geordie'. Joins Victoria Beckham and the other WAGs to support the England football team's World Cup campaign in Germany. Cheryl wins a survey to see which WAG received most press coverage. Afterwards she slams the others: 'I would die of embarrassment if I had to resort to taking my boyfriend's [credit] cards.'

July 2006 Marries Ashley Cole at the Sopwell House Hotel in St Albans. The following day the couple throw a big wedding extravaganza at Wrotham Park in Hertfordshire. Cheryl wears a Roberto Cavalli dress and *OK!* magazine reportedly pays £1 million for exclusive coverage of the day.

March 2007 Girls Aloud have their third number one with the *Comic Relief* single 'Walk This Way', a collaboration with the Sugababes. Cheryl turns down an offer from Simon Cowell to be a judge on *The X Factor*.

Jan 2008 Stories appear in the national newspapers alleging that Ashley has played away with a blonde hairdresser from South London.

Feb 2008 Cheryl goes on holiday to Thailand with Nicola and Kimberley. Flies to LA to complete video for will.i.am single 'Heartbreaker' as part of learning to street dance for the television programme *The Passions of Girls Aloud*. Pictured not wearing her wedding ring.

May 2008 Ashley accompanies Cheryl's mother, Joan, to the Girls Aloud concert in Birmingham. He sends balloons and flowers to his wife's dressing room and the couple embrace backstage.

June 2008 Begins filming as a judge on the new series of *The X Factor* after Simon Cowell persuades her she will be perfect in the role.

Aug 2008 The television public watch Cheryl for the first time on

The X Factor and she is an instant hit. Writer Tony Parsons says Cheryl has brought some honesty and unashamed emotion to Saturday night TV and that is why she is suddenly the nation's sweetheart.

Nov 2008 Girls Aloud's fifth studio album, *Out of Control,* is their first to hit number one.

Dec 2008 Alexandra Burke, the act Cheryl is mentoring, wins *The X Factor* and has the Christmas number one six years after Cheryl did the same with Girls Aloud.

Feb 2009 Girls Aloud win their first Brit Award – Best British Single for 'The Promise', which was their fourth number one. Cheryl says, 'This is the cherry on the cake.' She features on the cover of the prestigious *Vogue* magazine for the first time.

March 2009 Climbs Mount Kilimanjaro along with Kimberley Walsh and other celebrities in aid of *Comic Relief.* Ashley is arrested for being drunk and disorderly outside a London club.

April 2009 Named Best Dressed Woman by *Glamour* magazine and World's Sexiest Woman by *FHM.* Set to begin work on a solo album while Girls Aloud take a break in 2009.

June 2009 Girls Aloud end their British tour with two concerts at Newcastle's Metro Radio Arena. Goes on holiday with Ashley to the south of France. Begins judging auditions for her second season of *The X Factor.*

Oct 2009 Performs her first solo single, 'Fight For This Love' on *The X Factor* live results show and wins the approval of Simon Cowell. The song enters the charts at number one, selling nearly 300,000 copies, the fastest selling single of the year. The following week, her album, *3 Words,* also tops the charts.

Nov 2009 Sir Terry Wogan calls her the nation's sweetheart when she makes an appeal for donations during *BBC Children in Need*. The critics approve when she duets with Gary Lightbody of Snow Patrol on the band's classic ballad, 'Set The Fire To The Third Bar'.

Dec 2009 Her own television special, *Cheryl Cole's Night In*, is broadcast on the first night of *The X Factor* final. Her act, Joe McElderry, wins the show, a second consecutive victory for Cheryl. '3 Words', the title track from her album, becomes her second single and reaches number four in the charts.

Feb 2010 Sexual allegations involving Ashley Cole are published in the national press. Cheryl performs 'Fight For This Love' at the Brits but misses out on Best Single, beaten by former *X Factor* act, JLS. Announces her separation from Ashley.

Acknowledgements

One of the most enjoyable things about writing this book was getting the chance to explore Newcastle, a fine and sociable city that demands a return visit. I always enjoy going back to a subject's roots and Newcastle did not disappoint.

Many people have helped me with Cheryl's story. I have respected the wishes of those who did not want to be named and I hope they enjoy the book. My sincere thanks go to Andrew Bailey, Nupi Bedi, Clare Bulman, Hayley Conway, Michael Conway, Steve Gater, Valerie Hopper, Bernadette Lamb, Gail Mackay, Pat McKintosh, Margaret Waite, Peter White and Barry Wilmot. Thanks to Adam Jupp, the chief reporter of the *Evening Chronicle* in Newcastle, who told me all about his newspaper's excellent 'War on Drugs' campaign.

I particularly want to mention Jason Mack, who has had a very tough time but shared his memories of Cheryl with honesty and good humour. I hope this puts the record straight for you, Jason, and enjoy the fishing!

Television presenter Chris Park was hugely helpful in recalling the exciting days of *Popstars: The Rivals* and my old friend Kevin O'Sullivan offered great insight into *The X Factor*. Alison Sims provided invaluable research, while Jen Westaway did a fantastic job in transcribing all my tapes. Arianne Burnette once again did superb work copy-editing my original manuscript – our third book together.

At Simon & Schuster, my thanks to my editor, Mike Jones, for his enthusiasm and good advice; Sally Partington for supervising this edition; Rory Scarfe for expertly coordinating everything; Emma Ewbank for her striking cover design; Jo Edgecombe for overseeing production; Emma Harrow for publicity; and Grainne Reidy and Richard Clarke for looking after the all-important sales. I would like to say a particular thank you to Jonathan Atkins, who left the company while I was writing this book but was responsible for bringing me to S&S seven years ago.

My agent, Gordon Wise, is always at the end of the telephone to help and that's so important for an author alone with his PC. I have lost track of the number of birth charts Madeleine Moore has prepared for my books. They are always fascinating and memorable. Finally, I am grateful to Jo Westaway for her research, her patient support and for keeping me cheerful.

Select Bibliography

Ashley Cole, *My Defence* (Headline, 2006)
Girls Aloud, *Dreams That Glitter* (Bantum Press, 2008)
Girls Aloud, *The Official Yearbook* (HarperCollins, 2005)
Peter Robinson, *Popstars: The Rivals* (Granada Media Ltd, 2002)

Picture Credits

Index